Theology in the Service of the Church

Endowed by

TOM WATSON BROWN

and

THE WATSON-BROWN FOUNDATION, INC.

Theology in the Service of the Church

Essays Presented to Fisher H. Humphreys

To Trent, with very best wishes.

Fisher Humphreys

EDITED BY

TIMOTHY GEORGE AND ERIC F. MASON

MERCER UNIVERSITY PRESS
MACON, GEORGIA

1400 Coleman Avenue
Macon, Georgia 31207

First Edition.

MUP/ H761

Books published by Mercer University Press are printed on acid free paper that meets the requirements of American National Standard for Information Sciences—Permanence of Paper for Printed Library Materials.

Library of Congress Cataloging-in-Publication Data

Theology in the service of the church : essays presented to Fisher H. Humphreys / edited by Timothy George and Eric F. Mason. -- 1st ed.
p. cm.
Includes bibliographical references and index.
ISBN-13: 978-0-88146-114-5 (hardback : alk. paper)
ISBN-10: 0-88146-114-8 (hardback : alk. paper)
1. Baptists—Doctrines. 2. Theology. I. Humphreys, Fisher.
II. George, Timothy. III. Mason, Eric Farrel.
BX6331.3.T44 2008
230--dc22
2008008047

in piam memoriam

Father Stephen J. Duffy

(14 October 1930–29 March 2007)

Contents

Foreword

Thomas E. Corts

Our Creator did not allow us to choose our starting point nor to determine the path we follow, when and where the journey shall end. A young Fisher Humphreys offered himself to the Lord without a plan of location, vocation, discipline, or specialty, and with the Lord's guidance, he found his way—better, *his* way—to a life of significance as professor, preacher, writer, theologian, and friend. Among the greatest blessings of one coming to the end of his most active work-life is, looking back, to realize, that even with some pauses, interruptions, and wrong turns, you found the right road, and you made it!

Few at first realize how crucial it was that the right road for Professor Humphreys included a key role in establishment of Beeson School of Divinity of Samford University. In 1988 Samford University offered, and Ralph W. Beeson responded to, the idea that a degree-granting, minister-training center was needed in Alabama. Winds of controversy were blowing in all directions, churning up questions, and leaving in their wake a *chairos* moment for a divinity school as a strategic component of a Baptist university. If all truth is God's truth, why segregate young theologues to themselves, when their ideas and worldviews might be energized by the combustion of tempestuous secular culture and academic thought with the hot currents of scripture and theology?

As soon as Beeson Divinity School was a firm promise on the horizon—the first divinity school at a Southern Baptist university in modern times—young Dean Timothy George with distinguished Provost and Professor William E. Hull launched the quest for an established Baptist scholar—one with a warm, pastoral heart; an unyielding conscience; a capacity to accept other Christian traditions; and theological conviction. How many such individuals could be identified?

Would established scholars be venturesome to depart the security of denominational enclaves for the untested waters of a divinity school in a university setting? Could a major scholar-theologian find fulfillment as a participant in the idea-crossfire and the internal politics of a university where not every colleague is denominationally attuned? Could a recognized Baptist thinker find his audience in a setting of avowed evangelical, interdenominational commitment?

It is not melodramatic simply to point to the year 1988. Conflict was in the ozone of the Southern Baptist Convention, and it was affecting every state convention, but not always in the same manner. Storms arose first over who most believed the Bible, though no gauge has yet been invented to measure either the intensity of belief or the sincerity of the believer. Leadership was challenged and replaced. Books expressly addressing the conflict sought to explain. Claims were made of a justifiable purgation long overdue. Worry was that we were fixing what was not broken. Almost all agree: the foundations were shaken and the Southern Baptist Convention (SBC) would never again be the same.

Amid this contentious atmosphere, Professor Fisher Humphreys and his thoughtful and devoted wife, Caroline, chose to resettle in Birmingham, Alabama, bringing to Beeson and Samford their irenic spirits; their quiet hospitality; their innate kindness; and their brand of genuine, thoughtful Christianity. It was a leap into the unknown, for sure, but not unthinkable for people who long ago "decided to follow Jesus" instead of hopping on the most advantageous oncoming bandwagon.

Now, as he looks toward retirement, this celebratory volume pays thanks and tribute, touching on major themes of Professor Humphreys's life and character. He is not merely academic in his theology, so it is appropriate that "spiritual theology" be addressed. A capacious intellect and an understanding heart have made it easy for Professor Humphreys to consider other Christian and non-Christian traditions, yet his soul comprehends both the missionary call and the Savior's plea for unity. From his earliest days, Bible memory verses, sword drills, and scriptural songs have been part of Professor Humphreys's DNA, so biblical scholarship is bedrock. Alongside professorial duties; periodic preaching and lecturing; and responsibilities as husband, father, and grandfather, he has always been faithful to a local church, affirming the significance of the church of the past and prospects of the church for a glorious future. With a naturally curious mind, an inner sincerity, and an uncommon breadth of knowledge and understanding, he has been a joyously accepted colleague among Samford faculty of all disciplines and a helpful university citizen. He takes delight in theological themes of modern literature, but he also reflects on the integration of worship and theological expression through the arts. As a committed Trinitarian who has read and studied enough to know where he stands, Professor Humphreys has a deep appreciation for doctrinal preaching as the overflow of personal conviction, and he shares concern for basic doctrines; how the next generation will know them; and the role of his church, university, and divinity school.

Perhaps the theme most appropriate for those who know Professor Humphreys best is that of friendship. Of all the attributes we could pile onto his résumé, it is the one most characteristic of the man. In the fiber of his being, he has an unshakable willingness to accept differences, a disdain for bigotry and prejudice, and a devotion to the worth of the individual. These virtues combine with his naturally courteous and gracious spirit; his soft, easy manner; his ability to speak hard truths in gentle ways; his eagerness to listen—all make him the person you would most like to have with you if stranded on a deserted island.

My own testimony applies here. During thirty-two years at the head of two Baptist institutions of higher learning, no faculty friendship has meant more to me than that of Professor Humphreys. Over the years we have shared many group meals and, once or twice per academic year, a person-to-person lunch. Having lived in New Orleans and as a lover of quality in all things, he makes lunch a culinary adventure, an informational cafeteria, a devotional and inspirational refreshment with a little pastoral counseling and encouragement, the latter delivered with a stealth often unperceived until a good while afterward.

So, this volume is an appropriate expression of love, respect, and appreciation for one of the Lord's great gifts to the modern church and, especially, to Beeson Divinity School and Samford University. What he has meant to us in these important years is far more than credit hours of instruction and having filled a chair. When so many believers seek sound-byte theology, when commentators on the church are verbal pugilists, when spiritual hypochondriacs delight in merely describing their maladies, when front-running churchmen leave the race after moral injuries, when ministerial students aspire to test their "star" quality, when those who divide gain more attention than those who unite, and when marketing is more important than believing, Professor Fisher Humphreys came among us and taught, listened, cared deeply for each of us, and unfailingly reflected the love of the Lord Jesus Christ.

Lord, give us more!

Introduction

TIMOTHY GEORGE

The technical name for this kind of book is *Festschrift*, a German word that literally means "celebration writing." The essays in this volume have been written and brought together to celebrate the life and work of Dr. Fisher H. Humphreys, a noted Baptist theologian who has served as a minister of the gospel and a teacher in the church of Jesus Christ for nearly half a century. Since 1990 Humphreys has taught systematic theology at Beeson Divinity School of Samford University and this volume is presented to him, with affection and esteem, on the occasion of his retirement from full-time teaching responsibilities. This introductory chapter consists of two parts: a brief biographical overview and a short review of the essays contained in this volume.[1]

I first met Fisher Humphreys in the early 1980s when both of us were teaching at theological seminaries affiliated with the Southern Baptist Convention; he in New Orleans, and I in Louisville. Fisher had been invited to offer a two-week summer course at Southern Seminary and we became acquainted over lunch one day. I would later discover that Fisher is a connoisseur of fine cuisine, a gourmand who enjoys a great meal. The fare was simpler that day in Louisville, but I discovered in Fisher Humphreys a stimulating conversation partner, a theologian who read widely and thought deeply about great issues of the Christian faith, and also a person so winsome he was nearly impossible to dislike. I was impressed by his irenic spirit and by his humility and charity toward

[1] Biographical information in this chapter has been garnered from three sources: "Interview with Fisher Humphreys: A Conversation about Him, His Life and Contributions" by Timothy George, Beeson Divinity School, 4 May 2007; Fisher Humphreys, "The Wisdom of Friends" (sermon preached in Hodges Chapel of Beeson Divinity School, Fall 1995); and Fisher Humphreys, "Afterthoughts" (unpublished paper, presented at the Steely Colloquium, Wake Forest NC, Fall 2000).

those with whom he differed, even on important issues, and that included me. Here was a theologian deeply rooted in the Baptist tradition, but not in a narrow, exclusivistic way. I found in Fisher a person committed to the truthfulness of Holy Scripture, conservative in piety and belief, an evangelical devoted to the missionary work of the church but also a theologian committed to Christian unity and the ecumenical task of theology. We became friends. Soon thereafter, Beeson Divinity School was established as an explicitly evangelical, intentionally interdenominational graduate school of theology at Samford University. We were seeking to forge a new pattern of ministerial training, one respectful of the wisdom of the past but not bound to the prevailing paradigm of denominational politics. Fisher seemed to be a good fit for what we were trying to do, and I invited him to join our fledgling faculty. Over the years our friendship has deepened. I am honored to join with other colleagues and friends in presenting this volume to Fisher, who is not only a faithful teacher and a superb scholar, but also one of the finest Christians I have ever known.

Fisher Henry Humphreys was born in Columbus, Mississippi, in 1939 on the eve of the Second World War. He was the oldest of five children, one of whom died in infancy. Fisher's parents underwent a bitter divorce when he was only ten years old and he had little contact with his father after the separation. But his mother, Hilda Sharkey Humphreys, devoted herself tirelessly to support Fisher; his younger brother, Hunter; and their two sisters, Ruth and Dale. Fisher would later dedicate his book on *Nineteenth Century Evangelical Theology* (1983) to the memory of both of his parents.

In 1953 when he was fourteen, Fisher went to a Christian summer camp and met a counselor there named James (Nap) Clark. Nap Clark talked with young Fisher about his need for forgiveness and the importance of asking Jesus to be his Savior and Lord. Through the witness of Nap Clark, Fisher said, "I intentionally put my faith in Jesus the crucified and risen Lord." Fisher's description of Nap Clark's evangelistic approach is worth quoting because it reflects what would become one of the great qualities in Fisher Humphreys himself.

> I know exactly why I paid attention to Nap in a way that I had not paid attention to anyone before him. Nap not only

> talked to me; he listened to me. I don't know if he had read Ruell Howe, but Nap Clark was a great listener. I have tried to remember some of the things I talked to him about during and after that week at camp, trying out ideas, identifying my feelings, exploring my relationships with various people. Nap listened, and listened, and listened, for years. Nap's listening earned him the right to be heard.

Another influential person in Fisher's formation as a young Christian was Dick Shirz, an independent fundamentalist who organized a series of Bible clubs for young people around the state of Mississippi. In this setting Fisher learned to love the Bible and study it diligently. He also made a commitment to become a minister of the gospel and began to speak and preach. This was the era of Youth for Christ and Fisher once won a preaching contest that enabled him to travel to Winona Lake and preach to a large gathering there. Winona Lake was the home of the famous evangelist Billy Sunday. His formidable wife, Ma Sunday, still lived there when Fisher held forth as a teenage preacher at the Billy Sunday Tabernacle.

The world of youth camps, Bible clubs, and preaching contests gave Fisher a desire to learn the Scriptures and to grow as a Christian, but the crucible of his theological vocation was the First Baptist Church of Columbus. Fisher had been baptized as an infant in the Methodist church his mother had attended at the time, but his intensive study of the Bible convinced him of the need for believers' baptism. Upon the advice of his mother, he weighed this decision for one year before joining the Baptist church and being baptized during his first year of high school.

It is hard to exaggerate the importance of the First Baptist Church of Columbus in Fisher's subsequent life and commitment as a Baptist theologian. His pastor, S. R. Woodson, had a formal pulpit style and wore black pinstripe trousers and a black cutaway coat to preach in every Sunday morning. A graduate of Southwestern Seminary, Woodson counted the renowned preachers R. G. Lee and J. D. Grey among his peers in the ministry. His own preaching was biblically astute and theologically engaged at a time when Fisher needed this kind of challenge. This church was also strongly committed to the world missionary enterprise. Dr. and Mrs. S. B. Platt, a medical doctor and his wife, championed the cause of missions in the congregation and befriended Fisher Humphreys in his desire to serve the Lord and follow the call of ministry in his life. Fisher would later dedicate one of his books to the Platts and to the First Baptist Church of Columbus as a tribute to their influence and encouragement to him.

What Fisher would later call his "transition from fundamentalism to Baptist life" began during his high school years at First Baptist of Columbus, but came to an abrupt end at the close of his freshman year at Bob Jones University. Pastor Woodson had encouraged Fisher to attend Mississippi College, a Baptist institution in his home state, but other mentors pointed him toward the famous independent school in South Carolina. Thus, one day in summer 1956, Fisher arrived on the campus of Bob Jones University after hitching a ride on an eighteen-wheeler from Mississippi to Greenville. Fisher was fond of his teachers at Bob Jones and threw himself into the life of the campus. He studied Greek, acted in a class play, and enjoyed the emphasis on the fine arts. He also appreciated the fact that students from moneyed families and higher social standing were not given special privileges at the school. But he ran afoul of the rigid separationist ethos and the invective directed against evangelical ministers like Billy Graham and the Southern Baptist Convention (SBC) with which his home church in Mississippi had been affiliated. When students were asked to stand and pledge that they would never support Billy Graham or the SBC, Fisher refused to join. This led to a confrontation with the school authorities, including an interview with Dr. Bob Jones Sr. Fisher was not expelled from the school but, like Billy Graham himself, another former Bob Jones student, he decided to pursue a different path. After working for one year, he transferred to Mississippi College.

Working at an Air Force base in Columbus and at a television station in Jackson, Fisher earned money to help defray his expenses through college. During these years, two people had a special influence on Fisher. Joe Cooper, his philosophy teacher at Mississippi College, introduced him to the thought of Kierkegaard and helped him to connect issues of life and faith in a holistic way. Luther Joe Thompson, pastor of Calvary Baptist Church in Jackson where Fisher was a member and taught a Sunday school class, modeled the virtues of a scholarly pastor while also preaching with evangelistic ardor. These same qualities—a desire to pursue the life of the mind together with a commitment to communicate the biblical message of Jesus Christ in a persuasive and winning way—would shape Fisher's life and ministry across the years.

During his student days at Mississippi College, Fisher began to date a beautiful young woman named Caroline Nan Toler whom he had met several years before through friends in his youth group. Caroline and her family attended the First Presbyterian Church of Jackson and Fisher often went to church with her to hear the venerable pastor John Reid Miller. After Caroline graduated from Belhaven College, she and Fisher were married in 1963 and began their wedded life together in New Orleans where Fisher had already completed two years of seminary studies. Over nearly five decades of marriage, Fisher and Caroline have been deeply devoted to one another. Their life together has been blessed by two children, Stephanie Hoffman and Kenneth Humphreys, and by three granddaughters, Camille Grace, Kate Elizabeth, and Janet Margaret (Maggie).

In 1961 Fisher enrolled as a student at New Orleans Baptist Theological Seminary and took his first class in theology. His teacher was Samuel J. Mikolaski. Fisher had majored in classical languages at Mississippi College and had taken other courses in philosophy, ethics, history, and biblical studies. But he found a home in the discipline of theology and he knew it from the first day of coursework in Mikolaski's class. Fisher later described the impact Mikolaski had on him and the discipline to which he was inexorably drawn:

> I learned more from Dr. Mikolaski than from any of my other teachers, because I studied with him for a longer time and because his subject is the subject that I teach. From him I learned the importance of the doctrines that we share with all the Christians in the world and not just with our own Baptist or evangelical friends. From him I learned the promise of evangelical theology, which at that time needed, as Carl Henry has written, to repent of a theological faith that had produced so few theological works. Dr. Mikolaski was committed to a theology which was collegial, responsive, accountable, and done

> in and for the Christian community, but he was equally committed to a theology which insisted that it was making public truth-claims and was prepared to state and defend public criteria for those claims. He taught us that philosophy is a good servant for theology, but a poor master. Most important of all, he was committed to close links between theology, the Gospel, spirituality, and the life of the church. He followed the advice of one of his own theological mentors, P. T. Forsyth, who once wrote that if theologians will take care of the depth, the breadth will take care of itself.

Mikolaski saw great promise in Fisher Humphreys and arranged for him and his young family to pursue advanced studies at Oxford where Fisher became affiliated with Mansfield College. Fisher studied with the great patristics scholar Henry Chadwick, who directed his dissertation on "English Kenotic Christologies, 1889–1930," for which he was granted the Master of Letters degree in 1967. While at Oxford, Fisher also studied with the New Testament scholar George Caird, the theologian John Marsh, and the historian of doctrine F. L. Cross. Though Fisher had few contacts with Regent's Park College, a Baptist school at Oxford, he, Caroline, and baby Stephanie were regular attendees at New Road Baptist Church in the heart of the city. This congregation had an open membership policy in the tradition of John Bunyan and also a female associate pastor who was an excellent preacher. Fisher's support for women in ministry and his commitment to a broader type of churchmanship can be traced to these experiences abroad.

Perhaps the most important figure in Fisher's personal theological development was Leonard Hodgson (1889–1969), an Anglican theologian who was the Regius Professor of Divinity at Oxford for many years. Hodgson wrote with great clarity and penetrating insight, and Fisher was drawn to his many writings on the great themes of Christian theology such as the Trinity, the Incarnation, the atoning work of Christ, and ecclesiology. For some time Hodgson served as the secretary of the Commission on Faith and Order, and during an especially troublesome time during the Second World War, it was said that the entire ecumenical movement was housed in Hodgson's files at Christ Church, Oxford. Fisher's doctoral dissertation at New Orleans Seminary

(Th.D., 1972) was written on "God in the Theology of Leonard Hodgson."

Fisher learned much from Hodgson's eleven books and many essays and he has pursued some of the same major themes in his own theological work. But he also absorbed from Hodgson what might be called a proper sense of theological engagement. Hodgson was concerned with how one evaluates and interacts with other thinkers with whom one disagrees. Fisher explains Hodgson's views in this way:

> He pointed out that we human beings have a tendency to regard those who disagree with us in one of two ways. We assume that, if we have deep convictions and explain them clearly and a person still does not accept them, then that person is either unable to understand the truth or else unwilling to accept the truth. In other words, those who disagree with us are either ignorant or evil. Naturally, this entitles us to respond to them by either dismissing them as stupid or attacking them as willful betrayers of the truth. Hodgson insisted, however, that very intelligent, very honest people, sincerely disagree about things. He said that it is a part of growing up that we come to recognize that those who disagree with us may be as intelligent and as honest as we are trying to be.

For neither Hodgson nor Humphreys is such an analysis a pretext for relativism or lack of conviction, but it is a summons to civility, humility, and the kind of forbearance and gentleness the New Testament identifies with the fruit of the Holy Spirit.

In 1970 Fisher joined the faculty of New Orleans Baptist Theological Seminary where he taught for the next twenty years. During this time, he also received a master of arts degree in religious studies from Loyola University in New Orleans (1984), working with the late Professor Stephen J. Duffy. He also became the first editor (1975–1990) of a journal in theology and ministry published by the seminary, *The Theological Educator*. Fisher himself wrote many articles for this journal as well as numerous essays for other publications. He also published several significant books including *Thinking about God*, his masterful summary of Christian theology; *Speaking in Tongues* (with Malcolm Tolbert); *A*

Dictionary of Doctrinal Terms (with Philip Wise); and *The Death of Christ*, a major study of the doctrine of the atonement. During his faculty years in New Orleans, Fisher became widely known as a popular preacher and speaker at student gatherings, spiritual retreats, church conferences and in congregations of many denominations. Though he and Caroline always retained membership in a local Southern Baptist congregation, for eight years he served as the "permanent interim pastor" of Meterie Evangelical Church in New Orleans.

In 1990 the Humphreys family moved to Birmingham when Fisher became professor of divinity at Samford University's Beeson Divinity School. During the past two decades, Fisher has continued to speak in many different settings about issues of Christian faith, spiritual life, and theology. He has also continued to write prolifically producing books on Calvinism, fundamentalism, Southern Baptist theology, and a beautiful devotional study of the Christian life, *I Have Called You Friends: New Testament Images that Challenge Us to Live as Christ's Followers* (2005). In 2006 he served as an editor for a special issue of the journal *Perspectives in Religious Studies* bringing together a collection of essays by Baptist scholars on the doctrine of the Trinity. In 2007 he published *Baptist Theology: A Really Short Version* for a series sponsored by the Baptist History and Heritage Society. From his base at Beeson, Fisher has been an active participant in the life of Samford University. He has also been involved in the work of the Baptist World Alliance, the American Academy of Religion, the Christian Theological Research Fellowship, the National Association of Baptist Professors of Religion, and the Cooperative Baptist Fellowship. On two occasions he has served as theologian-in-residence (1998–1999, 2002) at the University of Alabama-Birmingham, where he offered courses and interacted with scholars on the theme of science and religion. In all of these contexts, Fisher Humphreys has shown himself to be an exemplary colleague, an engaging interlocutor, a careful scholar, a conscientious Christian, and a theologian in the service of the church.

Before turning to the essays in this volume, we must say a word about the influence Fisher has had on thousands of students across the years. Both at New Orleans and at Beeson, Fisher has poured his life into preparing God-called men and women for service in the church of Jesus Christ. I have met hundreds of Fisher's former students who are serving now as pastors, counselors, missionaries, chaplains, evangelists, and professors. Invariably they bear witness to a deepened sense of calling and spiritual transformation they gained through knowing and studying with Fisher Humphreys. In 1998 Fisher received Samford University's George Macon Award for Excellence in Teaching, and in 2003 he received the first Distinguished Teacher of the Year Award at Beeson Divinity School. This special recognition of classroom excellence was established in honor of Fisher by one of his former students, William T. Carlson and his wife Debra.

In the classroom, no less than elsewhere, Fisher has invariably shown respect and forbearance to those with differing views on controversial issues. Soon after Fisher had joined the Beeson faculty, one of our students became quite upset with his approach to the teaching of theology. He registered a stout complaint and eventually left our school in protest. But some years later, this same student returned to apologize to Fisher for his angry critique and to thank him for his patience and Christian demeanor in responding to his earlier outburst. I once heard a young theological student ask a very impertinent question to Dr. Gardner C. Taylor, one that bordered on disrespect. It was clear that the great preacher could have quashed the young man with a snappy retort. But he slowly, lovingly, and with much pastoral wisdom showed him the error of his ways, leaving the dignity of the student intact while reframing the discussion in a way that brought greater insight to the issue. Such wisdom is the mark of a great teacher and I have seen it displayed in Fisher Humphreys on more than one occasion.

How does Fisher understand his own calling and work as a theologian of the church? Several years ago, we asked every faculty member at Beeson Divinity School to share his or her spiritual journey in a series of chapel services devoted to this theme. Fisher spoke on "The Wisdom of Friends" and asked Kelly Reese, one of his students, to read Proverbs 8:1–21 as the text for his message. Fisher spoke about his family and the friends who had walked along beside him on his pilgrimage of faith. He also spoke about the church and declared that "there is no way that you can be a good Christian by yourself; you need the church." When he described his calling as a theologian, this is how he put it:

> For a quarter of a century, I have been trying to help God-called men and women to become trustworthy theologians. By *trustworthy*, I do not mean infallible, because that is not possible. I mean people who are conversant with theological issues, who are serious about important theological questions, who are sympathetic with our great theological heritage, and who can be counted on to be thoughtful when they talk about theology. I mean people who are not confused about theology, who also are not arrogant or meanspirited about theology, and who can speak of theology in ways that are biblical, pastoral, and quietly confident.

St. Paul once declared that the Christian message was "worthy of full acceptance" (1 Tim 1:15) commendable in its own right. The contributors to this volume agree that Fisher's self understanding of his own vocation as a theologian of the church also deserves to be commended. *Theology in the Service of the Church* is an appropriate rubric for the essays in this volume for it reflects Fisher's sense of the primary context of his life work, as he himself put it in the opening chapter of the revised edition of *Thinking about God*:

> My theology is church theology. I do thinking about God in the fellowship of the church. And I do it for the church. It is possible to do theology in settings other than the church and for persons other than the church. I appreciate the work of people who do their thinking about God primarily as scientists, or as therapists, or in the setting of a secular university. And I appreciate the work of those who write about God for the benefit of persons in other religions, or for those who doubt the existence of God. But my theology is written from within the fellowship of the church, and for the use of persons who are, like myself, committed to faith in Jesus Christ.

Each essay that follows illuminates some aspect of the theologian's calling from the standpoint of specific theological disciplines or from the intersection of theology with other areas of Christian thought and life. Together they constitute a tribute to a special friend who has lived out his calling as a theologian with humility, perseverance, and much wisdom.

Frank Thielman, Presbyterian Professor of Divinity at Beeson Divinity School, joined the Beeson faculty shortly before Fisher and they have shared adjacent offices for most of this time. In his essay, "Biblical Scholarship in Christian Theology: Can the Marriage be Saved?" Thielman explores the historic tension between two necessarily interdependent yet quite often bifurcated disciplines within the body of divinity. After exploring the historical developments that have led to the present impasse, Thielman offers his own constructive proposal for a better way forward. Thielman incorporates insights from the philosopher Alvin Plantinga and concludes that "the church has a *theological* interest in historically accurate exegesis because its theology is bound up with its history and because it stands under the authority of the Bible."

In "Back to the Future of Trinitarianism?" Curtis W. Freeman explores one of the major themes in Fisher Humphreys's theological work, the doctrine of the Trinity. Freeman shows that while almost all Baptists have been formally orthodox in their profession of Trinitarian belief, the doctrine of the Trinity has been consigned to practical irrelevance in the ongoing life and worship of most Baptist churches. He explores Humphreys's investigation of this theme and his case for retrieving Trinitarian faith and practice. Drawing on the recent revival of interest in Trinitarian theology among some Baptist theologians, among whom Humphreys has been a pioneer, Freeman sets forth a sevenfold program of Trinitarian ressourcement among Baptists today.

Bill J. Leonard is a distinguished Baptist historian and dean of Wake Forest University Divinity School. In his essay "Why Study Church History? Listening to Saints and Sinners," Leonard explores the crucial role history and tradition play in the life of the church and the theological work it is called to do. When theologians are ill informed about the Christian past, their work invariably becomes speculative, trendy, and idiosyncratic, just as church historians who ignore theology will offer an impoverished account of the Christian story. Leonard examines several fault lines in church historical methodology and shows how "church history helps persons who seek Christian identity know where they fit in the great ebb and flow of classic belief and practice and how specific identities have evolved across the centuries."

Stephen R. Harmon is a younger Baptist theologian whose work in ecumenical theology resonates with a major theme in Fisher Humphreys's teaching and scholarship. In his "Remembering the Ecclesial Future: Why the Church Needs Theology," Harmon presents a considered rationale for the ecclesial necessity of theology that emphasizes the call to Christian unity incumbent upon all Christians. "The church needs theology," Harmon writes, "because the ecclesial future disclosed in Scripture involves visible Christian unity, and unless its theologians function as stewards of the Christian memory, which is the living tradition to which all the currently divided churches are heirs, the church will be severely crippled in its movements toward this aspect of God's designs for it." Such a vision for theology must of necessity take the church seriously as its primary context and audience. Harmon commends Fisher Humphreys for doing just this in an exemplary manner.

J. Norfleete Day was a member of the inaugural class of Beeson Divinity School and studied theology with Fisher Humphreys before becoming his colleague as a teacher of New Testament and spiritual theology. In her essay on "Spiritual Theology for the Evangelical Church," Day examines both the contested history of the term spirituality and the role of the spiritual disciplines in spiritual formation. She encourages evangelicals to reclaim spiritual theology and its essential practices as foundational to the vitality and effectiveness of the evangelical church.

Christian theology is an eminently "practical" discipline in its task of undergirding and informing every aspect of the life and work of the church, including the task of proclamation. In his essay "Balancing Our Doctrinal Preaching," Robert Smith explores both the pastoral and prophetic aspects of the preaching ministry. Drawing from the wisdom of the African-American tradition, he calls for an approach to proclaiming God's transcendence and immanence that avoids the theological dangers of modalism and process theology.

Gary Furr is a pastor-theologian with a special interest in the intersection of theology, worship, and the arts. He and Fisher Humphreys have participated together in the Trinity Group, an informal gathering of pastors, missionaries, professors, and others whose friendship grew out of their shared interest in theology and its implications for all areas of life. In his essay for this volume, Furr finds a good discussion partner in the great English novelist and lay theologian Dorothy Sayers. He explores her book *The Mind of the Maker* and its delineation of Trinitarian reality as perfect love. This understanding of God has important implication for the meaning of worship and the artistic theological integrity it calls forth. Furr's conclusion challenges worship leaders to examine the motivation of their work: "The most damning judgment that can fall upon us is not whether people liked our worship or whether we felt better when it was done, but whether, at the end, we involved ourselves more deeply in the mystery that is God with us."

Wanda S. Lee had a distinguished career in the field of nursing before assuming her present role as executive director of Woman's Missionary Union, a post she has held since 2000. In her essay, "Into All the World: The Missionary God Who Calls and Sends," Lee presents a biblical and historical overview of the Christian missionary movement and concludes with a survey of the mission challenges facing the contemporary church. Her emphasis on "the missionary God" is in keeping with a theology of missions exemplified by the life and work of the great Baptist missionary pioneers William Carey and Lottie Moon. Wanda Lee's essay meshes with Fisher Humphreys's own lifelong commitment to the world Christian movement and his strong support for the missions education work of Woman's Missionary Union.

The chapter by the late Father Stephen Duffy, "That They May All Be One: The Unity That Is Ours and Not Ours," holds a special place among the collected essays in this volume. Father Duffy, a Roman Catholic priest and theologian, completed this chapter shortly before his death in March 2007. Duffy had been Fisher's teacher at Loyola University in New Orleans and was a good friend of Fisher and Caroline across the years. Father Duffy was a participant in the Southern Baptist-Roman Catholic Conversation that took place during the 1990s, and he drew on Humphreys's own work in an earlier phase of this ecumenical dialogue. In the chapter he provided for this volume, Father Duffy presents the call to Christian unity as rooted in the oft-time quoted words of Jesus in John 17:21: "That they may all be one...so that the world may believe." He reminds us that biblically-centered ecumenism has ever been, and will always remain, the impulse of the Spirit. Thus, it must be undergirded by mutual prayer, worship, and work done together in the name of Christ. Fisher Humphreys's theological work is permeated by a similar ecumenical spirit. In honor of Father Duffy and his special friendship with Fisher and Caroline Humphreys and as a tribute to his unstinting commitment to Christian unity, we have dedicated this volume in his memory.

Richard Land's essay, "Moving toward the Kingdom of Racial Reconciliation," was originally presented as a sermon during the International Summit against Racism sponsored by the Baptist World Alliance in Atlanta in 1999. Dr. Emmanuel McCall referred to this sermon as one of the finest messages on the theme of racial reconciliation he had ever heard from a Southern Baptist leader. Fisher Humphreys and Richard Land have been friends since their student days together in New Orleans, and since that time they have shared a common conviction about the need for Baptist Christians to confront the legacy of slavery, segregation, and racism. Fisher came to faith in Christ in the segregated Mississippi of the 1950s. In 1954 he attended an integrated Billy Graham crusade in New Orleans and this made a deep impression on him. Later, his teachers at New Orleans Seminary in the early 1960s, especially Frank Stagg, took a prophetic stance against the deep-seated segregationist policies of the day. Richard Land's stirring address reminds us that the price of racial reconciliation, like that of religious liberty, is eternal vigilance. He also reminds us that the kind of commitment to racial reconciliation that will bring about real transformation must be rooted in the truth of the Gospel itself: "A Christianity that forgets that its horizontal commission is to be ambassadors of reconciliation has forgotten the Incarnation, the Word made flesh that dwelt among us (John 1:14). Racism is a global problem and it has a global solution. That hope is found in the cross of our Savior."

Ralph C. Wood's fascinating essay, "'Jesus Thrown Everything Off Balance': Emily Dickenson, William Faulkner and Flannery O'Connor on the Necessity of Christian Radicalism in the Study of Literature" brings together his expertise in the study of Christianity and literature with the kind of radical Christian commitment inherent in the Gospel itself. As those who know Fisher Humphreys personally can attest, he loves movies, novels, and music and, like Ralph Wood, is alert to the subtle and oblique ways the Christian story often shows up in such unexpected places. Wood also refers to a public "debate" on the issue of Calvinism between Fisher and him (in which Bill Leonard and I also participated). All four of us were good friends before that discussion, and we remained such afterwards. While we certainly did not solve the perennial theological issues that have long swirled around this historic theological controversy in Christian thought, we did demonstrate, with Fisher taking the lead among us all, that one could discuss such important differences with civility and charity yet without compromise or loss of conviction.

Samuel J. Mikolaski's essay, "University, Seminary, and Congregation: Contexts for Theology," examines what he calls "the loss of Christianity as a hermeneutic in America" and proposes ways in which theology can recover something of its role as a mediating interpreter of the biblical worldview, especially among Christian colleges, universities, and seminaries. Mikolaski is an excellent person to write on this theme because he has served with distinction in all of these academic settings across the years. A native of Yugoslavia and reared in Canada, Mikolaski brings an international perspective to his theological reflection. Always concerned to relate theological studies to the ongoing life of a church, he is currently involved in the teaching ministry of Saddleback Church in California. As we have already seen, Mikolaski has had a formative influence on the theological trajectory of Fisher Humphreys, his former student and close friend of many years.

The concluding essay in this volume is "Friendship as a Theological Virtue" by Philip Wise, Fisher's former seminary colleague and lifelong friend. Wise acknowledges, of course, that friendship is not usually listed among the three theological virtues: faith, hope, and love. Still, he makes a good case for construing friendship in this way. Drawing both from the wisdom of the ancient Greek philosophers and the theological tradition of the church rooted in the Scriptures, Wise shows that genuine friendship consists of the greatest Christian virtues lived out in a genuine relationship of mutuality and care: "When we respond to God or to others with faith, hope, and love, we will have established the kind of relationship with others that Paul envisioned, a perfect friendship." He then demonstrates in a moving way how he has experienced such a reality in his personal relationship with Fisher Humphreys, his mentor and friend.

This volume concludes with a comprehensive annotated bibliography of the writings of Fisher Humphreys by my co-editor, Eric F. Mason. To peruse this bibliography is to see the range and breadth of Fisher's scholarly interest across the years and also to observe how he has written equally well for the scholarly community and popular readers. This bibliography will be a valuable resource for future scholars who will doubtless devote doctoral dissertations and book-length studies to the theology of Fisher Humphreys. Eric Mason, one of Fisher's former students at Beeson and a distinguished New Testament scholar in his own right, has been a superb helper to me in editing all of the essays in this volume. In this work we have both been ably assisted by Dr. B. Coyne, my research associate, whose expertise in preparing the volume for press has contributed much to its successful completion.

Looking back over his many accomplishments near the end of his life, the Latin poet Horace reflected on what he had done and what this might mean in years to come:

> I have erected a monument more lasting than bronze,
> More lofty than the regal structure of the pyramids;
> Which gnawing storm and impotent north-wind cannot destroy,
> Neither the innumerable succession of the years,
> Nor the flight of time, I shall not wholly die;
> The larger part of me will escape the tomb.[2]

No one who knows Fisher Humphreys personally could imagine that he would ever say anything like this about himself, for it is so out of character with his humility and his desire to follow the advice of St. Paul in preferring others more than himself. Still, those of us who do know and love Fisher Humphreys and who have considered with gratitude what he has meant in our own lives and to the cause of Christ will have no problem in thinking of his life's work (which, thankfully, still goes on

---

[2] Quoted in Fisher Humphreys, ed., *Nineteenth Century Evangelical Theology* (Broadman Press: Nashville, 1983) 415.

with vigor and joy) as constituting "a monument more lasting than bronze." It is a monument reflected in the topics surveyed in this book and reflected in the bibliography at the end—Fisher's teachings, writings, scholarly associations, and churchly commitments. All these accomplishments have been embodied in a Christ-like personality marked by generosity, hospitality, and genuine friendships, which, as Horace said, neither "gnawing storm" nor "impotent north-wind" will ever be able to destroy. For such a life and such a friend we give thanks to the Lord in whose love and mercy we all live.

Biblical Scholarship and Christian Theology: Can the Marriage Be Saved?

FRANK THIELMAN

Professor Humphreys, a cherished friend and colleague, has had a long running interest in biblical, and particularly New Testament, theology. He has not pitted his work as a systematic theologian against the work of biblical scholars but, with an intellectual fairness and charity typical of his character, has sought to build bridges between the two disciplines. It is with appreciation for his irenic spirit, and in the hope that he will have much company in years to come, that I would like to argue that the marriage between biblical scholarship and Christian theology, despite its checkered past, can be saved and even flourish.

I will begin by examining briefly the roots of the trouble and then will propose an easing of tensions. Reconciliation, I argue, can be achieved if theologians acknowledge the reliance of classical Christian orthodoxy on careful historical work and if critical historians understand the philosophical legitimacy of allowing basic insights to play a role in historical description. For this second point I call in the aid of a "marriage counselor"—the philosopher Alvin Plantinga, who, from a position outside the fray, asks biblical scholars to come to their philosophical senses.

The Problem from the Perspective of Biblical Scholars

A tense atmosphere in the relationship between the guild of Bible scholars and that of systematic theologians was already discernable in the now well-known inaugural lecture delivered by Johann Philipp Gabler in 1787. Gabler was burdened with the divisions among "all who are devoted to the sacred faith of Christianity" and united in their conviction that the Bible, especially the New Testament, is the "source from which all true knowledge of the Christian religion is drawn."[1] Although united on these important central convictions, Christianity is nevertheless plagued with dissension. Much of the blame for this sad state of affairs, Gabler argues, lies with a methodological confusion between the simple truths of religion ("what each Christian ought to know and believe and do in order to secure happiness in this life and in the life to come") and the sophisticated discipline of theology ("subtle, learned knowledge, surrounded by a retinue of many disciplines").[2]

Among the worst offenders in this confused state of affairs are biblical scholars and dogmatic theologians. The biblical scholars often confuse the enduring and universal religious truths contained in the Bible with the ancient theological clothing in which these truths were dressed by the biblical authors. The dogmatic theologians frequently clothe the Bible's universal religious truths with their inferior modern opinions.[3]

Gabler's solution calls for renewed methodological clarity on the distinction between biblical theology and systematic theology. The biblical theologian has the task of painstakingly separating religious truth from theological expression in the Bible and delivering the resulting distillate of universally valid religious truths to the systematic theologian. The systematic theologian may then engage in the legitimate and necessary task of expressing these truths in a contemporary idiom. Gabler seems optimistic that the marriage between the two disciplines can be saved as long as each spouse sticks to these properly assigned roles and dutifully resists undue interference in the other's business.[4]

A century later, however, William Wrede's influential essay titled "The Task and Methods of 'New Testament Theology'"[5] demonstrates

---

[1] John Sandys-Wunsch and Laurence Eldredge, "J. P. Gabler and the Distinction between Biblical and Dogmatic Theology: Translation, Commentary, and Discussion of His Originality," *Scottish Journal of Theology* 33 (1980): 134.

[2] Ibid., 136.

[3] Ibid., 135–38.

[4] Ibid., 142–44.

[5] Originally published in 1897 and available in *The Nature of New Testament Theology: The Contribution of William Wrede and Adolf Schlatter*, trans. and ed. Robert Morgan, Studies in Biblical Theology (London: SCM, 1973) 68–116.

that optimism has faded. This essay attempts to show that, despite protests to the contrary, New Testament theology as practiced in Wrede's time is largely a dogmatic rather than a historical enterprise. It limits itself to the New Testament canon not for historical reasons but because Christian dogma, settled by theologically driven church counsels, dictates that limitation. It favors an approach, moreover, that elevates "doctrinal concepts" and written arguments over "what was believed, thought, taught, hoped, required and striven for in the earliest period of Christianity."[6] Wrede was affiliated with Göttingen's history of religion school of thought and was far less interested in the relationship between the various abstract theological concepts of the New Testament authors than in the taste, smell, and feel of early Christianity.[7]

The problem, says Wrede, lies in the goal toward which New Testament theologians work. They intend to deliver the results of their supposedly historical investigations over to the dogmatic theologians who will then use them to instruct the church. This arrangement, however, is a recipe for disaster. As long as the New Testament theologian has the systematic theologian in view, he is "psychologically" inclined to work over the results of any historical investigation until those results conform to the systematic theologian's expectations. "Historical reality," however, "has its own laws," and so historians of early Christianity (which is what Wrede thinks New Testament theologians should become) cannot be burdened with a dogmatic goal.[8]

In Wrede's mind, the divorce of objective, historical study of early Christianity from systematic theology should be finalized. Gabler's counsel to observe separate roles but to maintain some relationship did not go far enough. All ties need to be severed.

In more recent times, Wrede's case for irreconcilable differences continues to find advocates. Wayne Meeks, for example, acknowledges that the "primary audience" for what New Testament scholars have to say will continue to be "believers" who consider the New Testament

---

[6] Ibid., 84; italics removed.

[7] On Wrede's life and work, see William Baird, *From Jonathan Edwards to Rudolf Bultmann*, vol. 2 of *History of New Testament Research* (Minneapolis: Fortress, 2003) 144–61.

[8] Ibid., 69, 73.

texts to be "sacred Scripture," but he is not sanguine about the church benefiting from the work of historical-critical scholars.[9] Little biblical scholarship, he says, is useful to believers, and historians of early Christianity are disinclined to communicate their results to an audience often hostile to their historical-critical method. Gabler's project of scholars handing over the distillate of their careful work to theologians who will use it to construct their theologies looks less possible as the years roll by. We might as well admit that this is the way the world is and break New Testament scholarship free from theological constraints once and for all. A good beginning would be the erasure from the guild's vocabulary of "the terms 'biblical theology' and, even more urgently, 'New Testament theology.'"[10] The reasons for this are reminiscent of Wrede: biblical theology focuses on doctrines rather than life as it is lived, and it tends to hide theological conviction behind the mask of historical research.[11]

To summarize, influential historians of early Christianity over the last three centuries have called for a separation of the study of early Christian history from theological reflection on the Christian faith. The nub of the problem is that the results of historical research cannot be dictated in advance by the expectations of theologians that their religious convictions will be confirmed. Should biblical scholarship be wed to Christian theological reflection? These observers would say that scholars of early Christianity need Christian theology only to the extent that those interested in Christian theology provide an audience for their work. Biblical scholarship must itself work independently from theological reflection, even when this requires the biblical scholar who is also a Christian to bracket his or her faith for the sake of unfettered historical analysis.

The Problem from the Perspective of Christian Theologians

As it turns out, some Christian scholars who value highly the theological tradition of the church also want a divorce, or at least a

---

[9] Wayne A. Meeks, "Why Study the New Testament?" *New Testament Studies* 51 (2005): 167.

[10] Ibid.

[11] Ibid., 168.

separation, from historical-critical biblical scholarship. The focus of these scholars lies on the priority of theological commitment in the Christian use of the Scriptures. They do not see the work of historical-critical biblical scholarship, at least in its current form, as necessary for the use of the Scriptures in Christian formation and theological reflection. Stephen E. Fowl (a New Testament scholar) and Robert W. Jenson (a systematic theologian) might be taken as representative voices for this position.

In a sophisticated and often insightful treatment of the issue, Fowl argues that Gabler's project failed, especially after it became linked to the history-of-religions framework that Wrede built for it. The failure occurred not only because the history-of-religions account of Israelite and early Christian religion was unconvincing historically, but also because it was not satisfying theologically.[12] Most biblical scholars did not want to limit themselves to historical description. They tended to move beyond history and exegesis to theological judgments. These judgments often took the form of adjudicating between the diversity of theological expression in the Bible on the basis of a canon within the canon or providing a taxonomy of important theological concepts within the Bible.[13]

All this, however, was flawed from the beginning. The whole enterprise worked out of the controversial presumption that texts have properties and that statements within those texts have fixed meanings. "Meaning," argues Fowl, "is a hopelessly ambiguous term, and the idea that texts have determinate meanings must consign centuries of Christian interpretation of Scripture, including much of the New Testament's use of the Old Testament, to the dustbin reserved for erroneous interpretation."[14]

The way forward recognizes that faithful Christian interpretation of Scripture involves a complex process of "underdetermined interpretation." This approach considers the interpretive process to be shaped by the interests the interpreter brings to the text. Interpreters

---

[12] Stephen E. Fowl, *Engaging Scripture: A Model for Theological Interpretation*, Challenges in Contemporary Theology (Oxford: Blackwell, 1998) 18.

[13] Ibid., 18–19.

[14] Ibid., 33–40.

with common interests can agree on both the purpose for which they are interpreting the text and the interpretive strategy they will follow.[15] Here the fellowship provided by the church, especially the local congregation, and the interpretive work of faithful Christians down through the centuries becomes crucial to the Christian use of the Bible: "Theological convictions, ecclesial practices, and communal and social concerns should *shape and be shaped by* biblical interpretation."[16]

How will such an approach, without the restraint of a text with a determined "meaning," avoid reading the Bible in self-serving and sinful ways? Fowl argues that if the Christian community cultivates a realistic appraisal of human sin, understands the necessity for forgiveness, knows the need for reconciliation, and engages in a charitable reading of those who disagree with them, it can avoid the pitfall of basically selfish interpretations of the biblical text.[17] The restraint of a text whose meaning is determined by historical-critical exegesis, even if it were attainable, would not therefore be necessary for a virtuous reading of the text.

This does not mean that the work of biblical scholars is useless for Christian interpreters—it certainly can be useful at certain moments in the interpretive process—but the goals of the professional biblical scholar and the goals toward which the church is working when it interprets Scripture are not compatible with each other. "There may not be outright enmity, but there is not much fruitful cooperation either."[18]

Robert W. Jenson finds a more systematic role for historical-critical scholarship in the interpretive work of the church, but it is a subsidiary role and one that, as with Fowl, must be carefully circumscribed. The value for the church of historical-critical work on its Scriptures is twofold. First, it prevents us from merely seeing a reflection of ourselves in Scripture, and so allows Scripture to speak to us (even if, in the end, we do not agree with it).[19] Second, it places some restraint on

---

[15] Ibid., 58–59.

[16] Ibid., 60.

[17] Ibid., 62–96.

[18] Ibid., 183.

[19] Robert W. Jensen, *The Works of God*, vol. 2 of *Systematic Theology* (Oxford: Oxford University Press, 1999) 278, 281–82.

allegorizing, especially the Old Testament, and this provides a check on impossible readings.[20]

Still, professional biblical scholarship is a dubious enterprise from the perspective of the church, and this is also the case for two reasons. First, professional biblical scholarship proceeds from the methodological assumption that the Bible is not unified, whether we think of the disunity between Old Testament and New Testament or the disunity between each of the separate texts that comprise the Bible. Although it is true that the Bible contains competing theological perspectives and perspectives from which the Christian may dissent, these are "inner differentiations" within a book that the church considers fundamentally unified at the level of narrative.[21] There is a coherent story in the Bible as long as the Bible is interpreted as a single book, but this way of interpreting the Bible is the church's domain, and the historical-critical method will have nothing to do with it. The minute we apply the method of the academic guild of Bible scholars to the church's Scriptures, they dissolve in our hands. The church is left with no Scripture to interpret, only a welter of ancient texts, fragmented into "shards," now available for anyone who is interested in them to inspect, but no longer the authoritative Scriptures of the church.[22]

Second, professional biblical scholarship fails to recognize that the people of God described in Scripture are continuous with the church of the present. God's people today do not stand at a distance from the people described in Scripture's story, but they are that people; they stand within that story and are part of its present unfolding. Biblical scholarship as it is performed in the academy, however, insists on distancing the interpreter of the present from the historical object of study and so brackets out of its method from the beginning one of the most important elements of Scripture for Christians.[23]

---

[20] Ibid., 283.

[21] Robert W. Jensen, *The Triune God*, vol. 1 of *Systematic Theology* (Oxford University Press, 1997) 32–33; Robert W. Jensen, "Scripture's Authority in the Church," in *The Art of Reading Scripture*, ed. Ellen F. Davis and Richard B. Hays (Grand Rapids: Eerdmans, 2003) 29.

[22] Jensen, *Triune God*, 58–59, including n96; Jensen, "Scripture's Authority," 27–29.

[23] Jensen, *Works of God*, 279–80; Jensen, "Scripture's Authority," 34.

In summary, it is not only historians of early Christianity who call for a separation of the historical investigation of the Christian Scriptures from the theological analysis of the church, but Christian interpreters of Scripture and systematic theologians are uneasy about the marriage. Biblical scholarship, at least as it is presently practiced in the academy, tends to rely on questionable hermeneutical strategies. Its methods, moreover, remove the Bible from the church both by dissolving it into useless fragments and locking God's people out of their own story.

A Proposal for Reconciliation

Despite the many calls for the separation of the two disciplines over the years, and despite my deep appreciation for the issues raised especially by Fowl and Jenson, there is still a case to be made that biblical scholars and systematic theologians need to be partners with each other in their tasks. At the risk of pedantry, I would like to make this case in two steps, arguing first that the church and its systematic theologians need to pay attention to biblical scholarship, and second, that biblical scholars need to listen to what believing Christians say about their Bible.

First, then, it seems necessary to recognize that Christianity is a religious movement with a profound investment in historical claims. The earliest preaching of the gospel focused on the crucifixion of the Jewish Messiah Jesus; his resurrection from the dead as the first resurrection of the general resurrection of the righteous; his future return with a mighty, heavenly army to establish his kingdom; and the theological significance of these astounding events (Gal 3:1; 1 Cor 15:1–5, 20; 1 Thess 1:9–10; 4:16). The truthfulness of this good news was linked from the first to the question of whether these events really happened or would happen (1 Thess 4:14–16; Gal 3:1; 1 Cor 15:12–20; Acts 1:3). This is why, in the New Testament itself, such weight is placed on credible, eye-witness testimony to the reality of these events (1 Cor 15:3–8; 2 Pet 1:16; Luke 1:2; 24:48; Acts 2:32; 3:15; 5:32; 10:39, 41; 13:31; John 19:35; 21:24; 1 John 1:1–3). This is also why opponents of Christianity and those who deviated from the theological teaching of the majority of Christians made such great capital out of "contradictions" between the church's four ancient narrative witnesses to Jesus and other "errors" in the Scriptures. Irenaeus, writing in the late second century, tells us that heretics speak of the Scriptures "as if they were not correct" or are "ambiguous" or "the truth cannot be extracted from them" (*Haer* 3.2.1). Celsus, writing at about the same time, spoke of Christians altering "the original text of the gospel three or four or several times over...to deny difficulties in the face of criticism" (Origen, *Cels* 2.27).[24] He may be thinking of the differences between the four gospels and claiming that Christians were embarrassed by them.[25] Augustine, writing about A.D. 400, and probably with the third-century philosopher Porphyry in mind, speaks of "certain persons" whose main charge against Christianity is that "the evangelists are not in harmony with one another" (*Cons* 1.10; *NPNF* 6:81).[26]

The list could go on, but enough has been said to state an important conclusion: long before the Enlightenment or late modern concerns with the possibility of "objective" history, Christians were fighting a life-or-death struggle with pagan detractors and theological heretics over whether the events proclaimed in the orthodox version of the gospel really happened. It would not do to claim that historical inquiry, particularly by unbelievers, could not damage the status of these texts as Christian Scripture or interfere with the right of Christians to interpret them as they wished. Irenaeus and Augustine sensed correctly that the orthodox church's Scriptures made historical claims and that Christians who wanted to remain credible and orthodox before a skeptical audience of pagans and heretics needed to do battle with their detractors on the common field of historical inquiry.

The gospel continues to make historical claims in our time, and because these claims lie at the root of its proclamation, the church must be willing to submit these claims to historical analysis. Moreover, because the earliest witnesses to the gospel's historical claims are texts contained in the church's canon, this analysis will have to be performed on Christianity's sacred Scriptures. To go even further, believers and

---

[24] Origen, *Contra Celsum*, trans. and ed. Henry Chadwick (Cambridge: Cambridge University Press, 1953) 90.

[25] Ibid., 90n2.

[26] On this, see Robert Wilken, *The Christians as the Romans Saw Them* (New Haven CT: Yale University Press, 1984) 144–45.

unbelievers can engage in historical analysis with roughly similar levels of competence, and so the church has little to fear and much to gain from the insights of even unbelieving historians. Like a meteor's crater in the desert, as C. F. D. Moule has aptly put it, the evidence that remains to us of the beginnings of the Christian movement reveal a massive event of overwhelming proportions centered on Jesus of Nazareth. Most of this evidential crater is made up of what Christians now call Scripture, and the most rigorous historical inquiry shows how reasonable Christian claims about the identity of Jesus are.[27]

Second, because the church has recognized its Scriptures as apostolically grounded testimony, they also function as the criteria by which the church's theological speculation must be judged. In light of various kinds of false teaching, Paul found it necessary to recall Christians to the tradition of the gospel that he and other apostles accepted as true and had handed on to them (2 Thess 2:1–2; 3:6; Gal 1:6–9; 2:6–10; 1 Cor 15:1–11; 1 Tim 6:20; 2 Tim 1:14). The "many deceivers" abroad who denied that Jesus had "come in the flesh" (2 John 7) led the Elder to tell the community over which he presided that their fellowship was built on the common conviction of the humanity of Jesus, a conviction based on the Elder's eyewitness testimony (1 John 1:1–3). Jude, in view of an especially insidious false teaching that had infected the churches, had to remind his readers of the apostles' teaching (Jude 3, 17). Second Peter, similarly, refutes those who scoff at the notion of Jesus' second coming (2 Pet 3:3–4) by recalling that this notion is based on apostolic eyewitness testimony (2 Pet 1:16).

Much later, Irenaeus became intensely annoyed with Marcion because of the disingenuous historical method he used to support his false teaching. Marcion selected one gospel out of the four (Luke), and mutilated it: "He persuaded his disciples that he himself was more worthy of credit than are those apostles who have handed down the Gospel to us, furnishing them not with the Gospel, but merely a fragment of it" (*Her* 1.27.2; *ANF* 1:352).

Again, examples could be multiplied, but this list shows that from the earliest days the church settled theological disputes by an appeal to

---

[27] C. F. D. Moule, "The Holy Spirit and Scripture," in *Forgiveness and Reconciliation and Other New Testament Themes* (London: SPCK, 1998) 220.

something roughly similar to present-day historical and exegetical methods. In the thinking of these early Christians, the church could refute "progressive" theologies that claimed Jesus was not really human (2 John 9) or scoffers who said there was no coming judgment and therefore nothing to fear from ethical irresponsibility (2 Pet 3:3–4) by appealing to the most historically reliable testimony about Jesus' teaching. The validity of this approach has not faded with time, even in an era when appeal to what "actually happened" and to texts with "meanings" seems hermeneutically unsophisticated.

Only in this way can the text, in the end, actually stand over us, correcting our tendencies to develop unfaithful theologies and to read the Christian Scriptures and the Christian tradition in self-serving ways. Cultivating forgiveness, reconciliation, and charity toward those with whom we disagree can, as Fowl says, go a long way toward preventing Christian communities from inappropriate readings.[28] In the end, however, the text can only actually stand over us, correcting our sinful tendencies and theological errors, if we can find out basically what happened and discover what the text essentially means.

The story of New Testament scholar and Tübingen professor Gerhard Kittel is instructive on this point. In the early twentieth century, Kittel was one of the world's most widely respected Christian scholars in the field of first-century Judaism.[29] From 1928 until 1945 he was the editor of the monumental, and still influential, *Theologisches Wörterbuch zum Neuen Testament.*[30] Much to the embarrassment of those of us who still find "Kittel" useful, however, he also joined Germany's National Socialist Party in 1933, was a member of the Nazi organization Reichsinstitut für Geschichte des neuen Deutschlands (National Institute for the History of the New Germany), and participated in an organization called Antijüdische Aktion (Anti-Jewish Action).[31] His

[28] Fowl, *Engaging Scripture*, 62–96.

[29] Wayne A. Meeks, "A Nazi New Testament Professor Reads His Bible: The Strange Case of Gerhard Kittel," in *The Idea of Biblical Interpretation: Essays in Honor of James L. Kugel*, ed. Hindy Najman and Judith H. Newman, Supplements to the Journal for the Study of Judaism 83 (Leiden: Brill, 2004) 515.

[30] Ibid., 534.

[31] Ibid., 516.

editorship of the *Theologisches Wörterbuch zum Neuen Testament* came to an end after four volumes because he was arrested by the French military in 1945 on the charge of war crimes.[32]

Kittel used his great learning in Hebrew and Talmudic studies to argue against the more violent expressions of anti-Semitism in the Nazi Party. Still, he thought the German *Volk* needed preservation from the corrupting effect of Jews living within their national borders, especially Jews who had assimilated to German culture. The mixing of the races, he maintained, did neither race any good. What was the solution to the present problem of racial mixture? Extermination and Zionism were impractical (and extermination would be wicked and unchristian), so the best solution, he said, was racial segregation, a policy that involved removing Jews from positions they currently occupied in education, government, and the professions.[33]

As late as December 1946 Kittel maintained from prison that his anti-Judaism was only an attempt to identify "sharply" the "presence of degeneration in modern as well as ancient Jewry." He claimed that he had engaged in nothing more than the kind of criticism that Jesus and Paul leveled at the Jews (citing Matt 23:15; John 8:40–44; and 1 Thess 2:15).[34]

Kittel's self-defense and the post-war testimonials of Jews who knew him during the war period reveal that he was, in his personal encounters with Jews, a decent and kind man and that he viewed his own scholarly treatments of the "Jewish question" as far more charitable than the virulently anti-Semitic researches of other Nazi Party members. It is reasonably clear that because these more reprehensible expressions of anti-Semitism formed his point of comparison, Kittel would have viewed himself and his interpretation of the Scriptures as forgiving and

---

[32] Robert P. Ericksen, *Theologians under Hitler: Gerhard Kittel, Paul Althaus, Emmanuel Hirsch* (New Haven CT: Yale University Press, 1985) 28; Meeks, "Kittel," 534. Kittel died on 11 July 1948 shortly after release from prison, and his editorial work passed to Gerhard Friedrich. Once complete, the project was eventually translated into English by G. W. Bromiley as the ten-volume *Theological Dictionary of the New Testament* (Grand Rapids MI: Eerdmans, 1964–1976).

[33] Ericksen, *Theologians under Hitler*, 56; Meeks, "Kittel," 516.

[34] Ericksen, *Theologians under Hitler*, 42–43.

conciliatory. He expressed dismay that such Jewish thinkers as Martin Buber disagreed with his views.[35]

Kittel needed something more than counsel to be charitable and forgiving in his reading of Scripture: he thought that he was doing those things. He needed instead to be reminded of two things, one historical and one exegetical: (1) Jesus and Paul were marginalized Jews speaking to Jews who were themselves marginalized by the dominant political power. They were not members of a powerful political party speaking to an oppressed minority. This historical distance makes a massive difference in how we appropriate the words of Jesus about the Pharisees and the words of Paul about the Jews today. (2) From Genesis to Revelation the movement of God's redemptive purposes includes the union, not the division, of races and nations. Hostility between these groups is a problem that the gospel overcomes, not a solution that it perpetuates (Gal 3:28; Eph 2:11–22; Col 3:11; Rev 7:9).[36]

Is such a "determined" reading of the text, however, even possible? Can we really speak of textual "meaning" without miring ourselves in hopeless ambiguity? This is not the place (nor do I have the ability) to mount a full-scale philosophical defense of the notion that we can more or less say what the biblical authors "meant" in any given passage.[37] It is necessary to concede that all interpreters approach the biblical text with presuppositions. It seems equally certain, however, that interpreters can, to the extent that they know themselves and their contexts well, account for their presuppositions in their exegetical and historical work and discipline their readings accordingly.[38]

---

[35] Ibid., 59–60. Ericksen, *Theologians under Hitler*, 29 comments that "Kittel reckoned himself on the side of the angels," and Meeks, "Kittel," 517 (cf. 543) says that it was a certain "culture of interpretation that made Kittel's paradoxical positions seem to him coherent."

[36] Jenson, *Works of God*, 278 is correct, therefore, to make room for some historical-critical reading of Scripture as a corrective to the tendency to deceive ourselves about what the text means.

[37] For such a defense, see Francis Watson, *Text and Truth: Redefining Biblical Theology* (Grand Rapids: Eerdmans, 1997) 95–126.

[38] On this, see Heikki Räisänen, *Beyond New Testament Theology: A Story and a Programme* (Philadelphia: Trinity Press International, 1990) 106–107.

The Christian church, therefore, needs the salutary restraint of historical inquiry into the meaning of its sacred texts in their original contexts. It needs this not for reasons related to intellectual freedom (*pace* Wrede) but for theological reasons. The gospel that calls the church into existence proclaims that certain saving events, such as the resurrection of Jesus from the dead, happened as certainly as Tiberius was Caesar, Pontius Pilate governed Judea, and Herod Antipas ruled Galilee. Without the occurrence of these saving events, there is no good news to proclaim. The church also needs to know what its Scriptures say if it is to resist interpreting them in selfish and heretical ways.

Historical method, by itself, however, can offer only a minimal account of what actually happened in the past. It seems to me that the failure of professional biblical scholars to realize this accounts for much of the frustration that both Fowl and Jenson so eloquently, and, I think, justifiably express. Fowl and Jenson know that the gospel is true, but they know this as a basic insight prompted by the Holy Spirit, not because historians of ancient religion have told them so.

Here, however, a scholar who is a philosopher and so something of a third party to the traditional debate between historians and theologians may help those who are nothing other than historians of religion to take seriously the claims of the Christian. Alvin Plantinga, in his book *Warranted Christian Belief*, makes the persuasive case that Christian faith in the existence of God or in the essential truthfulness of the Scriptures operates at the level of a basic belief similar in kind to the beliefs of most people that, for example, sensory perception and memory are reliable. When we look out the window and see a tiger lily in bloom we conclude that there is a tiger lily in the backyard, not on the basis of reasoned deduction but as a basic belief. When we remember a conversation with a friend, we trust that such a conversation actually happened, not because we have made a series of reasonable deductions proving such a thing as memory, but because we simply know that what our memory tells us is true. The reliability of our sensory perceptions and memory are basic beliefs, and it is not irrational or unreasonable to justify our knowledge by appealing to these basic beliefs.[39]

---

[39] Alvin Plantinga, *Warranted Christian Belief* (New York: Oxford University Press, 2000) 175–77, 413–14.

Neither is it irrational, argues Plantinga, to take into account a Christian's basic belief in the fundamental truthfulness of Scripture when subjecting the Scriptures to scholarly analysis. It is true that Ernst Troeltsch mounted an argument against such a notion that has become enormously influential, but from a philosophical perspective, his case is seriously flawed. Troeltsch believed that the historian of Christianity must adopt three methodological critera: criticism (that historical investigation cannot produce certain results), analogy (that all events are similar to all other events), and correlation (that every event has a cause).[40] The way he and others after him argue for this method shows that they think it necessarily brackets any appeal to God's intervention out of academically-responsible historical description.[41]

None of the three criteria, however, comes even close to offering compelling reasons for Christians to leave their faith out of account when reading their Scriptures. The criteria of criticism and correlation pose no problem for the Christian. Christians do not need historians to supply them with certain results. Since Christian faith is based in history, the historian could conceivably inform Christians of information that refuted historical claims central to their convictions, but the highly disputable and often contradictory results that historical-critical study of the Bible has so far yielded need not disturb Christian claims.[42] Similarly, the principle of correlation amounts to a platitude: all events have a cause. As long as God is not discounted from the beginning as a possible cause of some events, this principle poses no threat to traditional Christian faith. If God is discounted, the Christian may, with good reason, wonder why.[43]

If the Christian accepted the notion of natural law or natural necessity, then the criterion of analogy might pose a problem. Natural law, however, is a highly controversial philosophical notion, and it is not

---

[40] Plantinga, *Belief*, 391. Troeltsch's classic description of his approach in his essay "Historical and Dogmatic Method in Theology" (1898) is available in English in Ernst Troeltsch, *Religion in History*, trans. James Luther Adams and Walter F. Bense (Edinburgh: T & T Clark, 1991) 11–32.

[41] Plantinga, *Belief*, 393.

[42] Ibid., 391, 420–21. Here and occasionally elsewhere I am drawing inferences from Plantinga's argument rather than merely restating it.

[43] Plantinga, *Belief*, 391–92.

clear why the historian or the Christian should need to affirm this quaint seventeenth- and eighteenth-century notion.

Despite these problems, Troeltsch's method or variations on it continue to be defended among some biblical scholars. This defense, says Plantinga, usually takes three forms. First, proponents of the method claim that it is the only option open to moderns who participate in the present scientific community with its set of presuppositions. Second, they say that the internal prompting of the Holy Spirit is not a justified basis for knowledge about the matters on which the Bible speaks. Third, they claim that the approach of Troeltsch to the Bible is more inclusive than a faith-based approach because people of differing, contradictory, or no theological commitments can participate in it.

Plantinga has already shown at length that the second of these defenses is philosophically insupportable: a basic insight can form a rational warrant for belief. With respect to the first reason, he shows that the notion of a present scientific community unified around a series of modern presuppositions is a myth. Even if it were not, why would we want to follow a particular method simply because it prevented conclusions inconvenient to modern people? On the third point, Plantinga observes that a historical method that excludes God is actually less inclusive than one presupposing his involvement. Most people interested in the study of the Bible believe in God's involvement in historical affairs.[44]

Plantinga's argument is far more subtle and detailed than this brief summary has been able to indicate, but perhaps enough has been said to justify the conclusion that historians of early Christianity have something to learn from Christian theologians. Two lessons come immediately to mind.

First, biblical scholars who limit themselves to data gleaned and described using Troeltsch's historical method (or some slight variation of it) are not likely to garner much interest or support from most of the people interested in the biblical texts. These people, moreover, have good intellectual reasons for not finding such work attractive. Wayne Meeks describes the problem poignantly: "We [historical-critical New Testament scholars] find ourselves today approaching a state of complete

---

[44] Plantinga, *Belief*, 403–12.

isolation: within the university, lonely practitioners of a quaintly antiquated craft; in the larger world, distant voices scarcely heard within communities of faith and, in the noisy public realm informed by global corporate media, not noticed at all except when we say something truly outrageous."[45] Perhaps at least some of the problem lies with an attempt to exclude Christian faith from involvement in the craft as an unfortunate intrusion from the world of naive superstition into an otherwise intellectually respectable discipline.[46] Yet Plantinga has shown that Christian faith in the historicity of the central events recorded in Scripture is not irrational: it flows from a basic insight. Professors of religion at secular or secularizing educational institutions might dispute the truthfulness of this basic insight, but Plantinga's philosophical considerations should give them pause before they present the results of historical-critical biblical scholarship to their students as if these results render traditional Christian religious commitments intellectually unjustified.

Second, Christian theologians remind believing biblical scholars that they should not be embarrassed about their faith commitments as they go about their historical and linguistic work. They should also not feel entirely satisfied if their discipline only advances historical knowledge of ancient texts and never contributes to the articulation and deeper understanding of the Christian faith. It is probably not possible fully to separate their work as historians who handle the biblical texts from their faith as Christians who believe that the Bible is God's Word. Plantinga shows us, however, that such a separation is not, in the end, desirable. The church keeps the discipline of biblical scholarship afloat. Those of us who participate in the discipline owe the church the debt of making the results of our work available to it.[47]

---

[45] Meeks, "Why Study," 163.

[46] Jenson speaks of "the methodological irrationality and parasitism of late-modern academic biblical study" (*Triune God*, 58–59n96) and Plantinga of "elitism run amok" (*Belief*, 409). On the whole problem, see the perceptive treatment of Robert W. Yarbrough, *The Salvation Historical Fallacy? Reassessing the History of New Testament Theology*, History of Biblical Interpretation 2 (Leiden: Deo, 2004).

[47] Jenson puts it this way: "Biblical scholars who define their status as critics by their independence of church or synagogue end, as should have been

This does not mean that we give our theological presuppositions free reign and consider ourselves failures if systematic theologians cannot find some practical "application" for our work. The church has a *theological* interest in historically accurate exegesis because its theology is bound up with its history and because it stands under the authority of the Bible. The marriage, therefore, must endure.

---

antecedently obvious, with no entity to be the object of their scholarship" (*Triune God*, 58n96).

Back to the Future of Trinitarianism?

CURTIS W. FREEMAN

Just after the revised Baptist Faith and Message (BFM) had been approved by the 1963 Southern Baptist Convention, James Wm. McClendon offered a penetrating vision of the future of Trinitarianism in Baptist life. He suggested that with a few changes of terms the language about the Trinity in the BFM might just as well be used to describe "the structure of a denominational agency" or "the floor plan of a new church building."[1] No doubt the key to Baptists becoming the *de facto* established church of the South had more to do with organization and buildings than theology. But McClendon maintained that the guidebook tone of the confession, which reads like a quick tour through a theological museum, reflected a growing indifference to Trinitarian faith and practice. In many respects, the state of Trinitarianism among Baptists today is little different than it was four decades ago. When asked "What is the doctrine of the Trinity?" most Baptists are probably not far from Dorothy Sayers's catechism of the average churchgoer, which answers: "The Father incomprehensible, the Son incomprehensible, and the whole thing incomprehensible."[2]

This trend toward doctrinal lethargy notwithstanding, Baptists in America seem to recognize the importance of the Trinity as evidenced in the long-standing tradition of placing "Holy, Holy, Holy" as the first hymn in the hymnal.[3] Yet this apparent liturgical priority is not matched

---

[1] James Wm. McClendon, "Some Reflections on the Future of Trinitarianism," *Review and Expositor* 63 (Spring 1966): 150. McClendon examines the language from the then newly approved Baptist Faith and Message (1963 and 1925) as well as the New Hampshire Confession (1833). I would like to thank Fisher Humphreys for calling my attention to McClendon's article.

[2] Dorothy Sayers, *Creed or Chaos* (New York: Harcourt, Brace, 1949) 22.

[3] *The New Baptist Hymnal* (Nashville: Broadman Press, 1926), which was "prepared under the direct supervision of...The American Baptist Publication

with theological integrity. For example, in *The Baptist Hymnal* (1991), out of 666 hymns only twenty are Trinitarian (a ratio of approximately 1:32), but 268 of these 666 hymns are Christological (a ratio of approximately 1:1.5). Baptist worship currently tilts toward unitarianism of the Second Person, just as on occasions in the past it leaned in the direction of unitarianism of the First Person.[4] It seems that the Trinity remains for Baptists a doctrine to be held despite its apparent lack of theological coherence or practical relevance. What has been done to take up the challenge to retrieve Trinitarian faith and practice since McClendon's critique in 1966?

Baptist Theology and the Trinitarian Resurgence

For most Baptists and other evangelical Christians, the Trinity is an obscure teaching about an inscrutable mystery that must simply be believed. This doctrinal obscurity is wonderfully stated by John Leland, the post-revolutionary-era Virginia Baptist minister:

> There are three that bear record in heaven, the Father, the Word, and the Holy Ghost, and these three are one. This is a

---

Society...and The Sunday School Board of the Southern Baptist Convention," was the first to place "Holy, Holy, Holy" as the first hymn. It was followed by *The Baptist Hymnal* (Nashville: Convention Press, 1956); *The Baptist Hymnal* (Nashville: Convention Press, 1975); *The New National Baptist Hymnal* (Nashville: National Baptist Publishing Board, 1982); and *The Baptist Hymnal* (Nashville: Convention Press, 1991). The English Baptist hymnals have a more Trinitarian structure. The initial section of hymns that pertains to the call to worship is followed by sections on the Holy Trinity, God the Father, God the Son, and God the Holy Spirit. See *The Baptist Church Hymnal* (London: Psalms and Hymns Trust, 1900); *The Baptist Church Hymnal* (London: Psalms and Hymns Trust, 1933); and *The Baptist Hymn Book* (London: Psalms and Hymns Trust, 1962).

[4] G. Ernest Wright attributed the phrase "Unitarianism of the Second Person" to Elton Trueblood, who applied it to Christology at the first assembly of the World Council of Churches, which met in 1948 in Amsterdam, in *The Old Testament and Theology* (New York: Harper and Row, 1969) 24. However, two years earlier H. Richard Niebuhr delineated three unitarianisms in Christianity (i.e., of the Father, the Son, and the Spirit) in "The Doctrine of the Trinity and the Unity of the Church," *Theology Today* 3 (October 1946): 371–84.

> doctrine of revelation, for a confirmation of which, baptism is performed in the name of the Father, Son and Holy Ghost: but, like the ark of the Hebrews, it is too awful to be pryed into by curious eyes. When eternity can be fathomed and immensity measured—when creation can be accounted for, and the resurrection from the dead be philosophized—when the hidden mystery of God manifest in the flesh, and the guilty sinner being pardoned for the sufferings of an innocent Saviour, are clearly understood, then, and not till then, will limited creatures comprehend the incomprehensible doctrine of a three-one God. If the works of God are past finding out, surely the author of those works must be so.[5]

Leland was not the first Baptist, nor was he the last, to declare the Trinity an arcane but necessary doctrine. British Baptist pastor and theologian Andrew Fuller affirmed of the Trinity that "whether we can comprehend it or not, we are required humbly to believe it."[6] Alvah Hovey, president and professor of theology at Newton Theological Institution, made an even stronger admission: "We call the doctrine of the triune God a mystery, not so much because it is a *revealed* truth as because it is an *obscure* truth."[7] The "blind faith" attitude of Leland, Fuller, and Hovey illustrates the theological indifference toward the Trinity that is reflected in the twentieth-century Baptist confessions of faith.[8]

Although few recognized it at the time, McClendon's perceptive vision was being swept along an initial wave of Trinitarian resurgence.

---

[5] John Leland, "Thoughts" in *The Writings of the Late Elder John Leland*, ed. L. F. Greene (New York: G. W. Wood, 1845; repr., New York: Arno Press, 1969) 534.

[6] Andrew Fuller, *Letters on Systematic Divinity*, letter 9 in *The Complete Works of the Rev. Andrew Fuller*, 3 vols. (Philadelphia: American Baptist Publication Society, 1845; repr., Harrisonburg VA: Sprinkle Publications, 1988) 1:708.

[7] Alvah Hovey, "The Biblical Doctrine of the Trinity," in *Baptist Doctrines*, ed. Charles A. Jenkens (St. Louis: Chancy R. Barns, 1880) 362.

[8] For a more detailed account of this Baptist indifference to the Trinity, see my article "God in Three Persons: Baptist Unitarianism and the Trinity," *Perspectives in Religious Studies* 33 (Fall 2006).

D. M. Baillie attributed this renewed interest in the Trinity to two factors: the *Church Dogmatics* of Karl Barth, which began in the first *loci* with the revelation of the triune God, and the rediscovery of the social Trinitarianism of the Cappadocian Fathers.[9] Barth's *Dogmatics* appeared just as theological liberalism, which greatly reduced the significance of the Trinity, was reaching a state of bankruptcy.[10] For Barth, the doctrine of the Trinity is what "fundamentally distinguishes the Christian doctrine of God as Christian."[11] By placing an emphasis of the threefold character of God as Revealer, Revelation, and Revealedness, Barth returned the Trinity to the very center of theological reflection. He further strengthened the resurgence of Trinitarian theology by drawing resources from the biblical theology movement that provided theologians with a way of construing the Eternal Father, Son, and Spirit through the sweep of the biblical narrative as Creator, Reconciler, and Redeemer.[12] Barth inspired a new generation of theological reflections on the Immanent Trinity.[13] The Cappadocian emphasis on social relations in the Trinity established a second trend for retrieving the tradition of Trinitarian theology, which is represented in the work of

---

[9] D. M. Baillie, *God Was in Christ* (New York: Charles Scribner's Sons, 1948) 133–40. Bruce D. Marshall traces the twentieth-century renaissance of Trinitarianism to Karl Barth (on the Protestant side) and Karl Rahner (on the Catholic side) in "Trinity," in *The Blackwell Companion to Modern Theology*, ed. Gareth Jones (Oxford: Blackwell Publishing, 2004) 183–203, esp.

[10] Friederich Schleiermacher's placement of the Trinity in the conclusion of his *Glaubenslehre* indicated the marginality of Trinitarian theology in liberalism. Schleiermacher located the doctrine there because he believed the Trinity was "ecclesiastically framed" and "not an immediate utterance concerning Christian self-consciousness," in Friedrich Schleiermacher, *The Christian Faith*, ed. and trans. H. R. Macintosh and J. S. Stewart (Philadelphia: Fortress Press, 1976) 738–51, § 170–72.

[11] Karl Barth, *Church Dogmatics*, I/1, trans. G. W. Bromiley (Edinburgh: T. & T. Clark, 1975) 346.

[12] Barth, *Church Dogmatics*, I/1, 295–489.

[13] See T. F. Torrance, *Theology in Reconstruction* (London: SCM Press, 1965), *The Trinitarian Faith* (Edinburgh: T. & T. Clark, 1988), *Trinitarian Perspectives* (Edinburgh: T. & T. Clark, 1994), *The Christian Doctrine of God: One Being, Three Persons* (Edinburgh: T. & T. Clark, 1996), and *Karl Barth, Biblical and Evangelical Theologian* (Edinburgh: T. & T. Clark, 1990).

such theologians as Leonard Hodgson, Jürgen Moltmann, and John Zizioulas.[14] The Barthian emphasis on "modes of being" in the Godhead was offset by the rich personalism of the social Trinity, and the doctrine of *perichoresis*, in which there is a mutual permeation of each person of the Trinity by the others, held the three divine Persons in a communion of being.[15]

Subsequent revisions of the Baptist Faith and Message have not drawn significantly from the resurgence in Trinitarian theology, but some Southern Baptist theologians have.[16] Dale Moody's systematic

---

[14] Leonard Hodgson, *The Doctrine of the Trinity* (London: Nisbet, 1944); Jürgen Moltmann, *The Trinity and the Kingdom of God* (San Francisco: Harper, 1981); and John Zizioulas, *Being as Communion* (Crestwood: St. Vladimir's, 1985).

[15] The doctrine of Trinitarian *perichoresis* has its origins in the Fourth Gospel, in which Jesus says to the disciple community, "Believe me that I am in the Father and the Father is in me" (John 14:11). The eighth-century church father John of Damascus explained the Trinitarian relations in terms of *perichoresis* that suggested something of the circular character of the divine life. Moltmann states the doctrine of *perichoresis* simply: "The Father exists in the Son, the Son in the Father, and both of them in the Spirit, just as the Spirit exists in both the Father and the Son" (*The Trinity and the Kingdom of God*, 174–75). The personal characteristics of the divine persons distinguish them from each other find in *perichoresis* a unity that binds them one to another. Moltmann observes that "the doctrine of *perichoresis* links together in a brilliant way the threeness and the unity, without reducing the threeness to the unity, or dissolving the unity to threeness" (*The Trinity and the Kingdom of God*, 175). Later theologians of the West began to speak about the *circumincessio* of the Trinitarian persons, by which they meant that each person of the Trinity is contained in the others and (more actively) interpenetrates the others. It is in this active sense of interpenetration that *perichoresis* (and *circumincessio*) began to be understood as a dance. The word *perichoresis* is not derived from *perichoreuo* ("to dance around") from which we get our word choreography, but it became understood as a play on words. It took on the sense of the divine dance in which the Son indwells the Father, the Father contains the Son, the Spirit fills the Father.

[16] The only apparent revision of the Baptist Faith and Message 2000 pertaining to the Trinity was the addition of the word "triune" (an anti-modalism gesture?) to article 2 on God so that it reads: "The eternal triune God reveals Himself to us as Father, Son, and Holy Spirit, with distinct personal attributes, but without division of nature, essence, or being."

theology, *The Word of Truth*, published in 1981, contains a section on "the modes of God's being" (as an allusion to Barth?) in which he treated the Trinity in an economic and ontological perspective. Moody concluded that the doctrine of the Trinity was a logical development of biblical monotheism rather than a deviation, and he suggested that Trinitarian discussions in the history of the church retained the apostolic witness to "the oneness in the threeness and the threeness in the oneness."[17] Moody's insistence on a thoroughgoing biblical theology as the means of retrieving the apostolic origin of Trinitarian faith adapted well to historic Baptist biblicism, although his treatment of the post-apostolic writings does little to display the rich development in Trinitarian doctrine by the Cappadocians and other patristic theologians.

A decade after the publication of Moody's book, his former colleague James Leo Garrett published his own *Systematic Theology*, which contains an encyclopedic account of the biblical and historical development of Trinitarian faith. Garrett is conscious that the Baptist penchant for biblicism seems to lead to the sort of Trinitarian indifference described by McClendon, and he is aware that on occasion it has even been used to justify a functional unitarianism, as in the case of Frank Stagg, his former New Testament colleague at Southern Seminary, who seemed to conclude "from absence of the word 'Trinity' in the New Testament that there is no Three-in-Oneness taught in the New Testament."[18] Consequently, Garrett carefully describes how the Scriptures attest to the divine triunity, and after discussing the unitarian, modalist, and tritheistic alternatives to the Trinity, he offers a rich

---

[17] Dale Moody, *The Word of Truth* (Grand Rapids: Wm. B. Eerdmans Publishing Company) 120.

[18] Garrett cites Stagg as an example of how simple biblicism gets invoked in support of a unitarian view of God, in James Leo Garrett Jr., *Systematic Theology: Biblical, Historical, and Evangelical*, 2 vols. (Grand Rapids: Wm. B. Eerdmans, 1990) 1:271n28. Robert Sloan similarly argues that Stagg does not "take seriously enough the particularly Trinitarian language of the New Testament, given his hints that specifically *tri*-nitarian (as opposed to *bi*-nitarian or even other numeric models) language is not binding theologically," in *Baptist Theologians*, ed. Timothy George and David S. Dockery (Nashville: Broadman Press, 1990) 512.

account of the historical development of Trinitarian theology.[19] Yet as a confirmation that at the time of his writing the future of Trinitarianism was still in question among Southern Baptists, Garrett observed that none of their theological journals had published a thematic issue devoted to the Trinity.[20] Sixteen years after Garrett's book and forty years after McClendon's article, two Baptist periodicals issued thematic volumes on the Trinity in the same year, one of which was edited by Fisher Humphreys.[21]

It is difficult to name a Baptist theologian who has given more consistent or creative reflection to Trinitarian theology than Humphreys has throughout his career. His book *Thinking About God*, first published in 1974 and revised in 1994, contains a chapter on the Trinity as the capstone of Christian doctrines.[22] Like Barth, Humphreys contends that "the Trinity is the most distinctive doctrine in the Christian religion,"[23] but rather than beginning his theology as Barth did with an account of the revelation of the triune God, Humphreys considers the Trinity in the final chapter of his book. He explains that this placement of the Trinity at the conclusion of the doctrinal sequence is deliberate because locating it ahead of other doctrines makes it "seem superfluous."[24]

---

[19] Garrett, *Systematic Theology*, 1:262–88.

[20] Ibid., 288 n 54.

[21] *Perspectives in Religious Studies* 33 (Fall 2006), the journal of the National Association of Baptist Professors of Religion, and *The Southern Baptist Journal of Theology* 10 (Spring 2006), published by the Southern Baptist Theological Seminary.

[22] Fisher Humphreys, *Thinking about God: An Introduction to Christian Theology* (New Orleans: Insight Press, 1994) 235–57. His other major discussions of the Trinity may be found in *The Nature of God* (Nashville: Broadman Press, 1985) 128–39 and "Father, Son and Holy Spirit," *The Theological Educator* 12 (Spring 1982): 78–96. There is an abbreviated account in *A Dictionary of Theological Terms* (Nashville: Broadman Press, 1983) s.v. "Trinity," 125–28.

[23] Humphreys, "Father, Son and Holy Spirit," 78.

[24] Humphreys, *Thinking about God*, 11. Humphreys also places the Trinity as the capstone chapter of his book *The Nature of God*, 128–39. In a review article of Paul K. Jewett, *God, Creation, and Revelation: A Neo-Evangelical Theology* (Grand Rapids: Wm. B. Eerdmans Publishing Company, 1991), Humphreys takes issue with Jewett's placement of the Trinity in the discussion. Humphrey states, "It seems artificial to me…to put the doctrine of the Trinity ahead of the doctrines

Humphreys follows what he believes is a more systematic approach that treats the Trinity only after the revelation of God, the person of Christ, and the presence of the Spirit.

Although Unitarians and some Pentecostals admittedly deny the Trinity, Humphreys insists that it is still "one of the most universal beliefs in Christendom."[25] Yet despite the fact that the Trinity is an almost universally held Christian doctrine, he observes that modern Baptist theologians have paid surprisingly little attention to it.[26] For example, he characterizes the treatment of the Trinity by E. Y. Mullins as "unbalanced," noting that "Mullins devotes, out of the 2,000 pages in his six major books, only nine pages to this great teaching."[27] But Baptists are not alone in their impoverished Trinitarianism. Humphreys notes that evangelical theologians have not done justice to the doctrine either. He praises Paul Jewett's book *God, Creation, and Revelation* as an exception, saying: "His doctrine of the Trinity is strong enough that he is entitled to think of his theology as orthodox—something that, unfortunately, is not the case with some fundamentalist and evangelical theologies."[28]

Humphreys qualifies his assessment of Baptist and evangelical theology as insufficiently attentive to the Trinity by explaining that a weak Trinitarianism does not necessarily imply anti-Trinitarianism.

---

of the person of Christ and the Holy Spirit. Because he follows the tradition of placing the doctrine early, Jewett is obliged to deal in a preliminary way with Christology and the doctrine of the Spirit, and the result is not satisfying" (Fisher Humphreys, "A Neo-Evangelical Systematic Theology," *Perspectives in Religious Studies* 19 [Summer 1992]: 223).

[25] Humphreys, "Father, Son and Holy Spirit," 78.

[26] Though Trinitarian doctrine became marginalized among Protestant theologians in the nineteenth century, Humphreys's edited book on *Nineteenth Century Evangelical Theology* (Nashville: Broadman Press, 1983) contains fifty-six selections, two of which are on the Trinity. For a fuller account of the surprising eclipse of Trinitarianism in Baptist theology, see my article "God in Three Persons."

[27] Fisher Humphreys, "E. Y. Mullins," in *Baptist Theologians*, ed. Timothy George and David Dockery (Nashville: Broadman Press 1990) 330–50, esp.

[28] Humphreys, "A Neo-Evangelical Systematic Theology," 222–23 on Paul K. Jewett, *God, Creation and Revelation* (Grand Rapids: Wm. B. Eerdmans Publishing Company, 1991).

Indeed, Humphreys claims that Baptists and "the vast majority of Christians are Trinitarian in their faith and life, in the same sense in which the Christians of the New Testament were Trinitarian in their faith and life."[29] Christians, Humphreys maintains, confront the reality of the Trinity through a living tradition in which "we see God as triune out of the corner of our eye, as it were."[30] Those who contend that theology is shaped by Scripture alone rather than Christian tradition may flinch at this suggestion, but Humphreys explains that the most fundamental convictions about God are shaped by a living tradition that "is transmitted in worship, in hymns, in baptism, in the vocabulary of the church, and in formal confessions of faith."[31] Even sermons can be means of transmitting the tradition of Trinitarian faith. Yet preaching, Humphreys admits, is too rarely used as a means of articulating the doctrine of the Trinity, and the Trinitarian images in liturgy, hymnody, and spirituality have grown so dim among Baptists and other evangelicals as to be virtually imperceptible, especially when viewed "out of the corner of our eye."

Given that the full-orbed descriptions of the Trinity do not appear until the third and fourth centuries, Humphreys explains that Christians who adhere to a biblicist theology face a particular challenge: "If we believed, as many of our Roman Catholic friends do, that the traditions of the church were equally as revelatory as the Bible, then it would be quite easy to say that the doctrine of the Trinity is a revealed doctrine."[32] Christians who accept the supremacy of Scripture, however, cannot simply point to church tradition as the source of Trinitarian doctrine, but neither does appealing to biblical teaching alone yield satisfactory results. Humphreys proposes an alternative that mediates between biblicism and traditionalism by viewing the apostolic tradition as witnessed in Scripture. This approach attempts to come to terms with the fact that for generations before the New Testament was settled, the communities that produced the canon of Scripture sang hymns, proclaimed the gospel, baptized converts, celebrated the Eucharist,

---

[29] Humphreys, *Thinking about God*, 236.

[30] Humphreys, "Father, Son and Holy Spirit," 79.

[31] Ibid., 80.

[32] Humphreys, *The Nature of God*, 129.

prayed in the Spirit, and confessed the faith. Early Christians did not keep these practices because they were instructed in Scripture how to do so. Rather, because the canon was shaped by these practices, it reflects their observance, which was already firmly established, and explains why the New Testament gives surprisingly little instruction about how to keep these most basic practices.[33]

To display from the Scriptures how the faith and life of the earliest Christian communities was shaped by Trinitarian practices, Humphreys suggests the use of historical criticism. Such an examination, he contends, will reveal that "the community which produced the writings of the New Testament practiced a Trinitarian religion."[34] Humphreys identifies five practices that he thinks indicate the Trinitarian faith and life of apostolic Christianity. First, primitive Christians worshiped one God who they knew as the Father of Jesus Christ their Lord, and they lived a common life together through the Holy Spirit. Second, they proclaimed the *kerygma*, which announced the fulfillment of God's plan through the coming of Jesus and the presence of the Holy Spirit. Third, they baptized in the triune name of the Father, Son, and Holy Spirit. Fourth, they offered prayers and benedictions in which the three persons of the Trinity were invoked. Fifth, they confessed their faith by means of triadic formulas.[35]

Although some Baptists may believe that the Trinity is a speculative construct invented by people too much influenced by Greek philosophy

---

[33] Ibid., and "Father, Son, and Holy Spirit," 82–84.

[34] Humphreys, "Father, Son and Holy Spirit," 82. The suggestion that historical criticism might be an unlikely ally in recovering the Trinitarian theology of earliest Christianity is indeed ironic given that much of the energy driving historical criticism has been the interest in disengaging biblical and dogmatic theology. Humphreys does not provide a detailed account that demonstrates how historical critical analysis might support a Trinitarian reading of Scripture. C. Kavin Rowe may offer the sort of study Humphreys imagines. From the Lukan birth-infancy narrative, Rowe unpacks the implications for Trinitarian theology in the Gospel of Luke in "Luke and the Trinity: An Essay in Ecclesial Biblical Theology," *Scottish Journal of Theology* 56/1 (2003): 1–26. In another important article, Rowe displays how a Trinitarian hermeneutic operates more generally in "Biblical Pressure and Trinitarian Hermeneutics," *Pro Ecclesia* 11/3 (Summer 2002): 295–312.

[35] Humphreys, "Father, Son and Holy Spirit," 83–83.

and too little by the Bible, Humphreys argues, "This simply is not true."[36] He shows that "the people who developed the official Trinitarian doctrine were themselves people who shared a Trinitarian faith and life like the one we have seen in the New Testament churches."[37] If the Scriptures provide a historical witness to the Trinity as underlying the very foundation of apostolic Christianity, Humphreys wonders then why Baptists have produced so few books on the subject. As Leland, Fuller, and Hovey indicate, the answer is due in part to the perception that the Trinity is an impenetrable mystery. Humphreys makes no attempt to provide a rational justification for the divine three-in-oneness. Indeed, he doubts that many people find such philosophical arguments very helpful.[38] Instead he seeks to clarify what Christians mean when they confess their faith in the Holy Trinity. Drawing from Leonard Hodgson's work, Humphreys depends mainly on the social analogy to describe the mysterious unity of the three-person God as organic rather than mathematical. "God is one," he writes, "because of the powerful love which binds together Father, Son, and Holy Spirit."[39] Given that this love is most completely revealed in the death of Christ, about which Humphreys has thought and written much, and that he expresses an affinity for social Trinitarianism, it is puzzling that he does not reflect on the Trinitarian implications of the cross.[40]

---

[36] Humphreys, *Thinking about God*, 244.

[37] Ibid.

[38] Humphreys, *The Nature of God*, 133.

[39] Humphreys, "Leonard Hodgson," *Theological Educator* 40 (Fall 1989): 23–24. See also Humphreys, *Thinking about God*, 249–53 and *The Nature of God*, 133–37.

[40] Fisher Humphreys, *The Death of Christ* (Nashville: Broadman Press, 1978) and "The Mystery of the Cross," *Perspectives in Religious Studies* 14 (Winter 1987): 47–52. One prominent example of Trinitarian reflection on the cross is provided by Jürgen Moltmann who proposed the highly controversial view that Jesus' cry of dereliction was actually the expression of his abandonment, "which separates the Son from the Father," that is, a Trinitarian event—"within God"; see his *The Crucified God* (New York: Harper and Row, 1974) 151–52. This theopassionist Christology led Moltmann to explore an even more radically social Trinitarian account of the cross in which the Son loses his sonship, the Father loses his fatherhood, and the love that binds them becomes a curse. See Jürgen Moltmann, *The Trinity and the Kingdom* (San Francisco: Harper and Row,

On the whole, however, Humphreys suggests along the lines of McClendon's earlier critique that Baptists probably find the Trinity more irrelevant than irrational. To counter this indifference, Humphreys avers that a Trinitarian understanding of God is relevant to religious practice, Christian worship, evangelical preaching, ecumenical relations, orthodox theology, and human existence.[41] Indeed, he contends that the Trinity suffuses the whole of Christian theology and that without the Trinity Christianity would simply be unintelligible. Humphreys presents a strong case for retrieving Trinitarian faith and practice, although as he sadly admits that the doctrine of the Trinity is still viewed by many Baptists as a Roman Catholic doctrine. He recounts the story of a former student who preached a sermon on the Trinity, only to be confronted by one of the church deacons who asked, "Preacher, why are you talking to us about that Roman Catholic stuff?"[42] Yet with great patience Humphreys reminds his fellow Baptists that the Trinity is not a denominational doctrine. It is the view of God shared by all Christians, and he suggests that a more robust Trinitarian faith and life for Baptists lies on the road to their recovery of catholicity. Indeed, Humphreys candidly admits that a recovery of Trinitarian theology will require getting over the Baptist fascination with denominational identity. He confesses, "Although I am a loyal and happy Baptist and plan to remain thus all my life, I have a deeper commitment to the universal Christian heritage, to that which is catholic, than I do even to our beloved Baptist distinctives."[43] Is it possible that Baptists might retrieve a more Trinitarian faith and practice from the rich storehouse of the catholic tradition?

1981) 80. There are ample opportunities for Humphreys still to indicate the Trinitarian implications of his earlier work on Christology and the atonement, which it is hoped that he will do.

[41] Humphreys, *Thinking about God*, 253–56, *The Nature of God*, 137–39, and "Father, Son and Holy Spirit," 89–92.

[42] Humphreys, review of *The Catholicity of the Reformation*, ed. Carl E. Braaten and Robert W. Jenson, *The Catholicity of the Church*, by Avery Dulles, and *Soul of the World*, by George Wiegal, in *Perspectives in Religious Studies* 26 (Spring 1999): 95.

[43] Ibid.

Toward a Trinitarian Ressourcement among Baptists

At the same time that some Catholics were beginning to follow the direction of the Second Vatican Council by opening up theological windows to the outside world, others were exploring anew the vast storehouse of the Catholic tradition. The aim of this *ressourcement* movement was to return to the classic texts of Christianity with an eye toward a retrieval of the tradition and a renewal of the faith.[44] It is clear that Baptists have all but lost their connection with the Trinitarian faith and practice of historic Christianity and are in need of restoration. If there is to be a Baptist *ressourcement*, what are the contours along which such a movement might proceed? As Humphreys so simply stated, the way of Trinitarian renewal for Baptists lies in reconnecting with "the universal Christian heritage...which is catholic." When Humphreys published his 1982 article "Father, Son, and Holy Spirit," he commented that "Baptists have produced very few books about the Trinity."[45] Thankfully, that is no longer the case. Baptist theologians today are contributing to Trinitarian theological discussions more broadly as well as offering reflections addressed to their denominational family of origin. That Baptist theologians are already engaged in such serious work is a sign of a hopeful future for Trinitarianism among Baptists. What follows are the vectors of a Baptist *ressourcement* that is already in progress.

Recovery of the Biblical Narrative. Early Baptists accepted the doctrine of the Trinity based on a simple biblicism. Alluding to the warrant of 1 John 5:7, John Leland exclaimed, "That there are three that bare record in heaven, and that these three are one, I believe, because

---

[44] The ressourcement movement, sometimes known as "new theology" (or *La nouvelle théologie*) was connected with mostly French theologians, including Henri de Lubac, Jean Daniélou, and Yves Congar as well as with Swiss theologian Hans Urs von Balthasar. See Fergus Kerr, "French Theology: Yves Congar and Henri de Lubac," in *The Modern Theologians*, ed. David F. Ford, 2nd ed. (Cambridge and Oxford: Blackwell Publishers, 1997) 105–17. The series Ressourcement: Retrieval and Renewal in Catholic Thought, published by Wm. B. Eerdmans, is in the process of making many of the ressourcement writings available, some for the first time in English.

[45] Humphreys, "Father, Son and Holy Spirit," 92 n 5.

God has said it; but I cannot understand it."[46] After textual criticism revealed the Johannine Comma to be a spurious interpolation, Baptist theologians were left with no text that clearly set forth the doctrine of the Trinity. Although it took time for the scholarly opinion to trickle down to the popular level of preachers like Leland, the more learned ones turned to a plodding propositionalism to defend Trinitarian theology by presenting the "Scriptural facts" about the unity of God, the plurality of the Godhead, and the personality and deity of each person.[47] The return to biblical narrative in the theology of Karl Barth and such postliberal successors as Hans Frei and George Lindbeck has enabled theologians to move beyond propositionalism and historicism by construing Scripture as the story of the triune God.[48] The most prominent voice in the movement to recover biblical narrative as a means of reconnecting Baptists with classical Trinitarian theology is James Wm. McClendon's. A quick glance at the broad outline of volume 2 of his *Doctrine: Systematic Theology* indicates a deep Trinitarian structure that begins with the rule of God, proceeds to the identity of Jesus Christ, and concludes with the fellowship of the Spirit. McClendon contends that although "the Trinitarian doctrine does not appear in Scripture" the doctrine of the Trinity "was invented in order to encode and protect what does appear in Scripture, the one God who is truly

---

[46] John Leland, "Thoughts," 534.

[47] The most influential Anglo critic who showed the comma to be a spurious interpolation was Richard Bentley, the master of Trinity College Cambridge and the pre-eminent classicist of the day. Although the extant versions of Jerome's Vulgate and the *Textus Receptus* included the comma, Bentley determined after careful examination of the oldest and best manuscripts that it was in neither the original Greek or Latin texts. See *Dr. Bentley's Proposals for Printing a New Edition of the Greek Testament, and St. Hierom's Latin Version* (London: Printed for J. Knapton, 1721). For a description of how the critical work of Richard Bentley led to the exposure of the Johannine Comma in England, see my article "God in Three Persons," n 45. Arguments for the Trinity based on biblical propositionalism were invoked by Baptist theologians from John Gill to A. H. Strong, but without the comma they were left without clear biblical support for the doctrine.

[48] Hans W. Frei, *The Eclipse of Biblical Narrative* (New Haven: Yale University Press, 1974); and George Lindbeck, *The Nature of Doctrine* (Philadelphia: Westminster Press, 1984).

Israel's Father, truly eternal Word, truly life-giving Spirit."[49] Whereas the simple biblicism of the past contributed to an eclipse of Trinitarian doctrine, the recovery of biblical narrative has facilitated a Trinitarian ressourcement.

Retrieval of the Patristic Tradition. The often-invoked hermeneutical mantra "no creed but the Bible" arose in an era when such historic doctrines as the Trinity were presupposed to be the "clear teaching" of Scripture.[50] A century of relentless historicism (even in its more tame evangelical versions) has all but eroded this confidence. Whereas the biblicism embraced by Baptists often pushed toward a strict affirmation of *sola scriptura* and an equally staunch rejection of Christian tradition, a new generation of Baptists is finding value in retrieving the patristic tradition as a means of renewing faith and practice. D. H. Williams, like Humphreys, contends that the road to renewal for Baptists and other free church evangelicals lies in recovering a sense of catholicity by

---

[49] James Wm. McClendon, *Doctrine: Systematic Theology*, (Nashville: Abingdon Press, 1994) 2:320. McClendon continues, "The trinitarian doctrine, understood as an encoding of the biblical narrative of God, identifies God provided it is recognized as just that—an encoding meant to return us to its source" (Ibid., 321). Millard J. Erickson objects to the narrative-based Trinitarianism of James McClendon and Stanley Grenz in *The Evangelical Left: Encountering Postconservative Evangelical Theology* (Grand Rapids: Baker Books, 1997) 33–59. Erickson naively presumes that the common-sense approach of the Old Princeton theology is still intact and that establishing the Trinitarian doctrine is simply a matter of arranging the facts of Scripture. His book is misleadingly subtitled "A Contemporary Interpretation of the Trinity" but is in fact a throwback to the turgid propositionalism and retrograde rationalism of a bygone era (Millard J. Erickson, *God in Three Persons: A Contemporary Interpretation of the Trinity* [Grand Rapids: Baker Books, 1995]).

[50] William Tabbernee has shown that the rhetorical slogans "no creed but Christ" and "no book but the Bible," which originated with Alexander Campbell, were employed against the practice of (mis)using creeds and confessions to "fence the table" and not as a shorthand way of disregarding anything not "as old as the New Testament." Tabbernee demonstrates that Campbell was not opposed to the proper use of creeds as means of confessing the faith. See Tabbernee, "Alexander Campbell and the Apostolic Tradition," in *The Free Church and The Early Church*, ed. D. H. Williams (Grand Rapids: Wm. B. Eerdmans, 2002) 163–80.

reconnecting with the first five centuries of Christianity.[51] Williams finds it staggeringly ironic "that most evangelicals subscribe to a Nicene-Constantinopolitan Trinity and a Chalcedonian Christology, and read their Bibles with these theological 'lenses' as the truth."[52] Yet at the same time, they reject the normative status of the post-apostolic in which these orthodox doctrines were worked out. Williams is joined by other Baptists who echo this call for an appropriation of the patristic tradition.[53] British Baptist Stephen R. Holmes likewise argues that "serious Christian theology has almost always involved interaction with the earlier tradition."[54] Steven Harmon makes a compelling case for a "Baptist Catholicity."[55] Among other markers distinguishing catholic Baptists is the reception of "tradition as a source of authority."[56] Harmon shatters the historical amnesia of Baptists who do not remember that early Baptist confessions of faith drew extensively from the patristic tradition.[57] In a chapter devoted to the development of the doctrine of the Trinity, Harmon displays with great care how Christian theologians moved from the triadic narrative of the Bible to narrating the story of the triune God.[58] The retrieval of the patristic tradition like the recovery

---

[51] Similar to Humphreys, D. H. Williams recounts a story from his pastoral experience about being informed by a church deacon that "the study of the early creeds and councils is something Catholics or Episcopalians do, but true Christians need only uphold the complete authority of the Bible." See D. H. Williams, *Retrieving the Tradition and Renewing Evangelicalism: A Primer for Suspicious Protestants* (Grand Rapids: Wm. B. Eerdmans, 1999) 1.

[52] Ibid., 129.

[53] Williams is joined by three other Baptists (D. Jeffrey Bingham, Phyllis Rodgerson Pleasants, and E. Glenn Hinson) in calling for a retrieval of the patristic tradition in Williams, *The Free Church and The Early Church*.

[54] Stephen R. Holmes, *Listening to the Past: The Place of Tradition in Theology* (Grand Rapids: Baker Academic, 2002) 2.

[55] My essay "A Confession for Catholic Baptists" points in the same direction toward a recovery of catholicity in *Ties That Bind: Life Together in the Baptist Vision*, ed. Gary Furr and Curtis W. Freeman (Macon: Smyth & Helwys Publishing, 1994) 83–97.

[56] Steven R. Harmon, *Towards Baptist Catholicity* (Milton Keynes: Paternoster, 2006) 7–8.

[57] Ibid., 71–81.

[58] Ibid., 89–110.

of biblical narrative has provided a connection with the Trinitarian faith of historic Christianity.

Renewal of the Holy Spirit. As the first wave of Pentecostalism swept across America, the old-time devotion to Jesus made many Baptists suspicious about the new-fangled fascination with the Holy Spirit.[59] When the second wave of the charismatic movement lapped over the denominational and theological landscape, a few Baptist theologians tentatively entered the pneumatological waters.[60] Molly Marshall suggests that the theological drift that allowed the Spirit to become an object of too much worship and reflection may be attributed to the failure to anchor the Holy Spirit in the safe harbor of the Trinity.[61] Now that Baptists are adopting and adapting new forms of praise and worship

---

[59] Grant A. Wacker shows that the strongest anti-Pentecostal rhetoric can be found among radical evangelicals, which includes protofundamentalist Baptists, in "Travail of a Broken Family: Radical Evangelical Responses to the Emergence of Pentecostalism in America, 1906–16," in *Pentecostal Currents in American Protestantism*, ed. Edith L. Blumhofer et al. (Urbana and Chicago: University of Illinois Press, 1999) 23–49. As William C. Turner notes, African-American Baptists notably differ from the tendency of resistance to the Spirit among primarily white Baptists. Turner points to "the pneumatocentric" character of historic African-American Baptist faith, in *Discipleship for African American Christians: A Journey Through the Church Covenant* (Valley Forge PA: Judson Press, 2002) xv. Turner finds evidence for a convergence of the christological emphasis of the Baptists and the pneumatological focus of Pentecostals in the church covenant of National Baptists, which begins, "Having been led, as we believe, by the Spirit of God to receive the Lord Jesus Christ as Saviour; and on the profession of our faith, having been baptized in the name of the Father, and of the Son, and of the Holy Spirit, we do now in the presence of God, angels and this assembly, most solemnly and joyfully enter into covenant with one another, as one body in Christ" (Ibid., vi).

[60] One of the few positive assessments of the charismatic movement by a Baptist theologian was Dale Moody, *Spirit of the Living God: The Biblical Concepts Interpreted in Context* (Philadelphia: Westminster Press, 1968). Albert Frederick Schenkel narrates the reactions to the charismatic renewal by North American Baptists, in "New Wine and Baptist Wineskins: American and Southern Baptist Denominational Responses to the Charismatic Renewal, 1960–80," *Pentecostal Currents in American Protestantism*, 152–67.

[61] Molly T. Marshall, *Joining the Dance: A Theology of the Spirit* (Valley Forge PA: Judson Press, 2003) 6–7.

in the wake of the third wave of the Holy Spirit there is a growing sense of the need to incorporate this renewal into Trinitarian doctrine.[62] One indication of such a Trinitarian pneumatology is the retrieval of the ancient image of *perichoresis*, which envisions the reciprocal sharing of life among the members of the Trinity as a divine dance that calls humanity and all creation to participate in the life of the triune God. Stanley Grenz and Marshall's former student Mark Medley extend the use of perichoretic participation and social Trinitarianism to explore a relational understanding of human selfhood.[63] Paul Fiddes applies the model of Trinitarian relations to ecclesiology by describing how the church participates in the perichoretic life of the triune God who "does not need dependence [yet] freely desires to be dependent on us for the completeness of fellowship, for the joy of the dance."[64] Shifting from language of observation to participation, Fiddes develops a Trinitarian account of the gathered community that counters the popular heterodoxy that persons are isolated and self-sufficient individuals.[65]

---

[62] Clark Pinnock, *Flame of Love: A Theology of the Holy Spirit* (Downers Grove IL: InterVarsity Press, 1996) 22.

[63] Stanley J. Grenz, *The Social God and the Relational Self: A Trinitarian Theology of the Imago Dei* (Louisville: Westminster John Knox Press, 2001); and Mark S. Medley, *Imago Trinitatis: Toward a Relational Understanding of Becoming Human* (Lanham MD: University Press of America, 2002). Grenz's second volume in his series *The Matrix of Christian Theology* is titled *The Named God and the Question of Being: A Trinitarian Theo-Ontology* (Westminster: John Knox Press, 2005) and treats the being of God. His earlier book *Rediscovering the Triune God: The Trinity in Contemporary Theology* (Minneapolis: Fortress Press, 2004) surveys contemporary Trinitarian theology. Baptist theologian Roger E. Olson and Christopher A. Hall put together a "guide to theology" on *The Trinity* (Grand Rapids: Wm. B. Eerdmans, 2002), which is designed to provide a brief historical introduction to the subject with an annotated bibliography of works in English.

[64] Paul S. Fiddes, *Participating in God: A Pastoral Doctrine of the Trinity* (Louisville: Westminster John Knox Press, 2000) 108.

[65] Ibid., 46. Fiddes develops this Trinitarian ecclesiology more fully in *Tracks and Traces: Baptist Identity in Church and Theology* (Carlisle, Cambria: Paternoster Press, 2003) 70–82, in which he stresses the notion of covenant as the means by which the church gathers and is gathered. The Baptist/Free Church ecclesiology of the gathered community finds strong support in the similar account of Miroslav Volf, *After Our Likeness: The Church as the Image of the Trinity* (Grand

These pneumatological reflections are yet another hopeful sign of Trinitarian renewal among Baptists.

Reformation through Doxological Worship. The low ratio of Trinitarian hymns to the high proportion of Christological ones in contemporary Baptist hymnals is but one sign of the tilt toward a unitarianism of the Second Person in Baptist worship.[66] The preponderance of "Jesus is my boyfriend" choruses indicates that contemporary worship suffers (perhaps more severely) from the same tendency. How might Baptist worship be reformed toward a doxological expression of the *lex orandi* and a Trinitarian confession of the *lex credendi*?[67] A weekly singing of the *Gloria Patri* and the *Doxology* along with frequent singing of Trinitarian hymns might be a good place to begin. Contemporary Baptists might also imitate the example of their forebears whose hymnals included multiple Trinitarian doxologies.[68]

Rapids: Wm. B. Eerdmans, 1998). In his commentary on the Baptist Union of Great Britain report about the charismatic renewal, Fiddes interestingly does not situate these pneumatological reflections with reference to the Trinity. See Paul S. Fiddes, *Charismatic Renewal: A Baptist View* (London: Baptist Publications, 1980).

[66] Christopher J. Ellis comments that "the Lordship of Jesus Christ is central to worship because the Triune God has been revealed through him," in his *Gathering: A Theology and Spirituality of Worship in Free Church Tradition* (London: SCM Press, 2004) 240. He thus indicates that the christological emphasis of Baptist worship, though tilting in the direction of a unitarianism of the Second Person, may be redirected toward a more fully Trinitarian center.

[67] The old Latin tag *lex orandi, lex credendi,* though normally taken as a rule to stress prayer as the norm for faith, may also be reversed so as to emphasize the rule of faith as the norm for prayer. See Geoffrey Wainwright, *Doxology: The Praise of God in Worship, Doctrine, and Life* (New York: Oxford University Press, 1980) 218.

[68] Baron Stow and Samuel F. Smith, ed., *The Psalmist: A New Collection of Hymns for the Use of Baptist Churches*, with a supplement by Richard Fuller and J. B. Jeter (Boston: Gould and Lincoln, 1854); Basil Manly and B. Manly Jr., eds., *The Baptist Psalmody: A Selection of Hymns for the Worship of God* (Charleston: Southern Baptist Publication Society, 1851). *The Psalmist* has fourteen doxologies of which twelve are Trinitarian, and *The Baptist Psalmody* has sixteen of which fourteen are Trinitarian. Many of these same Trinitarian doxologies are included in Basil Manly and A. Brooks Everett, ed., *Baptist Chorals: Tune and Hymn Book* (Richmond VA: T. J. Starke, 1859). It is not clear how these

Such old doxologies as well as new Trinitarian hymns and choruses could be used to implement the principle of *lex orandi*, *lex credendi*. Reciting the ancient ecumenical creeds as confessions of faith is another means for the reformation of worship along the line of Trinitarian faith. A group of North American Baptists recently called for the recitation of one of the ancient ecumenical creeds each Lord's Day.[69] For centuries the Apostles' Creed in services of baptism and the "Nicene" Creed at observances of the Lord's Table have been used to confess a Trinitarian faith. Adherence to the seasons of the Christian Year also provides a Trinitarian rubric for worship: Advent-Christmas (the Father), Lent-Easter (the Son), and Pentecost-Ordinary Time (the Holy Spirit). Following the lectionary readings that correlate to the seasons of the Christian Year not only supplies a broad range of Scripture for use in worship beyond the sermon text, but more importantly, the lectionary provides a theological context for worship in the broad Trinitarian narrative of the Bible.[70] Many of these reform measures are being widely practiced by Baptists intent on embracing a more liturgical style of worship, but the reformation of worship need not be interpreted solely as a move away from the contemporary and toward the ancient. A return to a more doxological and Trinitarian pattern is cause for celebration no matter what the style.

Reintegration of Trinitarian Orthopraxy. One of the welcome themes in recent theology is the return to practice as a source of critical

---

doxologies were actually used in worship. It may be that in some churches they were sung in every service of worship and perhaps at several points in the liturgy. If so, these doxological punctuations would have had the effect of making Baptist worship more Trinitarian than unitarian.

[69] Curtis W. Freeman, Steven R. Harmon, Elizabeth Newman, and Philip Thompson, "Confessing the Faith," *The Biblical Recorder* (8 July 2004), http://www.biblicalrecorder.org/content/opinion/2004/7_8_2004/gc080704confess ing.shtml (accessed 26 June 2007). The document is also available on *The Baptist Standard* website at http://www.baptiststandard.com/postnuke/pdf/Confessing_ the_Faith_ Draft.pdf (accessed 26 June 2007).

[70] Steven Harmon has an excellent discussion of implementing the *lex orandi*, *lex credendi* principle through the retrieval of the patristic interdependence of worship and theology in *Towards Baptist Catholicity*, 151–77.

reflection.[71] Baptists, who from their beginnings found the language of practice to be useful in describing the attempt to live according to the apostolic pattern, will likewise find this neo-practical theology congenial to their appropriation.[72] McClendon observes, however, that practices are not theologically neutral: Whereas the promise "lies in their capacity to evoke and even to require skills of participants" (i.e., virtues), the threat "lies in the practices' capacity for monstrous distortion and disobedience to God's rule."[73] The early English General Baptist confession The Faith and Practise of Thirty Congregations, for example, makes no direct or indirect allusion to the Trinity—not even in the article on baptism. It is not surprising, then, that the non-Trinitarian practice of seventeenth-century General Baptists was soon followed by a unitarian theology.[74] Notwithstanding the reassurance that the weak Trinitarianism in contemporary Baptist life is not the same as anti-Trinitarianism, the better part of wisdom seems to lie in the reintegrating of Trinitarian practice. Such an approach recognizes that a lasting Trinitarian faith is not established in a once-for-all confession but instead becomes habituated through reiteration. The gracious action of the Father toward the Son is conveyed through sacramental practices by the Spirit. As John Colwell has compellingly argued, "The Trinitarian grammar of Christian theology gives structure and definition to the language of grace and mediation."[75] Humphreys and Williams have displayed how Trinitarian practices of worship, proclamation, baptism,

---

[71] Practices, as Dorothy Bass has defined them, are "those shared activities that address fundamental human needs and that, woven together, form…a life-giving way of life." See Dorothy C. Bass, *Practicing Our Faith* (San Francisco: Josey-Bass Publishers, 1997) xi, 2.

[72] For example, a General Baptist confession of faith written in 1651 was titled The Faith and Practise of Thirty Congregations; see William L. Lumpkin, *Baptist Confessions of Faith*, rev. ed. (Valley Forge PA: Judson Press, 1969) 176–88. The phrase "faith and practice" among Baptists became shorthand for right doctrine and orderly living in which orthopraxy was every much as important as orthodoxy.

[73] McClendon, *Doctrine*, 28.

[74] See my article "God in Three Persons."

[75] John E. Colwell, *Promise and Presence: An Exploration of Sacramental Theology* (Milton Keynes: Paternoster, 2005) 41.

prayer, and confession functioned in the early church.[76] Yet it remains to be seen how contemporary Baptists might go about recovering a Trinitarian orthopraxy. Steve Harmon gestures in the direction that such a reintegration might take in retrieving patristic practices.[77] Baptist ministers might begin by making it their practice to perform the doctrine of the Trinity when they baptize and lay on hands, offer prayers and pronounce blessings, confess sin and proclaim pardon, and make the sign of the cross and exchange the right hand of fellowship all in the name and the sign of the Father, the Son, and the Holy Spirit.[78] Their example would undoubtedly invite both congregational imitation and theological reflection. Trinitarian narrations in sermons, observance of communion, and even the polity of the church meeting may require more theological preparation so as to be performed in language that is fitting and faithful. Ministers seeking to reintegrate Trinitarian orthopraxy would do well, then, to adapt the rich resources of standard liturgical texts from other traditions (such as the Anglican *Book of Common Prayer)* or from their own heritage (like the British Baptist *Gathering for Worship)*.[79]

Revisioning with a Sanctified Imagination. Baptists, along with most others in the evangelical and free church tradition, suffer from the iconoclastic impulse of the Zwinglian reform that the finite is incapable of the infinite.[80] Given that as a whole Baptists have neither exemplified

---

[76] Humphreys, "Father, Son and Holy Spirit," 80–85; Williams, *Retrieving the Tradition*, 35–36 and 56–70.

[77] Harmon, *Towards Baptist Catholicity*, 159–77.

[78] Fiddes commends the practices of making the sign of the cross and baptism in the name of the Trinity as two important Trinitarian practices from the free church/Baptist heritage, in *Participating in God*, 43–44.

[79] *The Book of Common Prayer* (New York: The Church Hymnal Corporation, 1979); Christopher J. Ellis and Myra Blyth, eds., *Gathering For Worship* (Norwich: Canterbury Press, 2005).

[80] Zwingli distinguished sharply between images used as objects of worship and images as expressions of artistic creativity. He stated that "no one is a greater admirer than I of paintings and statuary; but those that offend piety ought not to be tolerated but to be abolished by unyielding command of the authorities," in Huldreich Zwingli, *Commentary on True and False Religion*, 29.II, ed. Samuel Macauley Jackson and Clarence Nevin Heller (Durham NC: The Labyrinth Press, 1981) 337.

the expression of artistic creativity nor encouraged the representation of religious devotion, what sense is there in thinking that their faith and practice might become more Trinitarian by revisioning with a sanctified imagination through artistic and religious images? McClendon offers a corrective word to Baptists who adhere to the iconoclastic principle *finitum non capax infiniti*. He suggests that a baptist theology of art does well when it "deems God not only beautiful but the beautifier of creation, deems God the world's original artist—sees redeemable creation as the scene of God's self-giving new creation, drawing for its life upon God's own life—Father, Son, Holy Spirit." And, he continues, "In plainer, baptist words, the story of God is by Christian conviction the world's Great Story."[81] This story has been told by the church with icons, stained glass, murals, statuary, illuminations, woodcuts, and symbols of every sort. Yet each telling, as the hymn-writer says, is "more wonderfully sweet."[82] That a proclivity for innovation, however, may produce orthodox improvisations such as three doors into the sanctuary—one for the Father, another for the Son, and a third for the Holy Spirit—or lead to heterodox degradations—like transforming trefoils into quadrafoils—is reason enough to pause and consider how the imagination might be sanctified by contemplation of the Trinity. It is important then to provide freedom for creative expression to arise out of the interplay with Trinitarian confession and contemplation. In so doing, the capacity for a sanctified imagination may be prepared to envision the beauty of the Trinity and construe the world as the story of the triune God.[83] Such revisioning with a sanctified imagination

[81] James Wm. McClendon, *Witness: Systematic Theology* (Nashville: Abingdon Press, 2000) 3:179–80. McClendon intentionally denotes the wider free church tradition with his reference to "baptists," using the lower case "b" to include such diverse groups as *Täufer* and Baptists to Pietists and Pentecostals.

[82] Katherine Hankey, "I Love to Tell the Story," in *The Baptist Hymnal* (Nashville: Convention Press, 1975) 461.

[83] In preparing a PowerPoint presentation that displayed the wide range of visual images used to depict the Trinity, I was surprised by the lingering presence of those images in my memory, which seemed to prompt my imagination to see the world anew with Trinitarian eyes.

confirms the mystery inscribed in the words of the same hymn: "the new, new song" is "the old, old story."[84]

Responsiveness to the Mission of the Triune God. Nothing is more central to the identity of Baptists than their commitment to follow the Great Commission: "Go therefore and make disciples of all nations, baptizing them in the name of the Father and of the Son and of the Holy Spirit" (Matt 28:19 NRSV). Yet this missional conviction is grounded not in human obedience but rather in the divine self-giving: the Father who sends the Son (John 17:3, 18) and gives the Spirit (John 15:26–27). Baptism is then the means through which disciples are commissioned to participate in the mission of the triune God. As Fiddes explains:

> Being plunged beneath the waters which represent the hostile forces of death and chaos (Ps 18:15–17), the baptismal candidate shares in the mission of the Son who is sent by the Father to be immersed into the bitterness and alienation of death; emerging from the water, raised with Christ to new life (Rom 6:4), the believer is taken up into the breath of the Spirit who opens new possibilities even in the waters of death, turning it into life-giving water so that she is born again of water and the spirit.[85]

John Colwell similarly offers a Trinitarian account that conceives of baptism as the means by which the promised gift of the Spirit is received. The Spirit is in turn the means of union with Christ who commands disciples to go and promises to be present with them in their going.[86] By thus participating through baptism in the life of the triune God, the church is formed into a community that is sent out to extend God's mission to the world.[87] McClendon explains that the goal of this mission, as Pentecost revealed, is "one new human race, redeemed and reconciled

[84] Hankey, "I Love to Tell the Story," 461.

[85] Fiddes, *Participating in God*, 44.

[86] Colwell, *Promise and Presence*, 124.

[87] Curtis W. Freeman, "Our Lord's Baptism (Matthew 3:13–17)" *Interpretation* 47 (July 1993): 285–89.

to God and thereby joined into one,"[88] thus bringing anew the "nations" of the Great Commission within the scope of this mission. Two Baptist theologians have offered extended Trinitarian reflections on the nations. Timothy George asks the question, "Is the Father of Jesus the God of Muhammad?" to which he replies both "yes and no." He explains that the answer is "Yes, in the sense that the Father of Jesus is the only God there is," thus gesturing toward the eschatological vision of the new humanity, but glancing back to the tragic confusion of Babel he continues that the answer "is also no, for Muslim theology rejects the fatherhood of God, the deity of Jesus Christ, and the personhood of the Holy Spirit."[89] For Mark Heim the Trinity provides a lens to glimpse the eschatological horizon of the one-peoplehood anticipated in Pentecost. Beginning with the presuppositions that salvation in Christianity is communion with the triune God and other creatures through Christ and that the Trinity provides a framework for understanding religious diversity, Heim contends that Christians may enter into deep conversation with followers of other religions and come to a fuller understanding of the inexhaustible depths of the riches in Christ.[90] Connecting the responsiveness of the church to the mission of the triune God is yet another indication of the ongoing Trinitarian ressourcement in Baptist theology.

Stanley Grenz was probably correct that when the story of theology in the twentieth century is told "the rediscovery of the doctrine of the Trinity...must be given center stage, and the rebirth of Trinitarian theology must be presented as one of the most far-reaching theological developments of the century."[91] But whether the work of the theologians will reflect the faith and practice of Christians in the pulpits and pews is another matter. As we look to the state of Trinitarianism in Baptist life forty years after McClendon's prospective vision, it appears that the disinclination of his fellow Baptists to move toward a more fully

---

[88] McClendon, *Doctrine*, 418.

[89] Timothy George, *Is The Father of Jesus the God of Muhammad?* (Grand Rapids MI: Zondervan, 2002) 69–70.

[90] S. Mark Heim, *The Depth of the Riches: A Trinitarian Theology of Religious Ends* (Grand Rapids: Wm. B. Eerdmans, 2001) 123–65.

[91] Grenz, *Rediscovering The Triune God*, 1.

Trinitarian future has in many respects continued.[92] What lies ahead is uncertain, and it is not an exaggeration to say that without radical theological redirection the Trinity may be at risk for more than a few of becoming an artifact of a bygone era. Will Baptists today be inclined to listen to the voices of ressourcement like Fisher Humphreys who nourish, invigorate, and rejuvenate Trinitarian faith and practice, or will it be back to the future in which the Trinity continues to grow increasingly irrelevant? We can only hope.

[92] McClendon, "Some Reflections on the Future of Trinitarianism," 156.

Why Study Church History? Listening to Saints and Sinners

BILL J. LEONARD

I have known Fisher Humphreys for almost thirty years, including a time when we were faculty colleagues at Samford University. Not only is he an outstanding scholar, ever exploring issues of theology and history, and a superb classroom teacher, but he is one of the most genuinely caring persons I have ever known. His integrity as scholar, minister, and friend is a model for all of us who know him. I am grateful to be a part of this volume in his honor, and even more grateful to be his friend.

Writing in the year 1890, William Whitsitt, president and professor of church history at the Southern Baptist Theological Seminary, Louisville, Kentucky, noted: "I am casting about to begin writing a work on American Baptist History. It is an [*sic*] Herculean task, and I must keep it all to myself. Baptist History is a department in which 'the wise man concealeth knowledge.' It is likely I shall not be able to publish the work while I live, but I can write it out in full and make arrangements to publish it after my death, when I shall be out of the reach of bigots and fools."[1]

From Whitsitt's perspective, writing church history, especially for the Baptists, was an endeavor fraught with danger. As he saw it, those who knew too many of the church's historical secrets would do well to keep those matters to themselves. If this is so, then simply studying the history of the church may be equally hazardous. It requires an individual to confront persons, issues, and ideas that could have significant, perhaps dangerous, impact on life, thought, and action. While the study of Christian history may at times be faith-affirming, it may also challenge an individual's most cherished beliefs, a sober reminder of the deep

---

[1] Thomas R. McKibbens, "The Life, Writings, and Influence of Morgan Edwards," *Quarterly Review* 11 (January–March 1976) 68.

divisions over faith and practice that have characterized Christian communities from the very beginning.

An answer to the question "Why Study Church History?" seems rather obvious. Of course persons inside and outside the Christian church should study its history to understand the origins and development of the world's largest religion. Christianity's enduring role in world history requires serious investigation sociologically, politically, and spiritually. Christians and non-Christians alike owe it to themselves to know something of the church's history in order to understand its influence and impact on the world.

Cultivating an appreciation for history in general and church history in particular is easier said than done, however. In fact, many people in today's society give limited consideration to historical studies or neglect them altogether. Some are no doubt influenced by a general anti-history bias that plagues much contemporary culture. They see historical studies as essentially "boring" or "irrelevant," an unending list of names, dates, institutions, and conflicts difficult to learn and soon forgotten. Still others may regard the church's history as a case study for verifying their respective viewpoints from a pious illustration of "God's saving activity in history" to a cynical indication of the church's enduring efforts to secure political and evangelical hegemony around the world. Those who go looking for historical proof texts will not be disappointed. Amid great moments of heroic faith and prophetic insight, there are multiple occasions when the representatives of Christianity seem a long way from the teachings of Jesus. Crusades, Inquisitions, anti-Semitism, and support for the slave trade are but a few of the "causes" promoted by Christians in Jesus' name. Internal conflicts, debates, and disagreements continue unabated. As the German reformer Martin Luther is said to have remarked, "The Church is like Noah's ark. Were it not for the storm without, you could not endure the stench within."

This chapter suggests that the study of history is important, indeed essential, for understanding the nature of the church and its mission in the world. In truth, nothing that the church does in contemporary society is untouched by historical influences. This essay explores those influences through five specific categories of historical investigation, tradition, identity, ideas, context, and individuals.

What is History?

Before asking, "Why study church history?" it is necessary to ask, "What is history?" That question involves the nature of historiography and the methods and mindset of those who write and comment on historical occurrences. David Bebbington reminds us that history "entails investigation, questioning, inquiry: [in fact] the word history is derived from the Greek word for 'inquiry.'" To study history, he says, is to investigate "whether an account of the past is firmly based on valid evidence."[2] Historical studies involve an actual event that is recorded, described, and interpreted for posterity.[3] Jacques Barzun and Henry F. Graff write that historiography involves the "method" of "fashioning written history." They suggest that "so close is the association in our minds between the event, the account of it, and the means by which the account is prepared that a consistent usage is difficult. The ideas overlap and prompt the speaker to use the most general term for the science, the art, and its substance: History."[4]

The study of history involves both the record and the analysis of specific events that occur in particular contexts. As Howard Grimes observes, history entails "the more or less scientific pursuit of truth and understanding."[5] This includes knowledge of the past in and for itself, as well as for insights useful in interpreting the present. Grimes concludes that "if history is only a chronicle of the past—a listing of who lived when and where—it *is* simple, though it may not always be easy to write because of the lack of accurate records. If, on the other hand, history is more than a mere chronicling of events, it begins to take on a complex character to the degree that interpretation enters into the process of writing history."[6] He insists that as soon as humans "began to reflect on the past and to record it, historical writing was born." As they "began to

---

[2] David Bebbington, *Patterns in History* (Leicester, England: InterVarsity Press, 1979) 4.

[3] Jacques Barzun and Henry F. Graff, *The Modern Researcher*, rev. ed. (New York: Harcourt, Brace & World, Inc., 1970) 48–52.

[4] Ibid., 49.

[5] Howard Grimes, *The Christian Views of History* (Nashville: Abingdon Press, 1969) 13.

[6] Ibid., 23.

reflect on the *meaning* of past events a philosophy of history, however crude, came into being."[7] Even the events that are written down and reported reflect a basic analysis of what seemed important in a particular time and place.

Most historical events are seldom preserved or described in any lasting way. Much of human history is lost to memory and recollection.[8] Likewise, the same historical incident may be described variously by those who observed it and those who write about it. Revisionism, the process reexamining historical analysis, is a constant task of historians.

To this day varying world cultures, religions, and institutions differ as to the nature and meaning of history itself. Many Eastern and ancient cultures reflect a cyclical approach to history in which nations, individuals, and life in general rest on a constant cycle of rise and decline, collapse and reformation. Hinduism and Buddhism are among those religions whose goal for individual life is to escape the cycle of reincarnation and lose the self in the center of all things, freed from the unending rise and fall of world history and personal re-embodiment. Those Western cultures with Judeo-Christian roots reflect a more linear approach in which history moves through periods of rise and decline but toward certain distinct ends. Judaism and Christianity stress that God—the author and creator of all things—brought history into existence and ultimately will guide it to a conclusion. Within that linear time frame, kingdoms rise and fall as history moves toward a purpose that only God fully knows and understands.[9]

---

[7] Ibid., 22.

[8] Technology—especially film and recording possibilities—has changed this dramatically, however. Photographs, recordings, and video technologies now permit nations, families, and individuals to record events large and small, personal and communal. Nonetheless, even visual records of historical events do not necessarily end debates as to the meaning and interpretation of those events.

[9] Bebbington, *Patterns in History*, 17–18. Bebbington describes three other views of history. The Enlightenment school supports the idea of progress as developed by human processes. The school of historicism places emphasis on "the growth of various cultures." Marxism is another school that historical process is the result of human effort to improve the life situation for all persons. See Bebbington, *Patterns in History*, 19–20.

Even those who agree on the importance of history and explore the varied theories of historical investigation wear many different "glasses" through which they understand the meaning of events and their place in the Divine scheme of things. Within these continuing divisions regarding history and its interpretation, there are significant reasons for examining the church's many stories and the impact they have on tradition, identity, ideas, context, and individuals.

History and Tradition

One powerful reason for studying Christian history concerns the church's function as a vehicle of tradition, the many ways in which beliefs and practices are passed on from generation to generation. In the first-century church, new traditions were established quickly as sources of unity and identity for the fledgling communities of faith. St. Paul wrote to the Corinthian church, "For the *tradition* which I handed on to you came to me from the Lord himself: that on the night of his arrest the Lord Jesus took bread, and after giving thanks to God, broke it and said: "This is my body which is for you. Do this in memory of me" (1 Cor 11:23–24 REB). Twenty centuries later, most Christian congregations continue to utilize those simple words when they observe the tradition known as the Eucharist, Holy Communion, or the Lord's Supper. Yet debates over the meaning of the tradition and the appropriate candidates for admission to "table fellowship" continue to divide churches worldwide.

The earliest Christians were heirs of many traditions passed on to them from Judaism. The four gospels indicate that Jesus and his disciples were consistent participants in the rites and rituals of the first-century Jewish communities. Luke's gospel says that Jesus attended the synagogue at Nazareth "regularly," even when he angered those who heard his commentary on certain Hebrew texts (Luke 4:16–30 NEB). When in Jerusalem, Jesus and his companions worshiped in the temple (Mark 11:11–27). At the same time, Jesus was frequently criticized by certain religious folk of his day for breaking with Jewish tradition in his eating habits (Mark 2:23–28), his Sabbath activities (Mark 3:1–6), and in the company he kept (Matt 11:18–19).

Early Christian worship reflected much of the Jewish liturgical tradition with readings from the "First Testament" (the Hebrew Bible), singing the Psalms, and commentary on the biblical text. The church "Christianized" a Seder-based meal as a perpetual tradition born of Jesus' last supper with his disciples. Yet the deepest break in tradition and the beginning of a new religion involved the decision to admit Gentiles (non-Jews) to the church without requiring them to become Jews in the process. St. Paul led that battle but still required Timothy to be circumcised before they traveled together (Acts 16:1–3). He rejected circumcision for Gentiles in general but demanded it in one specific instance "out of consideration of the Jews who lived in those parts" (Acts 16:3 NEB). The early Christians retained, rejected, and reformed numerous practices passed on to them from Judaism. The study of Christian history reveals similar tensions between preserving and rejecting traditions passed down to each generation.

Tradition has multiple meanings in the church. Alister McGrath suggests that it "can refer to both the action of passing teachings on to others...and to the body of teachings which are passed on in this manner." Tradition is both "a *process* as well as a *body of teaching*." It can also contain a "negative sense" concerning those "human ideas and practices which are not divinely authorized."[10] As Adrian Hastings notes, the "contrasts" in Christian tradition are diverse and decisive, covering a wide spectrum of belief and practice. He writes that Christianity:

> has been a rather unritualistic religion, both in its origins and in forms such as that of the Quakers, but it has also at times been reduced to a pattern of almost ceaseless ritual, whether in the monastic liturgy of Cluny or in a Byzantine cathedral. Christianity has been a very apolitical minority religion, yet it has been no less an imperial and persecuting one, just as it has acted as the other side of the coin to the nation-state. In some forms it is exceptionally activist, evangelistic and missionary, in others predominately monastic and contemplative; it has so lauded virginity and monastic life as to come close to rejecting

---

[10] Alister E. McGrath, *Christianity: An Introduction*, 2nd ed. (Oxford: Blackwell Publishing, 2006) 107.

> sex and marriage, and yet it has also in other circumstances appeared as committed above all to the social glorification of monogamy.... It has on one side produced the most lasting, centralized and complex ecclesiastical system of government in Rome and on the other has been intensely fissiparous, sectarian and multi-centered.[11]

These diverse traditions inform historic segments of the entire church of Jesus Christ. While many are rooted in Scripture, they have also evolved across the centuries as the church responded to new cultures, ideas, and controversies.

The relationship of Scripture and tradition is illustrated in the development of a non-canonical text known as the *Didache*, or *The Teaching of the Twelve Apostles*, probably written around the year 100 C.E. It indicates that there was already a common method for observing baptism, but that some communities of faith needed to negotiate that tradition in light of logistical difficulties. The document notes:

> Concerning baptism, baptize thus: Having first rehearsed all these things, "baptize, in the Name of the Father and of the Son and of the Holy Spirit," in running water; 2. but if thou hast no running water, baptize in other water, and if thou canst not in cold, then in warm. 3. But if thou hast neither, pour water three times on the head "in the Name of the Father, Son and Holy Spirit.": 4. And before the baptism let the baptizer and him who is to be baptized fast, and any others who are able. And thou shalt bid him who is to be baptized to fast one or two days before.[12]

This ancient work demonstrates how traditions develop and are modified by circumstances. Clearly, there is already a normative tradition for baptism—dipping the body in cold, running water with the

---

[11] Adrian Hastings, ed., *A World History of Christianity* (Grand Rapids: Wm. B. Eerdmans Publishing Company, 1999) 1–2.

[12] E. Glenn Hinson, ed., *The Early Church Fathers* (Nashville: Broadman Press, 1980) 30.

words of the Trinitarian formula (Father, Son, and Holy Spirit) spoken over the person being baptized. When the norm could not be followed because of extenuating circumstances the practices could be modified. Baptism by affusion (pouring) was permitted. The mode might change but the theological formula remained the same. Baptism was too important to delay or ignore even if the preferred standard was not available.

Christian history reveals the continuing tension between Scripture and tradition. Some Christian communities (Roman Catholic and Eastern Orthodox, for example) freely acknowledge the intricate relationship between Scripture and tradition, recognizing numerous rituals and doctrines that developed across the centuries as approved by church councils or the pronouncements of church leaders (popes and patriarchs). Martin Luther, John Calvin, and Ulrich Zwingli were among those sixteenth-century reformers who challenged many traditions of the medieval church regarding papal authority, the selling of indulgences, and the merit of the saints while placing renewed emphasis on *sola scriptura* and a return to the Bible as the foundational authority for belief and practice. Nonetheless, these reformers retained certain "catholic" traditions such as infant baptism and the intricate relationship between church and state and baptism and citizenship. More "radical reformers" such as the Swiss Brethren and Mennonites (Anabaptists) insisted that these "magisterial reformers" did not go far enough in replacing stultifying "man-made" traditions with dynamic biblical ideals. They repudiated the baptism of infants in favor of a church of believers who received baptism only after they had claimed Christian faith. Some even demanded freedom of religion for all, even heretics and atheists.[13]

In seventeenth-century England, various Protestants sought to purify the Anglican Church of all "trappings of popery"—those Catholic liturgical and hierarchical practices that seemed contrary to Scripture. The Puritan movement gave birth to various denominations including Presbyterians, Congregationalists, and Baptists. Members of the Society of Friends (Quakers) went even further, rejecting all "outward forms" of tradition—sacraments, vestments, an official clergy, and worship in

---

[13] Bill J. Leonard, *Baptist Ways: A History* (Valley Forge PA: Judson Press, 2003) 18–23.

"steeple-houses"—in favor of a renewed spirituality centered in the "inner light." They founded a new tradition grounded in the post-Pentecost church, anticipating additional sectarian debates over the nature of the church and the meaning of tradition.

Divisions over the nature of tradition continue to separate Christians in doctrine and practice the world over. The study of church history represents one way of understanding how traditions have been passed down, the meaning of tradition itself, and the role of Christian community in sorting out what should be preserved or jettisoned. Hastings comments, "An extraordinarily large amount of Church history is one of internal conflict, of disagreement about the nature of the tradition. There is no reason to think that this is going to cease and a realistic [study of] history has to give its full due to conflict and its underlying causes within the very nature of Christianity."[14]

History and Identity

Tradition is the vehicle for passing on identity, another significant resource for studying the history of the church. Individuals and faith communities utilize tradition as one way of inculcating identity, helping those who claim Christian faith to know who they are and where they fit in the church and in the world. Questions of identity ask: What really makes a Christian and what kind of Christianity best defines the nature of the Gospel and its implications for life, work, and worship?

Specific theological and regional identity is evident in the New Testament churches as illustrated in the book of Acts and the varied epistles. In Acts, divisions soon developed between Jewish-Christians in Jerusalem and its environs and certain Gentile-Christians living outside the "Holy Land." Acts 15:1–2 suggests that "now certain persons who had come down from Judea began to teach the brotherhood that those who were not circumcised in accordance with the Mosaic practice could not be saved. That brought them into fierce dissension and controversy with Paul and Barnabas. And so it was arranged that these two and some others from Antioch should go up to Jerusalem to see the apostles and elders about his question" (NEB). Christian identity at Thessalonica

---

[14] Hastings, *World History*, 3–4.

involved a concern for the immediacy of Christ's second coming. The eschatological speculations of the Thessalonians were so extensive that St. Paul apparently found it necessary to give information and caution about what they might and might not claim about the "end times" (2 Thess 4:13–5:11). At Corinth, Christians anticipated many of the later divisions in the church regarding apostolic and ministerial authority. St. Paul advises them to beware of "superlative-apostles" who apparently promoted "another Jesus, not the Jesus whom we proclaimed" (2 Cor 11:4–6 NEB) Thus the New Testament churches provide a classic illustration of the multiple identities present in even the earliest Christian communions.

And that was only the beginning. Significant controversies and disputes have raged in the church for 2,000 years as Christians differed over what beliefs and actions were acceptable. At certain historic junctures, those whose identity was different from norms set by Roman Catholics, Anglicans, or Puritans were burned, hung, exiled, or imprisoned. Claiming an unauthorized Christian identity could be dangerous. In more recent times, identity remains a source of spiritual strength and sectarian debate, dividing Christians from one another even as it gives them a place to stand in understanding and articulating the gospel. Sometimes that identity has humorous implications. Nineteenth-century Baptists expressed their distinctive identity in a hymnody that distinguished from their denominational competitors.

Not at the Jordan River,
But in that flowing stream,
Stood John the Baptist preacher
When he baptized Him.
John was a Baptist preacher,
When he baptized the Lamb.
So Jesus was a Baptist,
And thus the Baptists came.[15]

---

[15] William Warren Sweet, *Religion in the Development of American Culture 1765–1840* (New York: Charles Scribner's Sons, 1952) 158; and Leonard, *Baptist Ways*, 159.

Frustration with divisive identity and denominational debates has led some contemporary Christians to eschew "brand name" churches in favor of non-denominational congregations. Yet even these communions utilize unique forms of worship, ministry, and doctrine that distinguish them from other congregations and denominations.

The study of church history suggests that there really is no generic Christianity without specificity or particular identity. Sooner or later Christians are compelled to choose a place to stand, a way of acting and believing that relates to church polity, sacraments, preaching, spirituality, Christian education, doctrine, and other powerful dynamics. They claim a particular historical or contemporary approach that defines broadly or narrowly their kind of Christianity. Church history helps persons who seek Christian identity know where they fit in the great ebb and flow of classic belief and practice and how specific identities have evolved across the centuries.

Identity: Institutional.

Many Christians, perhaps the great majority, choose to express their connection with the church through particular institutions and/or denominations. They identify with the heritage of an explicit faith tradition that gives expression to their own Christian commitments. In many cases, the history of the church can be traced through studies of specific communities of faith, tracing the development of groups from Roman Catholic to Eastern Orthodoxy, from Protestantism to various sects and denominations. Institutional identity helps organize individuals and churches locally, regionally, nationally, and internationally.

The evolution of the papacy is one of the most intriguing stories in Christian history and centered in one of the most enduring offices of the church. Roman "primacy," born of questions of church authority and polity, globalism and politics, combine with specific forms of biblical exegesis (Matt 16:13–20) to create a classic illustration of the way in which the church sought to promote its vision in the world. Thus in 1215 Pope Innocent III could declare himself the very Vicar (representative) of Jesus Christ on earth, a title and authority popes still claim. He wrote:

> The Creator of the universe set up two great luminaries in the firmament of heaven; the greater light to rule the day, the lesser light to rule the night. In the same way for the firmament of the universal Church...he appointed two great dignities: the greater to bear rule over souls...the lesser to bear rule over bodies.... These dignities are the pontifical authority and the royal power. Furthermore, the moon derives her light from the sun, and is in truth inferior to the sun.... In the same way the royal power derives its dignity from the pontifical authority....[16]

Three hundred years later Martin Luther would write with brutal directness:

> Only think of it yourself! They must confess that there are pious Christians among us, who have the true faith, Spirit, understanding, word, and mind of Christ. Why, then, should we reject their word and understanding and follow the pope, who has neither faith nor Spirit? That would be to deny the whole faith and the Christian Church. Moreover, it is not the pope alone who is always in the right, if the article of the Creed is correct: "I believe in one holy Christian Church"; otherwise the prayer must run: "I believe in the pope at Rome," and so reduce the Christian Church to one man—which would be nothing else than a devilish and hellish error.[17]

Debates over the papal office galvanized Christians long before 1517 when Martin Luther posted his Ninety-five Theses. Then as now, persons inside and outside the Roman sphere divided over the office of the pope and its political and doctrinal claims. Yet even its most adamant critics must admit that the papacy remains Christianity's only truly global office, as reflected in the massive media attention to the death of

---

[16] Innocent III, "The Moon and the Sun," in *Sicut universitatis conditor. Ep. i. 401*, 1198, in *Documents of the Christian Church*, ed. Henry Bettenson, (London: Oxford University Press, 1966) 155–56.

[17] Martin Luther, "To the Christian Nobility of the German Nation," in *The Reformation*, ed. W. R. Estep (Nashville: Broadman Press, 1979) 130.

Pope John Paul II in 2005. The office and the church it represents serve as a source of identity for over one billion persons on the planet.

For modern Roman Catholics, institution and identity collided in the 1960s with the changes that accompanied the Second Vatican Council convened by Pope John XXIII in 1961. As a result, a variety of new liturgical options were offered to Catholic churches, often creating identity-confusion. Latin, long the only language used in Catholic worship, was essentially replaced by masses in the vernacular tongue of the specific nation, region, or congregation. Some churches were permitted to distribute Holy Communion in "both kinds," bread and wine, a break with a centuries old tradition in which the laity received only the consecrated bread. Priests no longer turned their backs on the congregation while saying mass but faced them across the altar.

While many welcomed these changes, others experienced significant institutional and personal crises. Some asked: If these ancient and distinctive traditions are no longer normative, then what does it mean to be Roman Catholic? Can the institution make these dramatic liturgical changes without undermining the very nature of Catholic identity altogether?

Church history is a case study in the way in which institutions develop, establish unique identities, and encounter trauma when the inevitable changes occur. Some participants celebrate institutional reforms as a necessary response to changing times, pressing needs, and new challenges. Others fear that institutional change represents compromise or betrayal of the original vision. This is one of the fascinating and inevitable elements of the life of any religious community.

Identity: Prophecy and Order

The relationship between change and stability reveals those inevitable tensions that historian Jeffrey Burton Russell calls "prophecy and order." He notes that religious communities often begin with a prophetic response to cultural, social, or religious norms that appear to undermine genuine faith. Dissenting/prophetic movements arise with a new voice of "thus saith the Lord," challenging institutional hegemony over religious identity and authority. Yet these radical movements may soon institutionalize to bring order and organization to their earlier dynamic and disseminate their ideas more systematically. This often leads to division, even schism, in the group as some members insist that the original vision has been lost and must be rekindled. Russell writes, "The Christian spirit has always been ambivalent toward this world. On the one hand, the spirit of prophecy, rooted in the tradition of Isaiah and Jeremiah, has insisted that this world...and its institutions, are under judgment.... On the other hand, the spirit of order has called for a progressive, creative, and often very moderate program of reshaping this world and its institutions on the model of God's world."[18]

The growth and development of many Protestant movements illustrates the continuing tension over prophecy and order in the history of the church. Even a brief survey illustrates the point. Anglicanism began as a reaction against Catholic global hegemony; Methodism began as a society inside Anglicanism. The Wesleyan Holiness movement began as a prophetic response to Methodist institutionalization, while the Pentecostal movement blossomed out of Holiness churches as a restoration of the power and impulses of the first Pentecost. Serpent-handlers and Jesus-Only Pentecostals consider themselves to be prophetic responses inside Pentecostalism. Each of these groups in its own way institutionalized itself in order to establish criteria for church governance, ordination of clergy, doctrinal clarity, and, of course, identity. Today's sect easily becomes tomorrow's denomination or religious institution. Knowing when and how to discern these forces is part of the study of church history.

Identity: Doctrine/Ideas

A study of church history is also essential as a way of tracing historical theology—the evolution of significant theological and doctrinal beliefs, mandates, and essentials. The study of historical theology details the unending quest for Christian truth born in Scripture but interpreted, expanded, and debated across the centuries. It is a survey of those great dogmas and ideas that have united and divided Christians to the present day. In other words, church history helps us understand

[18] Jeffrey Burton Russell, *A History of Medieval Christianity: Prophecy and Order* (New York: Thomas Y. Crowell Co., 1968) 1.

why Christians of various persuasions believe as they do, how those beliefs took shape, and how they are enacted in the ritual or liturgical life of Christian communities. Take for example the theological and doctrinal developments related to the Lord's Supper.

As noted earlier, the *tradition* surrounding the Lord's Supper begins with Jesus' admonition that "this is my body which is given for you. Do this in memory of me." These simple words shape the practice of Holy Communion, one of the most distinctive observances in the history of the Christian church. Yet this most identifiable of Christian rituals is surrounded by some of its most theologically-divisive doctrines.

Divisions over the Table of the Lord are evident early in the church's history. Some early Christians exalted the supper while insisting that it was only valid for those whose theology was appropriately orthodox. In a treatise known as *Against Heresies*, Irenaeus, the Bishop of Lyons (ca. 180 C.E.), wrote of the supper:

> How will they [heretics] allow that the bread over which thanksgiving has been said is the body of their Lord, and that the chalice is the chalice of his blood, if they say that he is not the son of the creator of the world…? For as the bread of the earth, receiving the invocation of God, is no longer common bread but Eucharist [thanksgiving] consisting of two things, an earthly and a heavenly; so also our bodies, partaking of the Eucharist are no longer corruptible, having the hope of eternal resurrection.[19]

Right belief was required of those who wished to receive the grace available at Christ's Table.

Debates over the meaning of Christ's words and their implications for the "mystery of the altar" continued until the great medieval philosopher Thomas Aquinas set forth a theological position that became Roman Catholic dogma regarding transubstantiation. This doctrine, approved by the Third Lateran Council of 1215, means that at the words of consecration by the priest ("This is my body; this is my blood") the bread and the wine are transformed in their "substance" into

---

[19] Irenaeus of Lyons, *Against Heresies*, in *Documents of the Christian Church*, ed. Henry Bettenson, 2nd ed. (London: Oxford University Press, 1966) 105–106.

the very body and blood of Jesus Christ. The appearance ("accidents") of bread and wine remain the same but the reality is changed. Thus believers literally "eat my flesh" and "drink my blood" as Jesus said they would. Aquinas writes: "And this is done in this sacrament by the power of God, for the whole substance of bread is converted into the whole substance of Christ's body.... Hence this conversion is properly called transubstantiation."[20]

Martin Luther questioned this doctrine but moved only a few steps away from it. He insisted that Christ was miraculously present spiritually and physically "in and through" the bread and the wine but that the elements were not transformed in any way. Christ's presence in the elements was a "Real Presence" but without the superstitious idea of transubstantiation.[21] John Calvin agreed with Luther's denial of transubstantiation, but differed with his view of Christ's presence in the supper. Calvin believed that that Christ was only spiritually available to believers since his physical being could only be in one place, "seated on the right hand of the Father" (Heb 10:12).[22] Ulrich Zwingli rejected these concepts with his belief that the supper was a memorial of Christ's death that nurtured his presence in the faithful hearts of the believing community of Christians.[23] The Society of Friends (Quakers) relinquished the external symbols of bread and wine altogether in order to feed on the inner light of Christ.[24] Anglicans, ever a *via media* amid these multiple traditions, included this phrase in the communion service

---

[20] Thomas Aquinas, *Summa Theologica, iii. Q.lxxv, Article IV*, in Bettenson, *Documents*, 208.

[21] Martin Luther, *The Babylonian Captivity of the Church*, in *Three Treatises*, by M. Luther (Philadelphia: Fortress Press, 1960) 139–52; and Bettenson, *Documents*, 276–79.

[22] John Calvin, *Institutes of the Christian Religion*, in Bettenson, *Documents*, 300–301.

[23] Jaroslav Pelikan, *The Christian Tradition: A History of the Development of Doctrine*, Five Volumes (Chicago: The University of Chicago Press, 1984) 4:196–203; and Sydney Ahlstrom, *A Religious History of the American People* (New Haven: Yale University Press, 1972) 72–83. Pelican and Alstrom offer introductory works that provide fine summaries of these varied views. Pelican is particularly clear on Zwingli's views.

[24] Robert Barclay, *The Chief Principles of the Christian Religion, as Professed by the People Called the Quakers*, in Bettenson, *Documents*, 359.

of the 1552 *Book of Common Prayer*: [*sic*] "Take and eate this, in remembraunce that Christ dyed for thee, and feede on him in thy hearte by faythe, with thankesgeuing."[25]

Ideas shape the meaning of Jesus' simple words of remembrance, body and blood, and life and death. We study church history to know something of the ideas that both unite and divide Christians around the world and across the ages.

History and Context

Perhaps we study the history of the church because we read the Bible and the newspaper, looking to the past for clues to the present. Church history offers a background for understanding context in the church and in the world. For example, the discovery of a collection of ancient manuscripts at Nag Hammadi reopened the study of Gnosticism, not simply as a heretical movement, but as one of multiple factions in the early history of the church that set forth varying visions of who Jesus was and what he meant in the world.[26] The novel *The Da Vinci Code*, with its thesis that Jesus and Mary Magdalene were married, played on many of those tensions, creating a furor in the public square and eliciting serious responses from critics and advocates alike.[27] The release of the *Gospel of Judas* in 2006 was widely discussed in the secular and religious press as scholars and other readers debated the impact of Gnosticism on some of the earliest Christian communities.[28] Media attention to those documents forced many persons to study church history.

The rise of the so-called Evangelical Right as a powerful political force in America has been widely discussed in the media with particular

---

[25] *The First and Second Prayer Books of Edward VI* (New York: E. P. Dutton & Co., 1952) 389; and T. M. Parker, *The English Reformation to 1558* (London: Oxford University Press, 1950) 118–34. Parker's classic work provides an excellent summary of the Eucharistic views of the various Reformation traditions.

[26] James Robinson, *The Nag Hammadi Library in English*, 3rd ed. (Leiden: Brill, 1988); and Bart D. Ehrman, *Lost Scriptures* (New York: Oxford University Press, 2003).

[27] Dan Brown, *The Da Vinci Code*, (New York: Doubleday, 2004) 467

[28] Rodolphe Kasser, Marvin W. Meyer, and Gregor Wurst, eds., *The Gospel of Judas* (Washington, DC: National Geographic, 2006) 185.

attention to concerns regarding prayer in schools, abortion, homosexuality, salvation, and elections. These reports have sent many individuals, Christian and non-Christian, to historical studies in order to understand something of the heritage of evangelicalism and its place in the church and the American Republic. In a work titled *American Gospel: God, the Founding Fathers, and the Making of a Nation*, Jon Meacham insists that "religion has always been woven into American politics." He concludes that "our finest hours—the Revolutionary War, abolition, the expansion of the rights of women, fights against terror and tyranny, the battle against Jim Crow—can partly be traced to religious ideas about liberty, justice, and charity. Yet theology and Scripture have also been used to justify our worst sins—from enslaving black people to persecuting Native Americans to treating women as second-class citizens."[29] To study the history of the church in America is to receive mixed signals about the religious nature of the culture and the use of religion in defending and denying freedom. Americans who read the signs of their own times would do well to know something of the religious ethos of Americans who faced similar dilemmas in earlier periods.

The influx of large numbers of non-Christians—Hindus, Buddhists, and Muslims—has renewed historical studies among those interested expanding their knowledge of Christianity in a pluralistic world. A concern for "spirituality" in various forms has led many people to pursue studies in the history of Christian monasticism, mysticism, and religious experience, even if they do not wish to join any particular church. Recently, a Benedictine friend remarked: "These days many people want to take a retreat at a monastery, but almost no one wants to become a monk!" Encounter with other religions or with diverse spiritual traditions has compelled many Christians to pursue the study of church history in order to know the background and meaning of practices they have long taken for granted.

---

[29] Jon Meacham, *American Gospel: God, the Founding Fathers, and the Making of the Nation* (New York: Random House, 2006) 13, 15–16.

History and Individuals

Finally, the study of Christian history is important because it introduces us to a vast array of individuals who have sought to follow Jesus Christ—strange, wonderful, committed, and sometimes downright crazy people who have shaped and been shaped by the gospel. They are the saints and sinners who have received that gospel and carried it in innumerable directions, bringing peace and wreaking havoc every step of the way. Even the briefest list illustrates the diversity and determination of persons whose lives are at once negative and positive, large and small influences on the church and its message. Polycarp, Perpetua, Augustine of Hippo, Francis of Assisi, Teresa of Avila, Julian of Norwich, John Hus, Martin Luther, John Knox, John Wesley, Peter Abelard, Ignatius Loyola, Jonathan Edwards, Jorena Lee, Mother Ann Lee, Joseph Smith, Sojourner Truth, Amy Semple McPherson, Billy Sunday, Billy Graham, Oscar Romero, Oral Roberts, Pope John XXIII, Jimmy Swaggart, Martin Luther King Jr., and Mother Teresa are considered prophets of one kind or another by significant groups of Christians. In many cases, the truths they professed were not simply in conflict, they were contradictory, although each claimed to have experienced the presence of Christ in profound ways.

They are also persons who knew brokenness, sinfulness, and common humanity in their successes and failures in the world. Polycarp and Perpetua welcomed, perhaps even sought, martyrdom. Augustine was ever haunted by the temptations of the flesh. The same could be said of Peter Abelard and Jimmy Swaggart. Francis, Teresa, and Julian were extraordinary mystics whose spiritual genius and eccentricity often bordered on the bizarre. Martin Luther had a terrible temper and John Wesley had a terrible marriage. Jonathan Edwards was fired from his first church and Joseph Smith was murdered while in jail. John Hus, Martin Luther King, and Oscar Romero were martyred by those who thought their religion had crossed political boundaries. Ann Lee, Sojourner Truth, Jorena Lee, and Amy Semple McPherson scandalized churches by daring to preach to men. Billy Graham has been attacked by Christian groups to his left and his right. Indeed, each of their stories is a fascinating case study in the nature of the church and the varied ways of hearing and living out the Christian faith. They reflect the strength and vulnerability of human beings, even those who seem overtaken by divine grace.

The Church as Saint and Sinner

Whether general or specific, there are manifold reasons for investigating the history of the church. In its most basic sense such a study is a confession that no one arrives at faith alone. Each is carried on the backs of unseen persons whose lives were at once sinful and saintly, full of selflessness and selfishness, in need and in search of grace. To study the church's history is to take seriously the strengths and weaknesses of the church itself, for the church, like the individuals who join it, is *simil justis et piccator*, as Martin Luther said, at once just and sinful. Perhaps that alone makes its story worth exploring, while Jesus tarries.

Remembering the Ecclesial Future: Why the Church Needs Theology

STEVEN R. HARMON

Following a Sunday morning worship service at the Baptist church where I served as part-time pastor while in college, a guest thanked me for conducting his mother's funeral service earlier that week and pressed an envelope into my hands. Along with an honorarium check, it contained a letter in which this member of an Assemblies of God congregation shared with me some words of encouragement he believed God had spoken to him during the funeral. Among other things, the letter exhorted me to remember during my years of preparation for ministry that God "does not want you to be imprisoned by the doctrines of man or the dictates of denominationalism." The man who kindly wrote these words to me instinctively held some of the same convictions about the sinfulness of ecclesiastical divisions that have motivated the modern ecumenical movement since the Edinburgh World Missionary Conference in 1910. In an earlier conversation with me he had offered his observations about some of the doctrinal differences between the Baptist tradition in which he had been raised and the Assemblies of God tradition of his adult experience. He took great delight in the essential agreements between the two denominations and attributed their disagreements to the limitations of human understanding. His words in the letter and in our conversation, however, also reflected a more negative perspective on the relation of theology to the worship, work, and witness of the church held widely not only among laypersons but even among clergy and other ecclesiastical professionals: doctrine, the product and object of the work of theological reflection, is merely human in origin in contrast to God's revelation and frequently serves only to confuse and divide Christians, distracting them from the real ministry of the church.

Such suspicions about theology's ecclesial utility are reinforced by the traditional curricular divisions in seminaries and divinity schools, where the future ministers of the church undertake biblical studies, historical studies, theological studies, and practical studies. The designation of the latter division as "practical theology" unintentionally implies that there is something less than practical about the courses in systematic theology. This chapter contends that the academic discipline to which Fisher Humphreys has devoted his life is indeed a practical discipline in the service of the church that is necessary for the pursuit of its mission, especially for its devotion to the end of the dominical vision of Christian unity expressed in Jesus' prayer in John 17:20–21 (NRSV): "That they may all be one...so that the world may believe."[1]

Theology's Manifold Service of the Church

Charges that theology is irrelevant or even injurious to the church and its ministry are not groundless. Some theologians have pursued theological reflection quite apart from active participation in embodied Christian community, sometimes in open antagonism toward the forms of Christian faith and practice that led them to be interested in theology in the first place. Theology done more consciously in the service of the church has sometimes exceeded legitimate polemical concerns and sought to justify the continuation of the separate ecclesial existence of various denominational expressions of the church, furthering its ongoing division. Theology continues to occupy a central place in the educational preparation of ministers, however, because across two millennia the needs of the church have occasioned the writing and teaching of theology.

Fisher Humphreys' fellow Baptist theologian James Leo Garrett Jr. identified seven major reasons for the necessity of systematic theology to the church. First, the *catechetical* reason: theology is "a proper extension of the teaching function of the Christian church." Second, the *exegetical*

---

[1] For an evaluation of the use of this ecumenical *locus classicus* in major ecumenical texts associated with dialogue between the Roman Catholic Church and other ecclesial bodies, see Hellen Mardaga, "Reflection on the Meaning of John 17:21 for Ecumenical Dialogue," *Ecumenical Trends* 34/10 (November 2005): 148–52.

reason: theology is necessary "for the integrated formulation of biblical truth." Third, the *homiletical* reason: theology is required "for the accurate clarification, the proper undergirding, and the helpful amplification of the gospel message that ought to be preached by Christian preachers and indeed of the total proclamation of the Word of God by all the people of God." Fourth, the *polemical* reason: the church depends upon theology "for the defense of Christian truth against error within the church or from quasi-Christian movements." Fifth, the *apologetic* reason: theology is done "either in response to the challenge of a leading philosophy in a given era, or in response to the entire cultural situation of the time, including prevailing criticisms of Christianity, or in response to questions about ultimate reality allegedly posed by humankind." Sixth, the *ethical* reason: theology functions "as the essential background for the interpretation and application of Christian ethics to personal and social needs and problems." Seventh, the *dialogic* and *missionary* reasons: theology contributes to "the proper encounter of Christianity with other major religions and...the more effective propagation of the Christian gospel among all human beings."[2]

The church certainly needs theology for all the reasons named by Garrett. Those needs are in the forefront of my own mind as I teach theology to future ministers as a discipline done in, with, and for the church. Yet in light of the confluence of three dimensions of my work as an ecclesial theologian—teaching theology to a denominationally diverse student body that includes members of a wide variety of Christian traditions in addition to Baptists, doing research in patristic theology, and occasionally serving as a Baptist ecumenist—I would add an eighth reason for the ecclesial necessity of theology, interrelated with the seven identified by Garrett: the *ecumenical* reason. The church needs theology because the ecclesial future disclosed in Scripture involves visible Christian unity, and unless its theologians function as stewards of the Christian memory, which is the living tradition to which all the currently divided churches are heirs, the church will be severely crippled in its

---

[2] James Leo Garrett Jr., *Systematic Theology: Biblical, Historical, and Evangelical*, 2 vols. (Grand Rapids: Wm. B. Eerdmans, 1990) 1:12–15 See also James Leo Garrett Jr., *Systematic Theology: Biblical, Historical, and Evangelical*, 2nd ed., 2 vols (North Richland Hills TX: BIBAL Press, 2000) 1:11–14.

movements toward this aspect of God's designs for it.[3] The church needs theology in order to remember the ecclesial future for which it works in the present and in order to conserve and cultivate the traditional doctrinal resources necessary for moving toward that future.

Theology and the Ecumenical Crisis of the Church

Most careful observers of the modern ecumenical movement agree that despite such dramatic breakthroughs in recent decades as *Baptism, Eucharist and Ministry* (World Council of Churches Commission on Faith and Order, 1982) and the *Joint Declaration on the Doctrine of Justification* (Lutheran World Federation and Roman Catholic Church, 1999),[4] interest in the classical ecumenical goal of a visibly united church in which there is full Eucharistic communion and common confession of the apostolic faith has declined so precipitously as to leave the future of this goal very much in doubt. Long-time proponents of "Faith and Order" ecumenism[5] are in general agreement in their identification of the factors that have contributed to the current ecumenical crisis. Recent publications by veteran ecumenists read almost like a common litany of lament in their rehearsals of the reasons for what they fear may be the demise of Faith and Order ecumenism.[6] In their preface to *The Princeton Proposal for Christian Unity*, Carl Braaten and Robert Jenson summarized

---

[3] Cf. Robert L. Wilken, "Memory and the Christian Intellectual Life," chapter 8 in *Remembering the Christian Past*, by Robert L. Wilken (Grand Rapids: Wm. B. Eerdmans, 1995) 165–80.

[4] World Council of Churches, *Baptism, Eucharist and Ministry*, Faith and Order Paper 111 (Geneva: WCC Publications, 1983); Lutheran World Federation and Roman Catholic Church, *Joint Declaration on the Doctrine of Justification* (Grand Rapids: Wm. B. Eerdmans, 2000).

[5] For a concise history of this approach to ecumenical engagement, see Jeffrey Gros, F.S.C., "Faith and Order in Historical Perspective," in *Faith and Order: Toward a North American Conference. A Study Guide*, ed. Norman A. Hjelm (Grand Rapids: Wm. B. Eerdmans, 2005) 23–31.

[6] E.g., William G. Rusch, "The State and Future of the Ecumenical Movement," *Pro Ecclesia* 9/1 (Winter 2000): 8–18; George Lindbeck, "Ecumenisms in Conflict," in *God, Truth, and Witness: Engaging Stanley Hauerwas*, ed. L. Gregory Jones et al. (Grand Rapids: Brazos Press, 2005) 212–28; Robert W. Jenson, "God's Time, Our Time: An Interview with Robert W. Jenson," *Chistian Century* 123/9 (2 May 2006): 31–35.

the factors that occasioned the work of the unofficial group of sixteen theologians and ecumenists from various Christian traditions who drafted the document:

> The Center for Catholic and Evangelical Theology called the group together following consultations which showed wide consensus that both the ecumenical movement itself and the churches' commitment to it were stalled in place. "Reception" by the churches of consensus achieved in dialogues is even more difficult than expected. Some key points of division have proven unexpectedly stubborn. The institutions of conciliar ecumenism are largely captive to a "new ecumenical paradigm" which subordinates the concern of the "faith and order" movement, for the visible unity of Christians, to social and political agendas which are themselves divisive. The wisdom of the first general secretary of the World Council of Churches, Willem Vissert's Hooft, "The World Council of Churches is either a christocentric movement or it is nothing at all," now carries little weight. Perhaps most distressing, the churches that once principally carried the movement have turned their energies to other matters, often to their own internal divisions...and few see the way forward.[7]

Since Braaten and Jenson wrote these words in 2003, "the way forward" has become even less clear for classical ecumenical interests in North America. In December 1999, seventy-five ecumenists, theologians, denominational leaders, and ministers broadly representative of Catholic, Orthodox, mainline Protestant, evangelical, and Pentecostal traditions issued "A Call to the Churches for a Second Conference on Faith and Order in North America." They hoped that the 1957 North American Conference on Faith and Order in Oberlin, Ohio, might be revisited in 2005 with a second conference more fully representative of

[7] Carl E. Braaten and Robert W. Jenson, eds., *In One Body through the Cross: The Princeton Proposal for Christian Unity* (Grand Rapids: Wm. B. Eerdmans, 2003) 6–7.

the church in North America.[8] In January 2001 an independent Foundation for a Conference on Faith and Order in North America was established to promote and hold such a conference. Following a planning consultation at the University of Notre Dame in October 2001, more concrete plans developed for a conference with the theme "The Church: Its Faith and Its Unity" to be held in New York City in September 2005. For a variety of reasons, including resistance by parties inside and outside the ecumenical establishment in the United States, the conference did not materialize.[9] A consultation in January 2006 examined the causes for the failure of the conference along with the factors that might yet make a similar venture possible. However, the board of the Foundation for a Conference on Faith and Order in North America dissolved the foundation in February 2006.

Among whatever factors are responsible for the paralysis of Faith and Order ecumenism in North America and beyond, surely the discipline of theology has made its own contributions to the widespread indifference to ecclesial division. Chief among them is an increasingly common abdication by academic theologians of their responsibilities to the catechetical needs of the church. Enamored with novelty in the interests of cultural relevance and academic respectability, many theologians have given more attention to the exploration of new philosophical frameworks for theology or the rethinking of Christian theology in light of the theory *du jour* than to careful stewardship of what "the church of Jesus Christ believes, teaches, and confesses on the basis of the word of God."[10] As a result, they have unwittingly helped form new generations of ministers who do not see catechesis as essential to the exercise of pastoral ministry and who therefore have not actively formed the members of their congregations in the teachings that have

---

[8] The text of the statement may be found in Hjelm, *Faith and Order*, 3–11.

[9] Jenson is forthright in his appraisal: "It was undone by mainline Protestantism's present indifference to and distraction from the whole matter, by evangelicalism's unconcern about separation at the Lord's table, and by deliberate obstruction from within the established ecumenical apparatus" ("God's Time Our Time," 33).

[10] Jaroslav Pelikan, *The Christian Tradition: A History of the Development of Doctrine*, vol. 1, *The Emergence of the Catholic Tradition (100–600)* (Chicago: University of Chicago Press, 1971) 1.

sustained the church through two millennia of challenges. This neglect of the catechetical dimension of the discipline of theology both exacerbates the existing ecclesial divisions and obscures the means by which they might be overcome. Joseph Small, coordinator of the Office of Theology and Worship for the Presbyterian Church (U.S.A.), observes:

> There have been times in the church's life when oppressive orthodoxy was a painful problem. Ours is not one of those times. Our problem is a *laissez faire* approach to dogma that produces ecclesial cacophony. The solution does not lie in a revival of oppressive orthodoxy, but in a fitting reception of the rule of faith coupled with suitable conversation about unsettled or ambiguous matters. The *regula fidei* does not squelch theological exploration in the church, but rather enables it.[11]

The ecumenical reason for theology as a discipline in the service of the church, then, depends especially upon proper attention to its catechetical rationale and to the relationship of theology as the explication of Christian teachings to other sorts of theologizing.

What Sort of Theology the Divided Church Needs

The church's current inability to make a common confession of the apostolic faith calls for a theology that makes a proper distinction between theological reflection that has the teaching of the church as its primary object, beneficiary, and set of parameters and theological reflection that carefully ventures beyond these parameters and creatively addresses other concerns while remaining rooted in the teaching of the church. In other words, the church needs a renewal of the writing and teaching of what used to be called "dogmatic theology"—not in the sense of the more recently acquired connotation of "dogmatic" as "asserting or imposing dogmas or opinions in an authoritative,

---

[11] Joseph D. Small, "Theology's Passive Voice," *Perspectives: A Journal of Reformed Theology* 20/9 (October 2005): 23.

imperious, or arrogant manner," but rather as a synonym of "doctrinal"[12] linked etymologically with the early Christian usage of the Greek adjective *dogmatikos* to refer to that which is "concerned with doctrine."[13] In this classical sense "dogmatics" designates a species of theology that reflects upon and gives expression to the church's teachings.

The program book for the annual meeting of the American Academy of Religion (AAR) provides ample evidence that many theologians who participate in that professional society are no longer concerned with this species of theology (along with more encouraging evidence that a growing number of theologians active in the AAR are in fact interested in dogmatics). [14] Yet from the age of the church fathers to those recognized as their modern equivalents, Christianity's finest theologians have been dogmaticians in the sense that they carefully distinguished between their efforts to give voice to the teaching of the church and their individual musings beyond it, even while exercising creativity in doing both dogmatic theology and theology of other sorts. Novelty and creativity do have a proper place within and alongside dogmatic theology. The dogmatic theologian is comparable to "the scribe who has been trained for the kingdom of heaven," who "is like the master of a household who brings out of his treasure what is new and what is old" (Matt 13:52 NRSV). The scribes, the theologians of Jesus' day, drew upon the traditional resources of the "old things" of the Torah but also brought forth the "new things" of the application of the Torah to the emergences of daily living centuries after the giving of the Torah. Just as the scribes "trained for the kingdom of heaven" connected these "old things" with the "new things" now experienced in Christ,[15] so the

[12] *The Oxford English Dictionary*, ed. J. A. Simpson and E. S. C. Weiner, 2nd ed. (Oxford: Clarendon Press, 1989) s.v. "dogmatic" (definitions A.2 and A.4).

[13] *A Patristic Greek Lexicon*, ed. G. W. H. Lampe (Oxford: Clarendon Press, 1961) s.v. "dogmatikos" (definition 3).

[14] The AAR Christian Systematic Theology section and Eastern Orthodox Studies and Evangelical Theology groups, for example, have maintained a rigorous focus on theology as the exploration of Christian doctrine.

[15] This reading of the role of the scribes in this enigmatic parable is influenced by Andrew T. Lincoln, "Matthew—A Story for Teachers?" in *The Bible in Three Dimensions: Essays in Celebration of Forty Years of Biblical Studies in the University of Sheffield*, ed. David J. A. Clines et al., Journal for the Study of

church's dogmatic theologians have creatively configured the "old things" of the traditional teachings of the church to address the "new things" of the life of the church in another time and place.

Origen (d. A.D. 254) is sometimes identified as the church's first systematic theologian on the basis of his coherent treatment of all the major doctrinal rubrics in a single work, *On First Principles*, something not accomplished in the extant Christian literature that antedates Origen. In the preface to that treatise, Origen declares that as Christian believers hold "conflicting opinions" on matters of great as well as trivial importance, "it seems necessary first to lay down a definite line and unmistakable rule (*regulam*) in regard to each of these, and to postpone the inquiry into other matters until afterwards."[16] Some of the apostolic doctrines are "necessary ones," while "there were other doctrines...about which the apostles simply said that things were so, keeping silence as to the how or why."[17] This distinction allowed a proper role for speculative theology as inquiry into "the how or why" that respects the broad boundaries of the "unmistakable rule." For Origen the apostolic rule included within an overarching Trinitarian structure a series of summary narrative affirmations regarding the oneness of the God of the Old Testament and New Testament who created all things and revealed himself in Jesus Christ; the preexistence, incarnation, virginal conception, crucifixion, death, resurrection, and ascension of Jesus Christ; the unity "in honor and dignity with the Father and the Son" of the Holy Spirit, who inspired the prophets and the apostles; the judgment of the soul after its departure from this world and the resurrection of the dead; the freedom of the human will and the reality of its struggle against the evil powers and assistance by the angelic powers; the creation of this world "at a definite time"—an affirmation of

---

the Old Testament Supplement Series 87 (Sheffield: JSOT Press, 1990) 107–108.

[16] Origen, *On First Principles*, I.pref.2; (Origen, *On First Principles*, trans. G. W. Butterworth [Gloucester MA: Peter Smith, 1973] 1–2); for the extant text of the passage in Rufinus' Latin translation, see Henri Crouzel and Manlio Simonetti, eds., *Origène Traité des Principes*,, Sources Chrétiennes 252 (Paris: Éditions du Cerf, 1978) 1:78.

[17] Origen, *On First Principles*, I.pref.3 (Origen, *On First Principles*, trans. Butterworth, 2).

creatio ex nihilo; and the divine inspiration of the Scriptures and the existence within them of both "obvious" and "hidden" levels of meaning.[18] These are the "first principles" to which the title of the treatise refers, and they provide guidance for the consideration of other matters. Origen carefully noted in his summary of the apostolic rule the points at which "no clear statement...is set forth in the Church teaching."[19] On such points—the nature of the resurrection body, precisely what sorts of creatures are the celestial bodies, and the extent to which God's saving work will be universally realized among rational creatures being notable examples—Origen was free to speculate, but always in an effort to relate them to the "elementary and foundation principles" in "a connected body of doctrine."[20] The later scholastic Origenists did not preserve this distinction between the "foundation principles" and speculation beyond them, for which failure their teachings were rightly anathematized in A.D. 553 at the Fifth Ecumenical Council (Constantinople II). Nevertheless, the church's first systematic theologian provides an ancient precedent for Joseph Small's contention that "the *regula fidei* does not squelch theological exploration in the church, but rather enables it."[21]

More recently the Swiss Reformed theologian Karl Barth (1886–1968), regarded by many as a "modern church father," rediscovered the centrality of dogmatic theology to the church's theological needs as a result of his encounter with the dogmatic theologians of post-Reformation orthodoxy. Daunted by the opportunity to teach a course in dogmatics in 1924 following the third academic year of his initial professorship at Göttingen, Barth—who lacked a doctor of theology degree, not to mention the second doctorate expected of professors in the German university system—was desperate not only for help in lecture preparation but especially for an approach that would help him and his students to read the Bible through the lenses of the church in a way not accomplished by any of the reigning theological paradigms. In the midst of a frenetic effort during the break between

---

[18] Ibid., I.pref.4–10 (Origen, *On First Principles*, trans. Butterworth, 2–6).
[19] Ibid., I.pref.7 (Origen, *On First Principles*, trans. Butterworth, 5).
[20] Ibid., I.pref.10 (Origen, *On First Principles*, trans. Butterworth, 6).
[21] Small, "Theology's Passive Voice," 23.

terms to work through the major dogmatic works of the patristic period and later, Barth happened upon the *Reformed Dogmatics* of Heinrich Heppe (1820–1879).[22] There Barth discovered a stage in the evolution of Protestant theology at which the breakthrough insights of Luther, Calvin, and the other early Reformers had been carefully evaluated by the church and incorporated into a truly "ecclesial hermeneutic." Although Barth went on to read other Protestant orthodox dogmaticians of the mid-nineteenth century, in particular the Lutheran theologian Heinrich Schmid (1811–1885),[23] Heppe remained the most influential, and the *Göttingen Dogmatics* that emerged from these lectures (delivered 1924–1926) reads like a running commentary on Heppe's *Dogmatics*.[24] Bruce McCormack has argued cogently that it was this discovery—rather than the much-cited later engagement with Anselm's thought in 1930—that marked the turning point that determined the ultimate shape of the *Church Dogmatics* published from 1932 to 1965.[25] In the prolegomena volume of the *Church Dogmatics*, Barth identified its genre as "regular dogmatics," which is "an enquiry into dogma which aims at the completeness appropriate to the special task of the school, of theological instruction" that prepares ministers to do their own independent theological work and so "must cover the whole field in respect of the range of concepts and themes that are significant for

---

[22] Heinrich Heppe, *Die Dogmatik der evangelisch-reformierten Kirche* (Elberfeld: R. L. Friedrichs, 1861); ET, *Reformed Dogmatics*, trans. G. T. Thomson (London: Allen & Unwin, 1950; repr., Grand Rapids: Baker Book House, 1978).

[23] Heinrich Friedrich Ferdinand Schmid, *Dogmatik der evangelisch-lutherischen Kirche*, 4th ed. (Frankfurt: Heyder & Zimmer, 1858); ET, *Doctrinal Theology of the Evangelical Lutheran Church*, trans. Charles A. Hay and Henry E. Jacobs (Minneapolis: Augsburg Publishing House, 1961).

[24] Karl Barth, *Unterricht in der christlichen Religion (1924–1926)* 3 vols., ed. Hannelotte Reiffen and Hinrich Stoevesandt, Karl Barth-Gesamtausgabe pt. 2, vols. 9, 10, 13 (Zürich: Theologischer Verlag, 1985–2003); partial ET, *The Göttingen Dogmatics: Instruction in the Christian Religion*, trans. Geoffrey W. Bromiley (Grand Rapids: Wm. B. Eerdmans, 1991).

[25] Bruce L. McCormack, *Karl Barth's Critically Realistic Dialectical Theology: Its Genesis and Development 1909–1936* (Oxford: Oxford University Press, 1997) esp. 23, 334–37, 349–50.

church proclamation."[26] While Barth did engage individual theologians across the history of the church as dialogue partners, he weighed the contributions of these partners in terms of their importance for "church proclamation" and in relation to the sources he considered even more authoritative: communal expressions of the dogma of the church in the form of creeds, conciliar decisions, and confessions.[27]

On a first reading, Barth's *Church Dogmatics* seems to be mostly concerned with the "old things" suggested by Matthew 13:52. Barth did not so much create a new theology as re-engage decidedly old expressions of theology, and much of the substance of the *Church Dogmatics* consists of extended fine print excurses in which Barth does biblical exegesis and mines the resources of the doctrinal tradition of the church. Yet in the manner in which Barth draws these "old things" into a coherent whole in the service of the proclamation of the church of his own age, the *Church Dogmatics* gives expression to "new things." A clue to the place of creative novelty in Barth's reclamation of dogmatic theology is supplied by the much-commented-upon juxtaposition of two portraits in his Basel study: John Calvin, the great Reformed theologian, and Wolfgang Amadaeus Mozart, the great classical composer. In light of this pairing of paintings, one might understand Barth the dogmatic theologian as a theological artist.[28]

As artists, musical composers normally work with certain givens that they did not themselves create: tones, keys, scales, rhythms, even formal and stylistic traditions that make the composition recognizable as music and as music of a certain type, and yet out of these given media the composer fashions something novel. Sometimes received media

---

[26] Karl Barth, *The Doctrine of the Word of God*, vol. 1 of *Church Dogmatics*, trans. G. W. Bromiley, 2nd ed. (Edinburgh: T & T Clark, 1975) pt. 1, 275–76.

[27] On this phenomenon in Barth's interaction with patristic dialogue partners, see Steven R. Harmon, "Karl Barth's Conversation with the Fathers: A Paradigm for *Ressourcement* in Baptist and Evangelical Theology," *Perspectives in Religious Studies* 33/1 (Spring 2006): 7–23, esp. 16 and 19; this article was revised and expanded as chapter 7 in Steven R. Harmon, *Towards Baptist Catholicity: Essays on Tradition and the Baptist Vision*, Studies in Baptist History and Thought 27 (Milton Keynes: Paternoster, 2006) 129–50, esp. 140 and 144–46.

[28] Cf. Theodore A. Gill, "Barth and Mozart," *Theology Today* 43/3 (October 1986): 403–11.

mandate fixed repetition, as in the baroque *passacaglia*, a dance form with a short melodic figure repeated over and over again and variations arranged around the fixed figure. In the *Passacaglia for Solo Violin* that concludes the *Rosary Sonatas* by Heinrich Ignaz Franz von Biber (1644–1704), for example, the violinist repeats the same four descending notes in each measure of the ten-minute-long piece, yet Biber's haunting ornamentations of the recurrent figure make this *passacaglia* anything but monotonous. Like the composer of a *passacaglia*, Barth worked with the Scriptures and the doctrines that he received from the church—unchanging "old things." In giving faithful voice to a tradition that he did not create, he nevertheless exercised a delightfully creative aesthetic sensibility in arranging the "notes" and "rhythms" of the tradition so that the *Church Dogmatics* offered the church "new things" in the form of artfully crafted theological compositions.

A renewal of dogmatic theology in seminaries and divinity schools, in which theologians would function primarily as catechists whose writing and teaching equips ministers to do catechesis themselves in local churches, will not consign the discipline of theology to antiquarian irrelevance, nor will it prevent those who do dogmatic theology from making *ad hoc* use of new developments in philosophy and social or literary theory to explicate Christian doctrines and ponder them in light of fresh perspectives. Rather, it will make available to the contemporary church the resources it needs to confess its faith with the oneness that the currently unbelieving world will find compelling in the ecclesial future envisioned by Jesus. Teaching the doctrines a specific ecclesial communion holds in common with all Christians, such as the Trinitarian character of God and the full humanity and full divinity of Jesus Christ, strengthens the basis upon which the divided churches may move closer to a common confession of the apostolic faith. Teaching the doctrines that a particular Protestant communion holds in common with other churches of the Reformation (and thus not with Roman Catholicism), as well as the doctrines unique to that denomination, helps foster clarity about the remaining doctrinal divisions and therefore contributes to the earnest ecumenical contestation of what it means to be the "one, holy, catholic, and apostolic church," an ecclesiological disputation that is necessary for seeking a visible unity of faith and order that is not merely an insipid affirmation of all existing differences as varying expressions of an invisible oneness.[29]

What Sort of Theologians the Divided Church Needs

The renewal of dogmatic theology in the service of the divided church will not come about merely through the adoption of a new set of methodological commitments by those who write and teach theology. Such renewal requires theologians who have been deeply formed by the church, who actively participate in its local ministries, and who in their vocational self-understanding are *ecclesial* theologians—teachers of the church as well as the academy, teachers of the church in its ecumenicity as well as its local and denominational expressions, teachers of laity as well as future clergy. The church has been hurt by theological teachers who pursue their careers as avenues of escape from engagement with the church in all its shortcomings. The church will be helped toward healing if we encourage students with promise for a ministry of theological education to live "in the ruins of the church" as ecclesial theologians, remaining in and devoting their lives to the service of the ecclesial communions of their nurture and calling, even if there is much that is undesirable about these ecclesial dwellings.[30] Fisher Humphreys has exemplified this sort of theologian; may there be others who follow in his steps.

---

[29] Fisher Humphreys has effectively utilized this ecumenical approach to defining Baptist identity in *The Way We Were: How Southern Baptist Theology Has Changed and What It Means to Us All*, rev. ed. (Macon GA: Smyth & Helwys, 2002) 15–58, and also in Fisher Humphreys, *Baptist Theology: A Really Short Version* (Brentwood TN: Baptist History and Heritage Society, 2007).

[30] This image is suggested by R. R. Reno, *In the Ruins of the Church: Sustaining Faith in an Age of Diminished Christianity* (Grand Rapids: Brazos Press, 2002). I remain convinced of the appropriateness of the book's thesis and argument, even if Reno himself subsequently came to view it as just the kind of theory serving to distance one from ecclesial concreteness that he had criticized in the book (R. R. Reno, "Out of the Ruins," *First Things* 150 [February 2005]: 11–16).

Spiritual Theology for the Evangelical Church

J. NORFLEETE DAY

I first met Fisher Humphreys in 1989 when he came to teach at Beeson Divinity School where I was a master of divinity student, although his reputation had preceded him. I had heard his former students singing his praises as a godly man and a gifted teacher. In my own divinity school sojourn, the dreaded systematic theology course was instead, thanks to Fisher, a stimulating, thought-provoking, and understandable learning experience. Ever since that time, he has been my touchstone regarding theological matters. When I encounter theological uncertainty or confusion, I turn to Fisher for clarity and insight. In addition to this pragmatic relationship, Fisher and Caroline have become valued friends. They bring joy and stimulation to every encounter. It is an honor to be included among those invited to celebrate Fisher's life and ministry by contributing to this volume.

Spiritual theology is an uncommon expression to evangelical Christians as well as to most Protestants, in general. Spiritual theology's history and use is primarily associated with Roman Catholicism. And yet the term encompasses the vital aspects of Christian living that are foundational to an evangelical expression of Christianity. Spiritual theology is that part of theology that defines the nature of spiritual life, formulates principles for its growth and development, and explains the process by which individuals advance from the beginning stage of spiritual life (conversion/justification) to its full and final perfection (glorification).[1] In its most basic definition, spiritual theology can be thought of as that branch of theology concerned with the principles and practices of living the Christian life.

---

[1] Adapted from Jordan Aumann, *Spiritual Theology* (Westminster MD: Sheed & Ward 1987) 22.

Divisions and subdivisions of theological endeavor were unknown in the pre-Enlightenment period; all theology was understood to be spiritual. Reflection about God was for the purpose of knowing God so that a person could lead a life that pleased and glorified God. The modern convention of theological specializations has led to distinctions in theological endeavor so that we now have systematic, moral, biblical, and spiritual theologies, to name only the most common divisions. Christian spirituality might be considered an equivalent expression for spiritual theology, but the simple and popular term spirituality is not a sufficient alternative. As Simon Chan notes, "Generally, *spirituality* refers to the kind of life that is formed by a particular type of spiritual theology. Spirituality is the lived reality, whereas spiritual theology is the systematic reflection and formalization of that reality."[2]

Proponents of evangelical theology have been conditioned to think of salvation as an ordered progression through three stages: justification, sanctification, and glorification. According to that scheme, spiritual theology can be thought of as that branch of theology concerned with the sanctification phase, or as it has been called, "the sanctification gap," because of evangelical emphasis on the first and third stages, often to the neglect of the middle stage.

The first stage of salvation (conversion/justification) is merely the beginning of the Christian life. The third stage (glorification) is achieved at death. But in the interval between these two stages—an interval of many years and the majority of life on this earth for most believers—there is the command to take up our cross and follow Jesus Christ. This stage of sanctification is for the purpose of *transforming* us into his likeness. It may be helpful to think of the first two stages—justification and sanctification—together. While in the justification stage we are *declared* righteous through God's gracious provision of Christ's righteousness imputed to us, the sanctification stage enables us to *become* what we have been declared to be. It develops in us the righteousness of God by the action of the Holy Spirit who now dwells in us.

The Bible makes it clear that our conversion experience does not constitute the entirety of our reconciliation with God. The grace that

---

[2] Simon Chan, *Spirituality Theology: A Systematic Study of the Christian Life* (Downers Grove IL: InterVarsity Press, 1998) 16.

initially drew us to respond to God's offer of forgiveness and restoration, subsequent to our justification, becomes operative in our lives to make us holy. We are called to follow Jesus as his disciples (Matt 16:24 TNIV),[3] to become holy as the God who called us is holy (1 Pet 1:15–16), and to be united with Christ that we might be conformed to his likeness (Rom 8:29). Because it is the life, death, and resurrection of Jesus that enable our restoration to relationship with God, the root of our Christian spirituality must be grounded in the experience of Jesus. Indeed, Jesus becomes our leader and our example as we embark on the pilgrimage of Christian living (Heb 12:2; 1 Pet 2:21).

The call to a union with Christ empowers us to share in his Spirit (1 Cor 6:17) so that we may be conformed to his image (Rom 8:29). It is this union with Christ that enables us to experience the new creation within us that God is making. In the words of Paul, "If anyone is in Christ, the new creation has come: The old has gone; the new is here!" (2 Cor 5:17 NRSV). Thus, our status of being "in Christ" makes it inevitable that we should want to be like him. The goal of our living becomes the transformation of our old selves into persons who are like Christ—in our attitudes, our actions, and our love.

Having entered into a personal relationship with Christ, we may desire to be like him, but we are unable to effect such a transformation by means of our own will and power. Paul testifies to the futility of such efforts in Romans 7:14–25. It is only by the work of the Holy Spirit that we grow in grace and become holy. Having been justified by partaking of the atonement provided by the shed blood of Christ, and thereby receiving the gift of the Holy Spirit, we enter into the lifelong process of sanctification (from the Latin *sanctus*, "holy").

While it is essential to affirm that sanctification is the work of the Spirit, it is equally important to understand that we are not merely passive recipients of the Spirit's efforts. Paul, in his letter to the Philippian Christians, makes it clear that our sanctification is dependent upon our cooperation with the work of the Spirit: "Work out your own salvation with fear and trembling; for it is God who is at work in you both to will and to work for his good pleasure" (Phil 2:12b–13). So God

[3] Bible translations are from *Today's New International Version* (Grand Rapids: Zondervan 2002) unless otherwise specified.

both instills in us the desire to grow in Christ-likeness and effects that growth as we cooperate with the work of the Spirit.

Because it spans our whole lifetime between conversion and death, the sanctification phase of our salvation has often been characterized as a journey or pilgrimage. There may be puncticular experiences that cause a quantum jump in our spiritual development, but the overall transformation is a slow and often invisible process. As John Tyson notes, "It is often a pilgrimage that proceeds steadily and incrementally as a Christian gives himself or herself more and more over to God's will and is correspondingly recreated more and more in God's character and likeness. The path toward godliness leads through participation in the 'means of grace' (such as Word and Sacrament) and 'spiritual disciplines' (such as prayer, fasting, and Christian service)."[4]

Our cooperation with the Holy Spirit's work in us occurs most visibly through the corporate practices of worship. Indeed, for evangelicals the most common spiritual practice is church attendance. Diogenes Allen allows that our experience of worship may lead "to the stirring of a desire for God's habitual presence, but...unless we have some explicit instruction in spiritual theology, we are not likely to recognize this stirring for what it is, nor know how to direct it."[5]

This reality indicates that we must understand the aim of our spiritual life. For John Calvin the goal was "to know God and to enjoy God forever."[6] But if that is our ultimate aim, how does that relate to the practical, quotidian goals of learning to control our emotions and love our neighbors? How do we, in plain and simple terms, learn to obey the two great commandments of loving God with our heart, soul, mind, and strength and our neighbor as ourselves? (Mark 12:28–34; Matt 22:34–38) To love God with heart, soul, mind, and strength means that every aspect of our being is centered on God and permeated with love for God. This sort of focus on God necessitates and eventuates increasing

---

[4] John R. Tyson, ed. *Invitation to Christian Spirituality: An Ecumenical Anthology* (New York: Oxford University Press, 1999) 3.

[5] Diogenes Allen, *Spiritual Theology: The Theology of Yesterday for Spiritual Help Today* (Cambridge MA: Cowley Publications, 1997) 15.

[6] John Calvin, *Institutes of the Christian Religion*, ed. John McNeill, trans Ford Lewis Battles, Library of Christian Classics 20 and 2 1 (Philadelphia: Westminster, Press 1969) 1:41

knowledge of God. According to Diogenes Allen, "In Christianity…it is the knowledge of God that produces likeness to God…but what enables us to know God and through that knowledge become like God is based on God's action, especially the act of becoming incarnate. Our entire life is drawn into the life of God by the presence of God the Holy Spirit who comes to us through our baptism into the death and resurrection of Jesus."[7] Because of our being made in the image of God, we long for fellowship with God, and as our fellowship grows and increases, our desire to will the will of God increases so that we act more as God acts.

While our conformity to the likeness of God in Christ is God's work, God does not violate our will or nature to affect it. If we resist the work of God's Spirit, our spiritual growth is stunted or lies fallow. If we wait passively for the Spirit's work, growth will take place in some measure. However, if we cooperate with the work of the Spirit by intentional actions and practices that make us sensitive to the Spirit's work, our spiritual growth is nurtured and accelerated.

God's ultimate purpose it to make us more like Jesus (Rom 8:28–29). God does this by the working of his grace in us that allows us to receive the benefits and power of Jesus. Our conformity to the likeness of Jesus is affected by God through the work of the Holy Spirit who empowers us to resist the sin to which we are prone in our humanity.

The sanctification that God brings about in our lives is the result of our being united with Christ through acceptance of the atonement he provides. As Paul expressed it in Gal 2:20: "I have been crucified with Christ and I no longer live, but Christ lives in me." So Christ's life becomes our life, and we gain the benefits of his standing with God and credit for his righteousness.[8] This "life exchange" is pictured vividly in an episode from John Bunyan's *Pilgrim's Progress*. Near the end of their journey the pilgrims discover a wonderful mirror. While there is nothing unusual about the front of the glass, on the back appears an image of the crucified Lord Jesus. Looking in the front of the mirror, one sees what any mirror would reflect—our true visual image, including the blemishes

---

[7] Ibid., 27.

[8] Anthony A. Hoekema, "The Reformed Perspective," in *Five Views on Sanctification*, ed. Melvin E. Dieter (Grand Rapids: Zondervan, 1987) 63–64.

and scars that mark our humanity. But if one looks through the reverse side of the mirror, one sees only the glory of the Son of God.[9] This imagery illustrates that our holiness is not a matter of what we personally achieve, but it is the result of God's gracious provision. God, in his grace, looks at us from the perspective that sees his holy Son in our place.[10]

The spiritual reality of Christ's life in us provides our definitive, or positional, sanctification, which means that God relates to us as he relates to his own Son. While we have a long way to go in attaining true personal holiness, God already accepts us on the basis of Christ's righteousness. In the words of Anthony Hoekema:

> Sanctification, therefore, must be understood as being both definitive and progressive. In its definitive sense, it means that work of the Spirit whereby He causes us to die to sin, to be raised with Christ, and to be made new creatures. In its progressive sense, it must be understood as that work of the Spirit whereby He continually renews and transforms us into the likeness of Christ, enabling us to keep on growing in grace and to keep on perfecting our holiness.[11]

As indicated previously, God's work of sanctifying us, making us holy, does not overlook our human will, our freedom to choose. This ability to choose is classically conveyed by Paul in Romans 12:2: "Do not conform any longer to the pattern of this world, but be transformed by the renewing of your mind. Then you will be able to test and approve what God's will is—his good, pleasing and perfect will." The transformation of which Paul speaks is at the heart of spiritual formation—"the intentional, sustained re-patterning of a person's life after the pattern set out by God when he created human beings in his

---

[9] See Bryan Chapell, *Holiness by Grace* (Wheaton IL: Crossway Books, 2001) 8.

[10] Ibid., 8.

[11] Hoekema, "Reformed Perspective," 77.

image, but made possible only by divine transforming power."[12] As Mel Lawrenz continues it:

> Every miracle of transformation in the Old Testament or in the life of Jesus is not a magic trick or divine razzle-dazzle, but rather the unveiling of his unique divine power to shape and reshape any element of the cosmos. Fishes and loaves may be multiplied, withered hands restored, dead eyes opened, a lake's surface made solid, a cloud shaped into a pillar, corpses enlivened. In each instance God signals, "I can transform anything in the universe I have formed."[13]

If God's intention is to grow us up to the fullness of Christ (Eph 4:11–16) and this growth is possible only through the action of the Holy Spirit working in and upon us, what is our role? Do we indeed have any responsibility other than passively submitting to this divine transformation? Paul's instruction in Philippians 2:12–13 indicates that we have a significant part in this transforming process, even though only God's power can bring it about: "Work out your own salvation...for God is at work in you." This seeming paradox is at the heart of spiritual formation. We cannot work out our salvation on our own, nor are we to sit passively by expecting God to do everything. We can intentionally engage in activities that facilitate God's work in us so that it is maximally effective. Thus, for hundreds of years Christians who have desired to facilitate this divine transforming action have practiced spiritual disciplines to make themselves attentive to God and to what he might be trying to teach them. These disciplines should never become legalistic, works-oriented activities. Rather, as M. Robert Mulholland observes, "Holistic spiritual disciplines are acts of loving obedience that we offer to God steadily and consistently, to be used for whatever work God purposes to do in and through our lives."[14]

---

[12] Mel Lawrenz, *The Dynamics of Spiritual Formation* (Grand Rapids: Baker Books, 2000) 145–46.

[13] Ibid., 146.

[14] M. Robert Mulholland Jr., *Invitation to a Journey: A Road Map for Spiritual Formation* (Downers Grove IL: InterVarsity Press, 1993) 103.

Discipline is not a welcome word in our twenty-first century culture. It tends to be equated with self-denial and structure in a culture that strives to be liberated from rules and imposed authority. Discipline implies limitations and restrictions that are not well received by self-indulgent post-moderns for whom pleasure and passion seem to be the driving forces in life. In reality, its root meaning is "training" or "instruction." Thus, a disciple is one who is being instructed or trained. Spiritual discipline is fundamentally training or instruction in matters of the spirit. Speaking in a Christian context, Dallas Willard notes that "a discipline for the spiritual life is...nothing but an activity undertaken to bring us into more effective cooperation with Christ and his Kingdom."[15] Or in the more picturesque language of Henri Nouwen, "Spiritual disciplines are nothing more and nothing less than ways to create room where Christ can invite us to feast with him at the table of abundance."[16] The word "practices" may sit more comfortably on our modern ears, but either term implies activities done consistently with intention, over an extended period of time, for the purpose of spiritual growth.

The so-called "classical" spiritual disciplines have taken shape and been tested and tried across hundreds of years of church history. Still, formulating a definitive list of disciplines would be something like compiling a complete list of spiritual gifts. It serves no useful purpose and is likely to overlook the creativity and imagination of God in uniquely gifting some individuals. While there are a few essential disciplines that should be part of every believer's pilgrimage, not every discipline is for every believer. The disciplines, other than the essential foundational and grounding ones, provide a smorgasbord from which individual Christians may choose as their particular temperament and personality prompt them. It is wise occasionally to vary the elective disciplines to keep freshness and vitality in the journey. It is also beneficial to work at practices that do not seem as comfortable a fit for us in order to allow God to stretch us and reveal himself to us in new ways.

---

[15] Dallas Willard, *The Spirit of the Disciplines: Understanding How God Changes Lives* (San Francisco: HarperSanFrancisco, 1988) 156.

[16] Henri J. M. Nouwen, "Foreword," in *Soul Feast: An Invitation to the Christian Spiritual Life* (Louisville: Westminster John Knox Press, 1995) x.

Spiritual Practices for Growth

Dallas Willard bases his list of disciplines on "those activities that have had a wide and profitable use among Disciples of Christ" and divides them into disciplines of "abstinence" and disciplines of "engagement."

Disciplines of Abstinence	Disciplines of Engagement
solitude	study
silence	worship
fasting	celebration
frugality	service
chastity	prayer
secrecy	fellowship
sacrifice	confession
	submission[17]

Even the briefest glance at these categories reveals that in today's world Christians are far more likely to participate in engagement disciplines than in abstinence ones. This insight is again reflective of our culture that has little or no interest in any sort of self-limitation. Nonetheless, abstinence is clearly biblical: "*Abstain* from fleshly lusts which war against the soul" (1 Pet 2:11); "Hold fast to what is good; *abstain* from every form of evil" (1 Thess 5:21–22); "For this is the will of God, your sanctification: that you *abstain* from sexual immorality (1 Thess 4:3).

Every believer can profitably engage in certain disciplines of abstinence. These disciplines involve denying ourselves, for a period of time, certain satisfactions of normal and legitimate desires. For Willard, "normal" desires include our basic drives or motivations, such as those for food, sleep, bodily activity, companionship, curiosity, and sex. But our desires for convenience, comfort, material security, reputation or fame, and variety are also considered under this heading."[18] These desires and their satisfactions are not wrong or sinful in themselves, but left undisciplined they can lead to many of the "deadly" sins recognized

---

[17] Willard *The Spirit of the Disciples*, 158.

[18] Ibid., 159.

throughout church history. The seven notorious sins—pride, envy, anger, laziness, greed, gluttony, and lust—are often the result of the undisciplined indulgence of our basic human desires. While the writer of Hebrews, in his exhortation to perseverance in the Christian life, does not mention specific sins, these are typical of the sins "that so easily beset us" (Heb 12:1) and that deter us in the life of faithfulness.

Disciplines of Abstinence

Solitude. Solitude is more than simply being alone. It is choosing to be alone with God so that we can be who we truly are and come to acknowledge this reality to ourselves and to God. It is as much a state of mind and heart as it is a place. We remove ourselves for a time from the distractions of the world and the responsibilities of community to reorient ourselves. It is a time to examine and confront what Kenneth Boa calls the "inner patterns and forces that are alien to the life of Christ within us."[19] Note also the words of Muholland: "In the classical Christian spiritual tradition...solitude is...beginning to face the deep inner dynamics of our being that make us that grasping, controlling, manipulative person; beginning to face our brokenness, our distortion, our darkness; and beginning to offer ourselves to God at those points."[20]

The New Testament portrays Jesus as frequently withdrawing for periods of solitude. He initiated his ministry by spending forty days alone in the desert (Mark 1:13). Before choosing his twelve disciples, he spent the night alone (Luke 6:12). After the long, inaugural day of his ministry in Capernaum, Mark's gospel records that "in the morning, while it was still very dark, Jesus got up and went out to a deserted place, and there he prayed" (Mark 1:35). As he faced the climax of his earthly ministry, his crucifixion, Jesus withdrew to the solitude of the Garden of Gethsemane (Matt 26:36–46). On each of these occasions and many more recorded in the gospels, Jesus sought solitude to be with his Father to be renewed and encouraged for the demands of his life and ministry.

Silence. Silence and solitude are soul mates; they are inseparable. Without silence there is no solitude. As Nouwen observes, "Silence

---

[19] Kenneth Boa, *Conformed to His Image: Biblical and Practical Approaches to Spiritual Formation* (Grand Rapids: Zondervan, 2001) 83.

[20] Mulholland, *Invitation to a Journey*, 138

completes and intensifies solitude."[21] Nor is silence merely the absence of sound; it is a quietness of the mind and spirit as well as of a space. This type of silence is not characterized by emptiness and absence as some might fear. Rather, it is a renewing fullness and presence—divine silence that is rich with the Spirit. Thomas Merton expresses the value of silence in a most elemental way: "My life is a listening, His is a speaking.... The sacrifice that pleases God is the offering of my soul—My silence, which takes me away from all other things, is therefore the sacrifice of all things and the offering of my soul to God. It is therefore my most pleasing sacrifice."[22] We tend to resist silence because it removes from us our ability to exercise control. Our silence allows God to take control and requires that we trust his control.

Fasting. The spiritual discipline of fasting, in its most basic use, is depriving oneself of normal food and drink for a period of time in order to be strengthened spiritually. It is an entirely biblical practice, and Jesus himself both practiced and taught it. In Matthew 4:1–4, John the Baptist records that following Jesus' baptism, he spent time in the wilderness where, "after fasting forty days and forty nights, he was hungry." Satan used this physical desire to tempt him, and Jesus' reply, quoted from Deuteronomy, is a strong argument in support of fasting: "People do not live on bread alone, but on every word that comes from the mouth of God." Jesus' instruction about fasting in Matthew 6:16–18 indicates that he expected his followers to fast: "*When* you fast..." (emphasis added).

The key factor in the effectiveness of fasting as a spiritual discipline is the motivation behind it. It must be more than a weight-loss scheme or an attempt at political manipulation. As James Earl Massey reminds us, "Fasting is important in Christian experience because it deepens within the whole self a sense of one's dependence upon the strength of God. Fasting is more than an act of abstinence. It is an affirmative act; it is a way of waiting on God; it is an act of surrender."[23] Fasting can also

---

[21] Henri J. M. Nouwen, *The Way of the Heart* (New York: Ballantine Books, 1981) 29.

[22] Thomas Merton, *Thoughts in Solitude* (New York: Farrar, Straus, Giroux, 1958) 69.

[23] James Earl Massey, *Spiritual Disciplines* (Grand Rapids: Francis Asbury Press, 1985) 66.

be extended to other forms of abstinence or denial of activities that distance us from God. In today's society that could include foregoing some of the time spent with entertainment and communication technologies (movies, DVDs, cell phones, internet) to spend more time with God. Thus Willard notes, "Fasting teaches temperance or self-control and therefore teaches moderation and restraint with regard to *all* our fundamental drives."[24]

Frugality. Frugality is perhaps best equated with Richard Foster's discipline of simplicity.[25] It relates to our attitude toward and use of our material resources, what Boa calls our "willingness to abstain from using these resources for our own gratification and aggrandizement."[26] In our self-indulgent, materialistic culture today, this discipline is perhaps the most difficult to reconcile. It requires a radical reversal of inward attitudes. According to Foster, the inward reality of simplicity, which results in the outward expression of simplicity, is characterized by three inner attitudes: what we have we receive as a gift, what we have is to be cared for by God, and what we have is available to others.[27]

Frugality or simplicity frees us from the tyranny of things and, in our contemporary culture, from the bondage of financial debt. Willard observes that "this kind of debt is often incurred by buying things that are far from necessary and its effect...is to eliminate our sensitivity to the needs of others."[28] The practice of frugality directs that we use our money for those things that are necessary and abstain from using it to indulge in luxuries and superficial gratifications. It encourages us to trust in God's provision for our lives and enables us to help others with our excess.

Chastity. Chastity has to do with the proper use of our sexuality and allows us to see the good of all with whom we come in contact, especially those of the opposite sex. It recognizes the legitimacy of sexual drives and provides a beneficial and appropriate context for their expression.

---

[24] Willard, *The Spirit of the Disciplines*, 167.

[25] Richard J. Foster, *Celebration of Discipline* (San Francisco: HarperSanFrancisco, 1978) 88.

[26] Boa, *Conformed to His Image*, 85.

[27] Foster, *Celebration of Discipline*, 88.

[28] Willard, *The Spirit of the Disciplines*, 169.

Secrecy. Secrecy simply means that we refrain from publicizing and boasting about our good deeds and qualities. It opposes self-promotion and depends upon God to provide whatever public notice of us is beneficial. It frees us from seeking the approval of others and keeps us content with God's approval.

Sacrifice. Sacrifice goes beyond frugality, which involves giving up our surplus, to giving up occasionally that which we would use to meet our basic needs. Its benefit is that it teaches us to trust God's provision for our needs.

Disciplines of Engagement

Concerning the disciplines, Willard writes, "The disciplines of abstinence must be counterbalanced and supplemented by disciplines of engagement. Abstinence and engagement are the out-breathing and in-breathing of our spiritual lives, and we require disciplines for both movements. Roughly speaking, the disciplines of abstinence counteract tendencies to sins of commission, and the disciplines of engagement counteract tendencies to sins of omission."[29]

Study. The relevance of study to the Christian life is implicit in Paul's second letter to Timothy when he asserts the values of Scripture: "All Scripture is God-breathed and is useful for teaching, rebuking, correcting and training in righteousness, so that all God's people may be thoroughly equipped for every work" (2 Tim 3:16–17). While spiritual reading and study may include many types of literature, Marjorie Thompson advises that "the primary focus of spiritual reading for Christians has always been Scripture with good reason. The purpose for which the Scriptures were written—presenting hearers with God's Word—and the purpose of spiritual reading—allowing ourselves to be addressed by God's Word—are completely consonant. They are suited to each other as a hand and a glove."[30]

It is essential to recognize that Scripture study and spiritual reading involve far more than simply reading for information, as we habitually do. Rather, this sort of engagement with the biblical text is for the

---

[29] Ibid., 175–76.

[30] Marjorie J. Thompson, *Soul Feast: An Invitation to the Christian Spiritual Life* (Louisville: Westminster John Knox, 1995) 19.

purpose of *formation* or *transformation*. It has to do with the renewing of our minds to which Paul calls us in Romans 12:2. By contrast with informational reading, when engaging in formational reading, the quantity of material covered is immaterial; the point is meeting God in the text. Formational reading functions like a depth charge; it allows the text to become the intrusion of God's Word into our lives. Formational reading allows the text to master us; we become servants of the word rather than masters of the text and we become shaped by it.[31]

This way of studying the word, however, also requires that we *meditate* on Scripture, as Willard notes: "Our prayer as we study meditatively is always that God would meet with us and speaks specifically to us, for ultimately the Word of God is God speaking."[32] The biblical warrant for Scripture meditation is found in the familiar words of Psalm 1:1–2: "Blessed are those…who delight in the law of the Lord and meditate on his law day and night." A well-established method for meditative reflection on Scripture is referred to by its Latin name *Lectio Divina*, which simply means "divine reading." While its practice in the Christian church was especially developed by Saint Benedict in the sixth century, Protestant figures, such as John Calvin and Richard Baxter, advocated a similar discipline. The four stages in this method are also referred to by their Latin terms: *lectio* (reading), *meditation* (meditation), *oratio* (praying), and *contemplatio* (contemplation).[33]

Worship and Celebration. Study and meditation on God's Word should lead naturally into worship and celebration. Thus Willard notes: "Worship must be added to study to complete the renewal of our mind through a willing absorption in the radiant person who is worthy of all praise.... In worship we are ascribing greatness, goodness, and glory to God.... Worship…imprints on our whole being the reality that we study."[34] Celebration completes worship as we respond to God's glory and greatness with our whole being and with the larger community of

---

[31] M. Robert Mulholland Jr., *Shaped by the Word: The Power of Scripture in Spiritual Formation*, rev. ed. (Nashville: Upper Room Books, 1985) 55–57.

[32] Willard, *The Spirit of the Disciplines*, 177.

[33] Detailed descriptions of these stages are available in numerous sources, including several of the works cited in this essay.

[34] Dallas Willard, *The Divine Conspiracy: Rediscovering our Hidden Life in God* (San Francisco: HarperSanFrancisco, 1998) 362–63.

believers. Again Willard: "Holy delight and joy is the great antidote to despair and is a wellspring of genuine gratitude.... Celebration heartily done makes our deprivations and sorrows seem small and we find in it great strength to do the will of our God because his goodness becomes so real to us."[35]

Service. Jesus' most radical call to service for those who follow him finds expression in his last night on earth before he was crucified, when he washed his disciples feet and instructed them to follow his example: "If I then, your Lord and Teacher, have washed your feet, you also ought to wash one another's feet. For I have given you an example, that you also should do as I have done to you" (John 13:14–15). Thus, every believer is called to the discipline of service.

Many acts of service come naturally to us as the simple kindnesses and courtesies we extend to one another as we go about our lives. These acts may enhance our ability to follow Christ, but service as a spiritual discipline is done for the purpose of training ourselves away from pride, arrogance, resentment, etc. Service of this sort does not come naturally to us and may even make us uncomfortable. Yet, it must be intentionally chosen as a means of honoring God and becoming more Christ-like. It seeks no recognition or reward from others, but finds its satisfactions in obeying Paul's instruction to servants: "Whatever your task, put yourselves into it, as done for the Lord and not for your masters, since you know that from the Lord you will receive the inheritance as your reward; you serve the Lord Christ" (Col 3:23–24).

Prayer. Prayer has the potential to be the most effective of all spiritual disciplines and is probably the one most practiced by Christians, but it is the one whose power to transform us is least appreciated. Jesus assured us that prayers are heard and answered when he said, "Ask, and it will be given you; search, and you will find; knock, and the door will be opened for you. For everyone who asks receives, and everyone who searches finds, and for everyone who knocks, the door will be opened" (Matt 7:7–8). Prayer brings us into communication with God and opens us to receive God's guidance, strength, love, and joy. As Herb Miller

---

[35] Willard, *The Spirit of the Disciplines*, 179, 181.

asserts, "Prayer facilitates spiritual growth by making Christ a guest in our mind, through the power of the Holy Spirit."[36]

Fellowship. Fellowship involves our sharing together with other believers in common activities of worship, Bible study, prayer, and service. Through fellowship we experience community with other Christians; this grows out of our fellowship with God. As Lawrenz observes, "Fellowship is one of the great mysteries of God's work. It only happens, though, when there is a real coming together. When that happens, we are shaped by each other, and as such, fellowship is a basic tool in the task of spiritual formation."[37] The result of such fellowship can be a delightful experience that includes mutual encouragement and inspiration as we share our life journeys as followers of Christ. Just as a coal removed from the fire becomes cold and lifeless, Christians without a Christian community and fellowship lose their vitality for growth and effectiveness. There is a direct connection between loving God and loving people so that just as strengthening our relationship with God strengthens our ability to love others, "strengthening our emotional connection to people can (under the right circumstances) strengthen our spiritual connection to God."[38]

Confession. Confession is an especially difficult spiritual discipline because it demands a transparency and vulnerability that reveals our sins and shortcomings. So long as our focus is on what others may think of us, we quietly cover our failures and lapses, convinced that everyone else is a better Christian than we are. Fear and pride keep us mute about our need for forgiveness and renewal. Therefore, the key to effective confession is understanding God's unconditional love for us and that the body of saints of which we are part is also a community of sinners. Although we naturally fear the disapproval of others, we are not alone in being sinful. Often the genuine, repentant confession of one will embolden others to cast off the load of their failures to experience forgiveness and freedom from them. The writer of James expresses clearly the call to the discipline of confession: "Therefore confess your

---

[36] Herb Miller, *Connecting with God: Fourteen Ways Churches Can Help People Grow Spiritually* (Nashville: Abingdon Press, 1994) 61.

[37] Lawrenz, *The Dynamics of Spiritual Formation*, 98.

[38] Miller, *Connecting with God*, 71.

sins to one another, and pray for one another, so that you may be healed. The prayer of the righteous is powerful and effective" (5:16).

Submission. Submission as a spiritual discipline may be a hard concept to grasp or embrace because it has been so abused in Christian circles. But in its biblically intended sense, it gives us the freedom to surrender our "rights" out of a spirit of respect and consideration for others. While it is possible for someone to be forced into submission, the biblical mandate is for Christians willingly to submit themselves, a manifestation of self-denial (e.g. Rom 13:1; Eph 5:21; Jas 4:7). The expectation of the one submitting is that the one submitted to will, in Christian manner, not misuse or take unfair advantage of such submission. Foster reminds us that "Scripture does not attempt to set forth a series of hierarchical relationships but to communicate to us an inner attitude of mutual subordination."[39] Therefore, submission is the result of following Paul's instruction in Philippians 2:3–5: "Do nothing from selfish ambition or conceit, but in humility regard others as better than yourselves. Let each of you look not to your own interests, but to the interests of others. Let the same mind be in you that was in Christ Jesus."

Conclusion

Not all spiritual disciplines are for everyone. However, those essential for every believer who desires to be like Christ are Bible study, prayer, worship, and service. Bible study keeps us open to God's insights and guidance for life. Prayer keeps us in communication with God and receptive to his teaching and correction. Worship provides the necessary outlet to express our praise and gratitude to God for who he is and what he does. Service reminds us that we receive God's blessings that we might be channels through whom God's blessings flow into the lives of others.

Spiritual theology explains what the Christian life is and the practices that characterize it. Spiritual disciplines provide proven practices that facilitate God's transformation of us into the likeness of Jesus Christ, through the agency of the Holy Spirit. Spiritual theology and its essential practices are foundational to the vitality and effectiveness of the evangelical church.

---

[39] Foster, *Celebration of Discipline*, 112.

Balancing Our Doctrinal Preaching

ROBERT SMITH JR.

Pastoral and prophetic: both callings reside within the heart of Fisher H. Humphreys. It is the pastoral quality that enables him to communicate comfort to the afflicted that need "the balm in Gilead." It is the prophetic trait that opens the way for him to speak truth to power while afflicting the comfortable who are "at ease in Zion." He has merged truth and love in his professorial ministry and understands the necessity of their inextricable relationship: truth without love can lead to spiritual boredom, while love without truth will lead to spiritual blindness. It has been a blessing for me to have observed him model these realities throughout the nine years I have served at Beeson Divinity School.

What time is it? The opening line of Charles Dickens's *A Tale of Two Cities* states, "These were the best of times and the worst of times."[1] In the Bible, the Chronicler reports, "The men of Issachar understood the times and knew what Israel should do" (1 Chr 12:32 NIV). The Germans often refer to a particular trend or psychological mindset as *zeitgeist*, "the spirit of the times." In the commonly used descriptive by Christians, Thomas Paine's diagnosis of his generation was that "these are the times that try men's souls."[2] The Latin phrase *carpe diem* is a challenge to our twenty-first-century doctrinal *sitz im leben*, or situation in life. The apostle Paul attempted to prepare the church of the *already* for the times of the *not yet* by indicating that "the time will come when men will not put up with sound doctrine. Instead, to suit their own desires, they will gather around them a great number of teachers to say

---

[1] Charles Dickens, *A Tale of Two Cities* (New York: Amsco School Publications, Inc., 1971) 1.

[2] Thomas Paine, "December 23, 1776" in *The Crisis* (Philadelphia: Independence Hall Association, 1999–2007), http://www.ushistory.org/Paine/crisis/c-01.htm (accessed 31 January 2008).

what their itching ears want to hear. They will turn their ears away from the truth and turn aside to fables" (2 Tim 4:3 4 NIV).

These are times when preaching has exchanged its birthright of sound doctrine for an unsatisfying bowl of doctrinal heresy. These are times when preaching has left Joseph's doctrinal bones in Egypt and made its trek to the Promised Land without them. These are times when preaching can no longer responsibly respond to Joshua's question, "What do these stones mean?" (Jos 4:6 NIV) because too many of its hearers know *what* they believe without knowing *why*.

If preaching fails to reclaim the mantle of sound doctrine and instead neglects the task of balanced doctrinal preaching, geology will be justified in protesting against preaching as the rocks cry out (Luke 19:40 KJV). God is sovereign and uses creation to amplify truth about himself: "The morning stars have sung together and the sons of God have shouted for joy" (Job 38:7 KJV); "the heavens declare the glory of God, and the firmament showeth 'his' handiwork" (Ps 19:1 KJV); "the mountains and the fields can break forth with joy" (Isa 55:12 KJV); "and the redeemed of the Lord must say so" (Ps 107:2 KJV). Preachers of Christian doctrine are resident theologians and are responsible for earnestly contending for the faith that was once delivered to the saints (Jude 3 KJV). Paraphrasing the admonition of Sandy F. Ray, pastors must take their bulldozer of preparation during the week to the mountain of sound doctrine, dismantle the doctrinal mountain until it is reduced to bite-size pieces, load the bite-size pieces into the dump truck of preparation, make a delivery to the church on Sunday morning, and serve the members messages that are doctrinally saturated.[3]

Preaching is operating in a time when it has forgotten its "alpha or beginning point." One of the musical dynamics of Paul Hindemeth was "wherever the musicians are in the playing of music they must always return to the tonic." By this he meant that if a musician was adding, embellishing, shifting, or riffing, the musician must remember to always return to the basic or fundamental music. George Arthur Buttrick, Lyman Beecher Lecturer on Preaching, years ago related an experience with a preaching audience. One of his preaching students had concluded

[3] Dr. Sandy F. Ray formerly was pastor of Cornerstone Baptist Church, Brooklyn, New York.

his sermon and awaited evaluative comments from Professor Buttrick. Buttrick's initial comments were piercingly truthful: "If the text had had smallpox the sermon would not have caught it." To transfer Hindemeth's advice to musicians and move it into the arena of preaching, wherever preachers are in the application of the sermon, they must always return to the pulsating heartbeat of the text's original intention.

During the Reformation Martin Luther rebaptized the term *ad fontes*. In its cultural context it meant going back to Greek and Roman sources of antiquity that had their zenith during the Renaissance. Luther sanctified the term *ad fontes* so that it took on new meaning and now referred to the church going back to its scriptural and spiritual roots: *sola fides* (faith only), *sola gratia* (grace only), *sola scriptura* (Scripture only), and *sola christus* (Christ only). Instead many modern preachers have gone back to *sola bootstrapa* (pull yourself up by your own bootstraps).

Former heavyweight champion of the world, Floyd Patterson, was interviewed by an ESPN correspondent. The correspondent knew that Patterson and the reigning heavyweight champion of the world, Mike Tyson, had similar backgrounds in their rise to the top of the boxing world. The correspondent asked Patterson, "If you had the opportunity to say one thing to Mike Tyson, what would it be?" After briefly hesitating Patterson said, "I would tell Mike to go back to his beginning and review the time when he ate food out of the garbage can and stole for food. This will help keep him from getting the big head."[4] Preachers must return to the tonic of the text if they are to experience balance in their doctrinal preaching.

In his book, *Working the Angles: the Shape of Pastoral Integrity*, Eugene Peterson noted that pastors are abandoning their calling. According to his observations, pastors still have their names on the church stationery, keep weekly office hours, and preach the Sunday morning sermon. However, they have transformed themselves from shepherds to shopkeepers. According to Peterson, the shops that the shepherds keep are their churches. Questions that concern them are: How can I keep the customers (members) happy? How can I package the goods (sermon) so that the customers (members) will lay out more

[4] Floyd Patterson, interview by ESPN, May 2005, Cincinnati OH.

money? How can I lure the customers (members) from my competitors' shops (churches down the street) to my shop (church)?[5] Paul reminds preachers that they are not to be peddlers of the gospel. In the words of Jesus, they are to be shepherds of the sheep who feed the Lord's sheep.

Biblical personalities who were greatly used by God had balanced ministries. David could sit down and write hymns, poems, songs, draw the blueprint for the Temple that he would give to Solomon, and then he would go out and kill a lion, a bear, and then slay the giant Goliath. David would encourage both the entering into the Lord's "gates" with thanksgiving for what the Lord had done and then proceeding into the Lord's "courts" with praise for who the Lord is. Habakkuk chose to sit in silence in the watchtower to wait to see what God was going to say and then sing praises to God with the knowledge that there may not be any cattle in the stall, crops in the field, grapes on the vine, or figs on the tree. Elijah gave a three-and-one-half year meteorological report to Ahab and Jezebel, king and queen of Israel, stating that it would not rain during those years, and disappeared from their presence. When Elijah reappeared, he called the drought off and challenged the prophets of Ahab and Jezebel to a showdown on Mount Carmel. Jesus could sleep during a storm and wake up and go into the Temple and create a storm by driving out the extortionists who were making his Father's house into a den of thieves when it was designed to be a house of prayer for all people (author's interpretation).

The Copernican Revolution was an indictment on both the secularist mindset of science and on the ecclesiastical mindset of the church. For centuries science and ecclesiology had believed and proclaimed that the earth was the center of the universe and that God had placed the sun to revolve around the earth. In his famous sermon, "The Sun Do Move," John Jasper, the captivating, self-taught preacher of Richmond, Virginia, was affected by this mindset. The Copernican Revolution had enough conviction and boldness to challenge the scientific mindset and the ecclesiastical mindset and say that both were wrong, for God had not placed the sun and the planets around the earth; rather, God had put the sun in the center of the universe, placed the

---

[5] Eugene H. Peterson, *Working the Angles: the Shape of Pastoral Integrity* (Grand Rapids: Wm. B. Eerdmans, 1987) 1.

eight planets in a merry-go-round pattern around the sun, and the planets have not collided since the birthday of creation.[6]

Doctrinal preaching is out of balance and needs to be called back to a state of balance. What is meant by doctrinal balance? Doctrinal balance is not to be measured by a centrist position, a medium or middle-of-the road position, or a halting or limping between two opinions (1 Kgs 18:21 KJV). Doctrinal balance is better described than defined. Eugene Peterson provides great insight in relation to describing balance through his use of the triangle metaphor to describe a pastoral ministry of balance. Peterson points out that the three lines of a triangle are obvious, but the three angles are essential. The three angles bring the three lines together to form a triangle. Without the three angles there is no triangle. For Peterson, the pastoral ministry is triangular in its configuration. The three lines of the pastoral ministry that are the most obvious and the most discussed ministries are preaching, teaching, and administration. These ministries get the most attention. The three angles that are less visible and less discussed are prayer, reading Scripture, and spiritual direction. These three angles of private ministry buttress, support, and enable the three lines of public ministry to become more effective.[7]

Transcendence and Immanence Meet

The first line of balanced doctrinal preaching is formed at the angle where transcendence and immanence meet. Transcendence refers to the truth that God is above us, and immanence asserts that God is with us. Both Henry Mitchell in *Black Church Beginnings* and James Evans in *We Have Been Believers* establish the fact that Africans did not come to America as unbelievers or atheists.[8] Africans believed in the Most High

---

[6] Reverend John Jasper (1812–1901) gained national fame in 1878, when he first preached his famed "Sun Do Move" sermon at Sixth Mount Zion Baptist Church in Richmond, Virginia. He later delivered the sermon more than 250 times and once before the entire Virginia General Assembly. See http://www.library.vcu.edu/jbc/speccoll/vbha/6th4.html.

[7] Peterson, *Working the Angles*.

[8] Henry H. Mitchell, *Black Church Beginnings: The Long-Hidden Realities of the First Years* (Grand Rapids: Wm. B. Eerdmans 2004). James H. Evans Jr., *We*

God. However, believing that God was above them, they recognized that there was distance between deity and dust, divinity and humanity. The titanic theological struggle was bridging the gap between the *aboveness* of God and the *withness* of God within the unity of one God. How could the same God be both above humanity and dwell with humanity simultaneously? This was the African theological dilemma. Upon being uprooted from their homeland of Africa and transplanted to the soil of America, Africans would adjust and modify the teachings of white Christianity, and white Christianity would assist them in clarifying what they already believed; they had not yet acquired the theological language to articulate what they believed. They would later come to express that the Most High God had a Son and that God in his Son, Jesus Christ, could come out of God and become human without forfeiting his deity. In this mysterious, inscrutable, and inexplicable process God would become human without losing God's divinity. Theologically speaking, this dynamic is known as the incarnation. "The Word 'became' flesh and tabernacled with human beings and they beheld his glory, the glory as of the only begotten Son of the Father, full of grace and truth" (John 1:14 KJV). The Son God who came from Father God in the incarnation is the Son God who was forsaken by Father God during the crucifixion. The cry of dereliction reverberated throughout the three realms of earth, heaven, and hell: "My God, my God, why hast thou forsaken me?" (Mark 15:34 KJV). In his book, *Kurze Erklärung des Römerbriefes* translated in 1959 as *A Shorter Commentary on Romans* of 1919, Karl Barth dropped a bombshell on the theological world.[9] For a century liberalism had been amplifying the immanence of God and had lowered the volume of the transcendence of God until it was practically muted. Liberalism anesthetized Christians and made them practically immune to the transcendence of God. The awesomeness of God had vanished from the screen of their minds. Barth led the theological resurgence to reclaim the doctrine of the transcendence of God. Several decades later Barth recognized that although he had sufficiently emphasized the

---

have Been Believers: An African-American Systematic Theology (Minneapolis: Fortress Press, 1992).

[9] Karl Barth, *A Shorter Commentary on Romans*, trans. D. H. Van Daalen (Richmond VA: John Knox Press, 1959).

doctrine of the transcendence of God, he had underemphasized the doctrine of the immanence of God.[10] He became very intentional about balancing the two in his preaching and writing.

Open theism and process theology indirectly attempt to sever the transcendence and immanence of God, and "what God has joined together let no one separate" (Matt 19:6). Through their theological mindsets they attempt to reverse the process of creation and make God in the image of humans when God has made humans in the image of God. Theoretically speaking, these two theologies handicap the *Wholly Other*. This is particularly true in the doctrinal category of the omnipotence, or the all-powerfulness, of God. Omnipotence contends that there is nothing that God cannot do. With God all things are possible, declares Jesus (Mark 10:27 KJV). In *Why Bad Things Happen to Good People*, Rabbi Harold Kushner writes in response to the death of his child.[11] His conclusion is that God sat with his family as a mourner at the funeral service and wept with the family, for God had done everything that God could do prior to the death of the child. Such a doctrinal position flies in the face of the omnipotence of God. For example, Jesus stood at the deathbed of the twelve-year-old daughter of the synagogue ruler, Jairus, who had just died. He told her to rise. She rose and death died. Jesus met a funeral procession on its way to deposit the body of a young man in the Nain cemetery. He was the only son of his mother and she was a widow. Jesus touched the top of the coffin and told the son to rise. He rose and death died. Jesus showed up at the Bethany cemetery four days after the funeral had taken place. He called Lazarus by his name. Lazarus rose and death died. In the eschaton Jesus will call the saints from their graves and they will rise. Death will die a final death and will be no more!

These theologies also impair the doctrine of the omnipresence, or the "everywhereness," of God, and the doctrine of the omniscience, or the "allknowingness," of God. The doctrines of omnipresence and omniscience argue that God is in all places at the same time and knows everything there is to know about everything. There is no place where

---

[10] Ibid.

[11] Harold S. Kushner, *When Bad Things Happen to Good People* (New York: Shocken Books, 1981).

God is not. God is so immense spatially that whenever he moves anywhere in the universe, God has to bump into himself! There is no knowledge about anything that God does not have. Isaiah asserts that God knows the end before the beginning began (Isa 46:10 KJV). However, process theology and open theism challenge the divine "everywhereness" of the omnipresence of God and the "allknowingness" of the omniscience of God by contending that God cannot be in the future or know the future because the future is still unborn and resides within the womb of the "not yet." Yet God is the only one who both dwells in the future and knows the future. God demystifies the mystery of the future, unscrews the inscrutability of the future, and figures out the unfigurability of the future. In the descriptive phrase of Rudolf Otto in his essay, "The Wholly Other," God is the *mysterium tremendum* or the "tremendous mystery."[12] The British hymnist William Cowper correctly assessed the God of mystery: "God works in mysterious ways; His wonders to perform. He plants His footsteps on the sea and He rides on every storm."[13] Moses asked Yahweh, "If I am going back to Egypt, the place of my birth and the country where there has been a warrant for my arrest for years, who shall I say sent me?" Yahweh replied, "Tell Pharaoh that I Am sent you" (Exod 3:14 ESV). When someone says "I am," the listener expects the speaker to provide additional information. A sentence seems incomplete when it ends with the words "I am." However, when God says "I Am" it is a complete sentence by virtue of the fact that God is complete within God's self, for God is the self-existent God. God is the God who lives up to his claim to be "I Am who I Am." God is one noun and three adverbial phrases simultaneously existing in the three tenses of past, present, and future. Although it is grammatically incorrect to articulate God's "I Am-ness," it is doctrinally sound. God is "I Am was." God is before time and even before pre-existent eternity. God is "I Am is." God is not in time; time is in God. God is the "Eternal Now." God is "I Am will be." God is on the other

---

[12] Rudolf Otto, "The Wholly Other in Religious History and Theology," in *Religious Essays: A Supplement to the Idea of the Holy*, ed. Rudolf Otto and Brian Lunn (London: Oxford University Press, 1931).

[13] William Cowper (1731–1800), *Worship & Rejoice* (Carol Stream IL: Hope Publishing Company, 2001) 65.

side of the future. God sees from the perspective of God's own eternality [*sub specie aeternatatis*].

Process and open theism theologies are insufficient for suffering and disinherited people. They need a God who is not in the process of becoming or developing. They need a God who "is" and a God who controls all processes. Oftentimes oppressed people do not have the technical theological language to relate the divine attributes of God. Borrowing the language of the Negro spiritual, African Americans regularly referred to the omnipotence of God as one who "had the whole world in his hands." They understood the omnipresence of God as one who "was so high that you can't get over him; so low that you can't go under him; so wide that you can't get around him; you must come in at the door." They comprehended the omniscience of God as one who could be acknowledged in a Negro spiritual: "Nobody knows the trouble I see; Nobody knows but Jesus. Nobody knows the trouble I see; Glory hallelujah."[14] Isaiah announces the omnipotence of God:

> Hast thou not known? Hast thou not heard, that the everlasting God, the Lord, the Creator of the ends of the earth, fainteth not, neither is weary? There is no searching of his understanding. He giveth power to the faint; and to them that have no might he increaseth strength. Even the youths shall faint and be weary, and the young men shall utterly fall: But they that wait upon the Lord shall renew their strength; they shall mount up with wings as eagles; they shall run, and not be weary; and they shall walk, and not faint (Isa 40:28–31 KJV).

The psalmist embraces the omnipresence of God: "Whither shall I go from thy spirit? Or whither shall I flee from thy presence? If I ascend up into heaven, thou art there: if I make my bed in hell, behold, thou art there. If I take the wings of the morning, and dwell in the uttermost

---

[14] Director of the New York Music School Settlement for Colored People, J. Rosamond Johnson's arrangement of *Nobody Knows the Trouble I See* for voice and piano was published in 1917. It was eventually published in *The Book of American Negro Spirituals* (New York: Viking Press, 1925) and *The Second Book of Negro-Spirituals* in 1926. See http://www.rachelbartonpine.com/mus_notes.htm.

parts of the sea; Even there shall thy hand lead me, and thy right hand shall hold me" (Ps 139:7–10 KJV). Isaiah, the psalmist, and Jesus extol the omniscience of God: "Before they call, I will answer; and while they are yet speaking, I will hear" (Isa 65:24 KJV); "All the days ordained for me were written in your book before one of them came to be" (Ps 139:16 NIV); and "Your Father knows what you need before you ask Him" (Matt 6:8 NIV).

How do process and open theism theologies respond to the truism of James Russell Lowell? He says, "Truth forever on the scaffold; wrong forever on the throne. But the scaffold sways the future; and behind the dim unknown standeth God in the shadows keeping watch above His own."[15]

How do process and open theism theologies respond to the eschatological hope of the Methodist pastor and hymnist, Charles A. Tindley? He says, "Harder yet may be the fight, Right may often yield to might; Wickedness a while may reign, Satan's cause may seem to gain. There is a God that rules above; With hand of power and heart of love. If I am right He'll fight my battle, I shall have peace some day."[16]

Spirit and Word Meet

The second line of balanced doctrinal preaching is formed at the angle where Spirit and Word meet. The Spirit of God and the Word of God were married in pre-existent eternity. The opening verses of Genesis 1 established this fact: "In the beginning God created the heavens and the earth. Now the earth was formless and empty, darkness was over the surface of the deep, and the Spirit of God was hovering over the waters. And God said, 'Let there be light' and there was light" (Gen 1:1–3 NIV). The prophet Ezekiel stood in the desolate valley of dry bones with no visible reason to believe that any transformation would occur through his preaching. However, after preaching to these dry bones he witnessed them making noise, forming skeletal frameworks; and being covered with tendons, flesh, and skin. Finally, God commanded Ezekiel to preach the Word to the four winds and tell them

[15] James Russell Lowell, "The Present Crisis," *Yale Book of American Verse*, ed. Thomas R. Lounsbury (New Haven CT: Yale University Press, 1912).

[16] Charles A. Tindley (words and music), "I'll Overcome Someday," 1901.

to breathe upon the corpses. Ezekiel obeyed God. The Word of God was accompanied by the *ruach* or the Holy Spirit of God, resulting in the raising of these corpses back to life (Ezek 37:9 NIV). Simon Peter, who had denied his Lord three times following the arrest of Jesus, stands up on the Day of Pentecost, fifty days past that hauntingly unforgettable evening, and boldly preaches the Word. The spoken Word by Peter had been preceded by the divine presence of the Spirit in the form of cloven tongues of fire and the rushing mighty wind. After the sermon had been delivered, about 3,000 persons were saved and added to the church.

Doctrinal preaching is facing a false dichotomy: Spirit of God or Word of God. This dichotomy has produced a serious dilemma. Churches are lining up on one side or the other. Some take pride in being "Word churches" and others take pleasure in being "Spirit churches." A pioneer in the Christian Missionary Alliance church movement, A. W. Tozer, commonly acknowledged throughout the breadth of his writings that if God took the Holy Spirit out of the world, many churches would continue to do the same things twenty-five years after the Spirit's exit and never notice the difference. In Stephen Olford's work, *Anointed Expository Preaching*, he argues that "*the sin* of the Old Testament Jew was the rejection of God as Father; *the sin* of the New Testament was the rejection of God as Son; *the sin* of the contemporary church is the rejection of God as Spirit. God as Father is God without human skin. God as Son is God who comes with skin. God as Spirit is God who gets inside of our skin."[17] James Forbes, in his book *The Holy Spirit and Preaching*, charges the contemporary church for being "Holy Spirit shy" or embarrassed by the movement of the Holy Spirit.[18]

Some Christians resist and resent being called charismatic. The Greek from which the English term charismatic is derived is *charisma*, which means "favor bestowed, gift."[19] In essence every believer in the church is a charismatic in that God has bestowed upon every believer in

---

[17]Stephen F. Olford with David L. Olford, *Anointed Expository Preaching* (Nashville: Broadman & Holman Publishers, 1998) 29–30.

[18] James Forbes, *The Holy Spirit and Preaching* (Nashville: Abingdon, 1989) 21.

[19] BADG: Frederick Danker, ed., *A Greek-English Lexicon of the New Testament and Other Early Christian Literature* (Chicago: University of Chicago Press, 2000) 3rd ed.

the body of Christ a gift that is to be used to edify the church (1 Cor 14:26). Every member has received a spiritual gift by God's grace for the purpose of glorifying God and edifying the church. Pastors who are comfortable with the members of their churches checking their minds in the vestibule and entering into the sanctuary mindlessly prepare the worship atmosphere for spiritual excesses and biblically-unwarranted emotional experiences. Preaching becomes incessant testimonies given from the pulpit that are totally divorced from the text and promises put on their lips without a "thus saith the Lord" certitude.

Before one can confidently say "thus saith the Lord," one has to know "what saith the Lord." Many churches have *Ichabod*, "the glory of the Lord has departed," written across the front entrances of their buildings because there is no Word being delivered inside the buildings. God promises to bless his Word about himself, but not necessarily our words about him. In the song, "Brethren We Have Met to Worship," George Atkins lyrically voices the inseparability and the unified indispensability of the presence of the Spirit of God and the Word of God engaging the people of God in their praise to God: "Brethren, we have met to worship, And adore our God the Lord; Will you pray with all your power, While we try to preach the Word? All is vain, unless the Spirit of the Holy One comes down; Brethren, pray and holy manna, Will be showered all around."[20]

Where Christology within an Intratrinitarian Community Meet

The third line of balanced doctrinal preaching is formed at the angle where Christology within an intratrinitarian community meet. Christ inextricably resides within the divine triune community. In mathematics, one plus one plus one equals three. This is correct arithmetic, but it is erroneous theology, for it evokes the thought of three gods, which is a contradiction to the *shema*—"Hear O Israel: The Lord our God is one Lord" (Deut 6:4 KJV).

---

[20] George Atkins (words), "Brethern, We Have Met to Worship," 1825, set to Holy Manna by William Moore.

Modalism is a heretical doctrine that was condemned by the church over sixteen centuries ago. It teaches that God put on three masks: one mask in the Old Testament as Father, another mask in the New Testament as Son, and a third mask in the present world today as the Holy Spirit. If God is viewed modalistically, one implies that there was a time when God was not Father because he did not have a Son until the first century A.D. when Jesus, the Son of God, was born in Bethlehem. This implies that God was not Father on the first day of creation. As Jonathan Edwards has believed the "triune God never acted apart from God's self as existing in a sweet and holy society and forever known Himself as Father, Son and Holy Spirit." The doctrine of the Trinity is the corrective for the heresy of modalism. Instead of modalism's one plus one plus one equals three, the doctrine of the Trinity posits that God is simultaneously working within God's self as Father, Son, and Holy Spirit in the dynamic of one times one times one equals one.

The picturesque portrayal of the creation in James Weldon Johnson's *God's Trombones: Seven Negro Sermons in Verse* is striking and engaging. After nearly seven decades it continues to be read with great interest and appreciation for both its poetry and its theology. However, there is a glaring defect in its imaginative theological anatomy. Johnson suggests that the stimulus behind God's making a human being was that God was lonely: "I am lonely; I will make a man."[21] There has never been a time when God was lonely. Although humans are not indispensable for the divine completeness, God still desires dispensable creatures so that God may share himself with them. Neither creation nor humans added anything to God, for God was complete before God ever gave the divine creative fiats, "let there be" and "let us make."

The song that once appeared on the first page of several of denominational hymnbooks was "Holy, Holy, Holy! Lord God Almighty." Perhaps the relegating of this song from page one to several pages toward the back of several of our denominational hymnbooks may be more than a numerical move; it may portray a theological move to indicate a flawed or lessened understanding of Christology within an intra-trinitarian community. With profound theology combined with lyrical

---

[21] James Weldon Johnson, *God's Trombones; Seven Negro Sermons in Verse* (New York: The Viking Press, 1927) 17.

musicality, Reginald Heber demonstrates the unity of the Triune community: "Holy, holy, holy! Lord God Almighty! All Thy works shall praise Thy name in earth and sky and sea; Holy, holy, holy! Merciful and mighty; God in three persons, blessed Trinity!"[22]

"Balancing our Doctrinal Preaching" was previously published in *Doctrine that Dances* (Nashville: Broadman & Holman, 2008) 127–140. It is published here with permission.

[22] Reginald Heber (words) "Holy, Holy, Holy," 1826, set to Nicaea by John B. Dykes, in *The Baptist Hymnal*, ed. Wesley L. Forbis (Nashville: Convention Press, 1991) 2.

Theology, Worship, and the Arts: Dorothy Sayers and the Trinity

GARY FURR

It is a privilege for me to be able to contribute to this *Festschrift* for Fisher Humphreys. He has shaped generations of pastors and leaders of churches through several outstanding qualities. First, he brings to his work a keenness of mind and devotion to the discipline of theology. Second, he has always had a great ability to get to the simple essence of matters. Friends and students always know that when Fisher is asked a question, he will often stop—his mind recalling, evaluating, and distilling the possible answers—and then he will usually be able to say, "There are essentially four (or two, or his favorite number, three) reasons for that," and you will say, "That's right." Finally, he embodies the truths he teaches. I have never known a theologian who lives out humility and Christian charity better than he or she can describe it more than Fisher Humphreys.

My relationship with Fisher has been different from most. All of my education and early experiences in ministry came before we ever met. We were often at Baptist meetings together, but we did not actually meet until I was invited to join a theology group (the Trinity Group) that he had started. The entrée into the group was an invitation from someone who knew you and required a Ph.D. in theology. Through the years it included pastors, missionaries, seminary and college teachers, and others, but at its intellectual center was Fisher Humphreys. Twice annually we met for two days to talk books, theology, ideas, and life. Fisher's thinking shaped my own profoundly during those meetings. I was inspired to see theology as vitally connected to my daily work as a pastor and to be a better theologian for the sake of my people.

Further, Fisher Humphreys helped me to see that theology was not an exotic realm where specialists spoke of indecipherable mysteries that excluded the average person. Theology, to the contrary, fails when it does not connect understandably with the real life issues of the living, worshiping church.

Theology, the Arts, and Worship in Tension

I have spent most of my adult life in two worlds—academic theology in my education and thought life, and the local church with its practical demands and areas of lived theology. The tension between the two is great, but it is also where the most fruitful theology is done. Nowhere has this been more interesting and perplexing to me than in the area of worship.

We find ourselves embroiled in debates over styles of worship that divide congregations. Many thoughtful laypersons struggle with worship that is sometimes disconnected from their living experience. Worship leaders wrestle with how to address the needs of such vastly different personalities and understandings represented in even the smallest congregation. While the culture expresses profound interest in spiritual matters and mysticism, it does not seem to translate into involvement in the lives of local congregations and their worship of God.

Our debates about worship are often confused—focused too little on substance and too much on styles and preferences. The better theological writing on the subject sees this theological poverty in the current conversation.[1] Often, the appeal to theology is seen as an appeal to return to "traditional" or more liturgical worship, but that is not a necessary conclusion. The theological question is not about what we use in worship so much as theological integrity in the use of the arts, words, symbols, and media.

There have been more than enough outstanding efforts to define worship. Suffice it to say that worship, like missional identity, is one of the core realities of the people of God. It is that intentional practice in

---

[1] See Ronald P. Byars, *The Future of Protestant Worship: Beyond the Worship Wars* (Louisville: Westminster John Knox Press, 2002); see also Don E. Saliers, *Worship as Theology -Foretaste of Glory Divine* (Nashville: Abingdon Press, 1994); and for a Baptist perspective, see Christopher Ellis' fine work, *Gathering: A Theology and Spirituality of Worship in Free Church Tradition* (London: SCM Press, 2004); also Milburn Price and Gary Furr, *The Dialogue of Worship* (Macon GA: Smyth & Helwys Press, 1998).

which we gather together in the corporate awareness that God is in our midst. We give attention to God and listen for God's direction. We remember our faith and recite it together. We sing our joy and pain. We reflect together on the world and our mission in it. All these and more are parts of the glorious mystery that is worship.

My interest is in finding some theological resources from faith itself to help us in an area where the pain of our differences seems most deeply experienced—that of the use of the "arts." In the larger sense, of course, we struggle over all of the "media" of worship—music, which version of the Bible should be used, whether creeds are appropriate, the right way to baptize, who should be admitted to the Lord's Table, and whether sermons and prayers should be written and planned or spontaneous and heartfelt. The list is almost endless and forms a tense history.

Much of our recent conversation about worship, however, is specifically about music and the use of other artistic media in worship. Are there theological criteria that can help us as the church decipher "good" from "bad," or is it all simply a matter of recognizing relative tastes, preferences, and the utilization of the arts in a neutral fashion as a cultural or linguistic medium?[2]

Dorothy Sayers and the Mind of the Maker

Some humility among all the combatants for musical supremacy would be welcomed, but there is also no need for us simply to resign ourselves to a mass consumer culture to direct our worship. All worship styles can be done poorly or done well. Nothing is more awful than worship done with the wrong motivations, poor planning, or with no respect for the artistic use of its media.

---

[2] For a good summary of these competing styles, see Paul Basden, "'Something Old, Something New': Worship Styles for Baptists in the Nineties," in *Ties That Bind: Life Together in the Baptist Vision*, Gary A. Furr and Curtis W. Freeman, ed. (Macon GA: Smyth & Helwys, 1994) 171–90. He later expanded this into book form in *The Worship Maze: Finding a Style to Fit your Church* (Downers Grove IL: InterVarsity Press, 1999). I agree with Byars in *The Future of Protestant Worship*, though, that at their core, we have two general and competing directions in Christian worship in America today—those that generally appeal to the notion of tradition and those that weigh more heavily in the direction of relevance to the present (which are labeled "contemporary").

While I do not propose to solve this issue for all time, I do think that theology can play a helpful role for the church as it seeks to worship faithfully. I will focus on a rather creative proposal by a laywoman of the twentieth century who was a successful secular writer. Dorothy Sayers is well-known to the larger world as a writer of detective stories in the mid-century era. To Christians she is remembered as a contemporary of C. S. Lewis and J. R. R. Tolkien and an intense thinker about matters of faith.[3]

Of greater interest to this chapter is her work on the theology of creativity called *The Mind of the Maker*.[4] That it has not received wider attention from theologians is interesting, but perhaps it is because she was not a part of the academy. One theologian of a generation ago, however, recognized her understanding of the Trinity in the book to be one of the three most original and suggestive proposals of the twentieth century on the subject.[5]

The Mind of the Maker does not purport to be an exhaustive theology of the Trinity. Instead, Sayers argued that the creeds and Christian doctrine explain other areas of reality to us. Therefore, they might be helpful to us in understanding other things besides doctrine.

Sayers believed that the doctrine of the Trinity helped her better understand the creative process. There is, she says, a "threeness" and yet oneness inherent in every work of art. Every book or work of art—visual, musical, or whatever—as a created reality has three dimensions. She calls these "Idea," "Energy," and "Power."[6]

A work of art exists first as idea. Artists are often at a loss, she says, to explain where their concept or creation as idea came to them. It comes intuitively, suddenly, unexpectedly in many cases. And many

---

[3] See Mary Brian Duncan, "Dorothy L. Sayers: A Christian Humanist for Today," *The Christian Century* (14 November 1979): 1114–20; and Barbara Reynolds, "The Importance of Being Dorothy L. Sayers" (colloquium, Taylor University, 2006).

[4] Dorothy L. Sayers, *The Mind of the Maker* (New York: Harcourt, Brace and Company, 1941; rev.: Harper San Francisco 1968, 1987).

[5] Henry P. Van Dusen, "The Trinity in Experience and Theology" *Theology Today* 15/3 (October 1958) 377–386. The other two theologians cited by Van Deusen were Karl Barth and Fisher's mentor Leonard Hodgson.

[6] Sayers, *The Mind of the Maker*, 35–45.

artists work out the play or the concept in their mind long before it is put to canvas or paper. So there is the creation as idea, which corresponds to the eternal Father.[7]

Eventually, though, the book must be written or the drawing done. Here we meet the artistic equivalent of the Son. The word becomes flesh and enters into space-time. An author, says Sayers, may say, "My book is finished—I have only to write it." But until it is written, it lacks incarnation. Sayers says this is the artistic work as energy, for now the reality of an idea takes shape in the world and unleashes its power there.[8]

Finally, though, there is also the creation as it is experienced and enjoyed by others. Sayers calls this "Power," and it corresponds to the Holy Spirit. She distinguishes this from "Energy" in that in "Power" the idea expressed by the energy (or "Activity," as Sayers puts it) is communicated to other readers and elicits a response in them. Once it is expressed, the energy is already unleashed upon the world. It makes the author a reader of her own book.[9]

While the student may understand these aspects of creative work as separate for analytical purposes, these three are one. She writes:

> Lastly, "these three are one, each equally in itself the whole work, whereof none can exist without other." If you were to ask a writer which is "the real book"—his Idea of it, his activity in writing it, or its return to himself in Power, he would be at a loss to tell you, because these things are essentially inseparable. Each of them is the complete book separately; yet in the complete book all of them exist together. He can, by an act of the intellect, "distinguish the persons" but he cannot by any means "divide the substance." He cannot know the Idea, except by the Power interpreting his own Activity to him; he knows the Activity only as it reveals the Idea in Power; he knows the Power only as the revelation of the Idea in the Activity.[10]

---

[7] Ibid., 37–38.
[8] Ibid., 38–42.
[9] Ibid., 40–41.
[10] Ibid., 41.

The defects of any artistic work relate to failures in one of these three dimensions. If the process of creation is too heavily focused on one aspect to the detriment of the others, the work will have problems.

Sayers's proposal is ingenious and leads to some reflections that are extremely important to her understanding. First, creative process implies the idea of freedom—both the freedom of God and the freedom of creatures. Though an author completely "creates" a fictional character, that character nonetheless has a certain limited "freedom," even though the author is theoretically free to do as she pleases with him. In fact, the author respects the freedom of characters as a story develops.[11]

Second, the idea of integrity is implied in that freedom. Characters in a written work, for example, have their own integrity even though they are completely "mental" creations of the author. The author can, in one sense, do as he or she pleases. Yet in another sense, if the characters are to be "true" to the creation willed by the creator, the author cannot do so without damaging their integrity. The reader can sense when a character is not "true" to itself. There is artificiality and disconnect with the work's "reality," and the entire work suffers and fails.[12]

Third, implied in Sayers's notion of the Trinitarian structure of life is her concept of work. Work is very important, for it is in our work that we "make" things as God does. We are continually—and usually obliviously—creating all the time. In a real sense this "creating" of ours is not true creation. Only God the Creator truly "creates" *ex nihilo* (out of nothing) as we would put it in theology. Artists know the difference.[13]

We who create art (and this includes what we do in worship leadership) actually take existing realities already "created" (notes, words, melodies, images, visions, artistic media, etc.) and "make" something new of them. Our work is the continual reshuffling of combinations of this resplendent and fathomless creation of God's into new possibilities, which God also willed and yet did not actualize in the mystery of giving us who are creatures something joyful, happy, and meaningful to do with our lives.[14]

---

[11] Sayers, *The Mind of the Maker*, 63–67.
[12] Ibid., 68–70.
[13] Ibid., 26–28.
[14] Ibid., 29–30.

God the Creator intends for us to experience our work as the joy of making. Sin did not bring work into the world—it poisoned it and robbed it of the joy that was inherent in "making." Post-fall work became addictive, idolatrous, tedious, and laborious. Whatever has gone wrong with our work (and our "works") has happened in contradiction to its original intent by God.[15]

Fourth, Sayers's understanding of art and the role of the artist in creation is crucial to our understanding of what worship is and should be. Toward the end of the book, Sayers says that artists have much to teach us all about life. It is not that all artists lead good lives, but at least in their art they have something to say about life. The artist must "surrender" to the medium he or she is using if the artist is ever to create something tangible and not just "have it in one's head." This takes imagination, commitment, and faithfulness to the creation's own "integrity."[16]

We live in a world that wants to treat life as problems to be solved. Yet it is clear that the harder we try to "fix" things in the world, the more problems we seem to have. We address the great problems of humanity—war, hatred, poverty, and injustice—as though we could solve them.[17]

Sayers implies that the artist can help us here "since the artist does not see life as a problem to be solved, but as a medium for creation."[18] That is, a creation—or a life—has certain possibilities in it. The point of creating at all is not whether that creation *can do everything, but whether it will live up to its potential.* There is something we can "make" of a life, whatever problems or limitations it has. There is still the possibility, through imagination and hope, that something wonderful can be made of it.

The point, then, is not to master, control, or even to fix life. It is, finally, to explore life as a wonder and a possibility and "to cooperate with it in love."[19] This is why we need art and artists in the world. Life

---

[15] Ibid., 217–225.
[16] Ibid., 181–87.
[17] Sayers, *The Mind of the Maker*, 181–87.
[18] Ibid., 185.
[19] Ibid., 186.

without the artistic imagination is just solving one dilemma after the other with no larger frame of reference. We can make life matter not only from material gifts and abilities we have, but from suffering, death, sin, pain, troubles, and failures we encounter.

Our job is to not shrink from life but step up to it and live it with courage and faith, knowing that God is with us in the endeavor. If Sayers is right, every human being is, in one's own life, an artist. The medium is the life one has been given.

If we apply this to worship, we begin to see that there is not only a theological standard for worship but also an artistic one, though it can be argued that these are one and the same. In worship the media includes the entirety of the congregation—their lives, hearts, minds, and responses. This is in addition to other gifts God gives us, such as Scripture, the church, theology and doctrine, the Christian story, and above all the presence of the Holy Spirit, as well as more mundane "media," such as music, drama, and our worship spaces.

Sayers certainly gives a powerful perspective from which worship leaders might begin to think about what they do. Clearly, the act of leading worship is not unlike writing a story, molding clay, or painting an imaginative canvas—except it is the ever—interesting task of involving other human beings as the medium. Moreover, when we construct liturgies or prepare corporate events, we are also engaged in a process that corresponds easily to the Trinitarian reality that Sayers envisions.

Finally, Sayers fully understands Trinitarian reality as perfect love. The Triune God did not create because God was lonely and needed us. Rather, God created the world because *that's what love does. Love expands, shares, and extends perfect communion and community*. So instead of the dead, empty, lifeless universe that randomly spawned life trapped in a dead system (as in atheistic understandings), the Father, Son, and Spirit expressed the Trinitarian love by making a universe, a world, life, and human beings.

The creation is itself the love of God carried out as the ultimate (and really *only)* true artistic creation. And as a part of that creation, God created the bounds of integrity for the creatures and respects it, even to the point of permitting the loss of union with the love of the Father, Son, and Spirit.

This last point ties to a serious affirmation made by Fisher Humphreys in a little book he wrote many years ago, *The Nature of God*. Fisher wrote that Father, Son, and Holy Spirit lived together from eternity in love. That love was, he said, perfect and uninterrupted happiness. He writes, "One day the Father said to the Son and the Spirit, 'This love is too good to keep to ourselves. Let's create some people and share our love with them.' So they did. And that is how the world began."[20]

The end of all true worship is the deeper discernment of the love of God. The fruit of worship will inevitably lead to decisions to live lives commensurate with that love.

So what can we call this "Trinitarian Structure as Worship?" I would suggest that if all the realities Sayers suggests are true, then worship is the free creative work of the people of God to intentionally give their attention and connect to the fullness of the love of the Triune God.

No style issues are resolved here, nor should they be. Worship is a theologically grounded and centered artistic work of, by, for, and with God's people. Its aim is to connect them with the reality of the perfect union of God's own life. It gives attention and helps focus.

To understand our worship as work is to offer a serious critique to one of the cultural temptations for the contemporary worship movement in America. It is tempting to make worship something other than the giving of something, a sacrifice of ourselves, something as work (creative work, to be sure!). If we yield to this temptation, our worship may become merely entertainment, which people may enjoy and move on, unchanged. Like all other aspects of life in a consumer culture, we may try to reduce worship to one more commodity that must be marketed to wary buyers.

On the other side, so-called traditional worship cannot escape critique. The creative work of the people of God is to be faithful to the Trinitarian God who is revealed to us in Jesus Christ. The creative dimension asks us to be responsible to re-form, remake, reapply, and revisit. It is not enough to "perform" well if it lulls us into lethargy.

---

[20] Fisher H. Humphreys, *The Nature of God*, Layman's Library of Christian Doctrine 4 (Nashville: Broadman Press, 1985) 128.

The Trinitarian vision of perfect communion expressed as missional love would seem to call us to a radically different attitude toward one another and a completely different perspective on this "work" we are doing week by week. Too many churches operate like everything else in the worlds of their members with subverting agendas, power politics, unrestrained egotism, and the absence of a truly spiritual dimension.

In the presence of the Trinitarian vision of community, we have a vision of love that is not sentimental, for it has a cross in its memory. It is love that knows that its worship is absolutely essential for its life and continued survival. The purpose of worship is to invite us into the depths of the love of God and out into the deep purposes of God. It seems incompatible that people who truly touch this great mystery of love could disrespect one another in their weekly work of expressing it.

Sayers and Kierkegaard

There is an interesting convergence between Sayers's view of the Trinitarian nature of being and Søren Kierkegaard's oft-cited analogy for worship found in his book *Purity of Heart Is to Will One Thing*.[21] The book, which Kierkegaard says was inspired by reflection on the office of confession, represents a relentless pursuit of the individual's spiritual quest for a unified will. Double-mindedness is the enemy of this quest. In almost infinite variety, humans in their sinfulness avoid the powerful call of God to concentrate their mind and energies upon what is before them at the moment.

This capacity for evasion happens in worship that humans render to God as well. Kierkegaard compared worship to a drama. He said that Christians tend to think of the congregation as the audience, the worship leaders and the preachers as the actors, and God as the scriptwriter or the prompter offstage. But in fact, says Kierkegaard, God is the audience of worship, and the congregation, worship leaders, and preachers (all of us) are the actors. It is a helpful metaphor because it pushes us toward

---

[21] Søren Kierkegaard, *Purity of Heart Is to Will One Thing: Spiritual Preparation for the Office of Confession*, trans. Douglas Van Steere (New York: Harper & Brothers, 1938). Reprint 1956.

active participation. Worship leaders are the prompters, preachers are the actors—God is the audience of our worship.[22]

But this model does not say enough about God's involvement and presence in the worship event itself. God is also author of the play and one of the actors with us on the stage. It is true that God as the audience of our worship represents the dimension of God as the transcendent Lord. But Sayers's book is an interesting complement to this metaphor.

We may think about a play, she says. As we noted earlier, she says the author may conceive the idea, finish it, and say, "My play is completely finished. I have only to write it."[23] There is perfect unity/union of these three in the creative act. So we might say that the play is not simply an idea that actors try to bring to life for the enjoyment of the audience. According to Sayers, when the curtain goes down, the audience goes away with their own energy and reaction to the experience and may continue to reflect on the experience as a whole.[24]

When we see a great play, like Shakespeare's *Hamlet*, "we behold the eternal power of an idea, incarnate again and again, that has the capacity to 're-present' itself each time an audience hears the words as the actors present them and give inflection and nuance. And then, even though it has been read, critiqued, and performed countless times since it was first presented, it can be experienced by people for the first time with great force as though it were a fresh creation. It is new to *them*."[25]

This amplifies our understanding of Kierkegaard's concept of worship as drama. For we realize that in "creating" worship we are not creating at all. We are merely offering ourselves and our talents, energies, voices, and work to the script written from all eternity by God.

This might be a helpful correction to the obsession with novelty that sometimes pervades American worship, something that has more to do with our cultural loathing of boredom and stability than it does with our need to find "breakthroughs." The relatively recent adulation of adolescence that the baby boomers introduced in our marketing society has caused us to believe that the need of the rebellious adolescent to

---

[22] Kierkegaard, *Purity of Heart Is to Will One Thing*.

[23] Sayers, *The Mind of the Maker*, 42.

[24] Ibid., 115–16.

[25] Ibid., 116–18.

push back against elders somehow requires the church to come up with something "new" that will accommodate this unhappiness.

Instead, we might consider thinking about why our worship is uninteresting in the first place. It is true that it might not be well "incarnated." Our notions and ideas may be noble, but we may have not done the hard work of connecting with the realities inherent in the story we are presenting. But this reflection might just as well lead us to think about the "medium" of the worshiper. Has he or she come to participate in worship fully ready to enter the mystery? How do we "prepare" for that?

Plays, says Sayers, may suffer from defects of understanding of the Trinity. Heresy can appear even in the creative process. There is important work to do, the work of love. The creator must love his or her creatures. Sayers means several important things by love. First, there is a respect for the freedom and integrity of the creation.[26] As a writer she understood that an author can fail his or her creatures in a play or book by sentimentally failing to let their true being carry out to its end. With sentimentality there is loss of energy and power. To truly love one's creation is to permit it its own integrity, including the risks of freedom, the willingness to sacrifice and take risks with it, and to know that genuine creation implies the willingness of the creator to "surrender" to the creation.[27]

In artistic work, this means that we accept the possibilities of our creation, whether it be letting the character in a book be true to his or her flawed being (and suffer its consequences) or whether we acknowledge the qualities in a piece of earthen clay and mold it accordingly. "Surrender," in this sense, is not "acquiescence"—as we are prone to think of surrender—but "embrace."

To surrender is to enter fully into the truth of one's creation. Surrender is not the emptying of one's passion. It is entering fully into that passion. Theologically, it is easy to see the flaccid failures of much contemporary "spirituality" in which "surrender" is a tragic and superficial obliteration of one's "selfhood"—but only in a self-delusional sense.

---

[26] Sayers, *The Mind of the Maker*, 64–68.

[27] Ibid., 75–80.

Genuine surrender is the full embrace of self—not selfishness, but acceptance of oneself as a given. Sayers writes, "A passion of this temper does not resign itself to sacrifice, but embraces it, and sweeps the world up in the same embrace. It is not without reason that we feel a certain uneasy suspicion of that inert phrase, 'Christian resignation'; an inner voice reminds us that the Christian God is Love, and that love and resignation can find no common ground to stand on."[28]

Surrender is the surrender of love—it is passionate embrace. If this is so, and if I might take the liberty to extend this notion to our worship, the "problem" of worship is not a problem of forms and musical tastes. It is the loss of passion—in worship planners, in worshipers, and in human lives. Conversely, the recovery of worship in our time will mean the rediscovery of this energy and power and the rediscovery by all those who worship of what it means to "surrender ourselves" in the moment of worship.

We do not have to conjure energy and power artificially. Where the presence of Christ is with the church as the Holy Spirit is, there is life. The deeper and more troublesome questions about our worship are about the states of our respective souls. But at the least, worship planners must begin to think about their work this way—that it is a weekly drama in which our highest artistic sensibilities are required.

This does not, oddly enough, mean we ought to reinvent the wheel every Sunday. There are different aspects of creativity. There is the creative process of bringing something novel into being, something more rare than one would think! There is also the very honorable creativity of breathing new life and identification into the familiar. Repetition is not off limits, but lifeless repetition is.

This Trinitarian view of creative process can be an enormously useful way for worship leaders to think about their humble little "creations" week after week. It gives opportunity for theological reflection and perspective on what they are trying to do in the first place.

The worship leader who has too many "ends" in mind (such as forcing the whole drama toward a predetermined response in the people) can be guilty of failing to do the hard work of incarnation and of failing to respect the power of the Spirit to move afresh. Worship does not

[28] Ibid., 136.

require manipulation, and manipulation, however impressive, is not worship. There *is* a theological basis for worship.

Ultimately, Sayers's book is a powerful invitation to see ourselves as artists of God. If this seems daunting to us, it need not be. In the simplest way, it suggests that the "basis" for evaluating our worship is not something we must conjure—it is inherent in the life we already share in Jesus Christ. The living God—Father, Son and Holy Spirit—is the reality of our lives.

Reflections on Sayers's book invite us to ask different questions of our worship plans: Is this true to life? Have we respected the integrity of our participants? Have we loved them and honored the ways they express themselves in our planning? Have we done the hard work of crafting our ideas, of giving them intrinsic integrity as we express them, and of allowing the space for what the Spirit will do among us? Have we avoided the safety of integrity and the heresies that result from our imbalances of idea, energy, and power?

The Trinity is often seen as a "problem" in Christian life and worship, a mystery that we acknowledge but do not understand. The genius in Sayers's view is that the Trinity is a clue to understanding life.

Concluding Reflections

Perhaps what is most wrong with worship in our time is not marketing, cleverness, or relevance. Instead, it is a lack of artistic and theological integrity, and the loss of energy and power that comes with poor art. It is not the introduction of mystery in worship that is a problem—it is our trivialization of mystery and our poor handling of it in our midst.

The "standard for judging worship," if it is to be judged at all, is the same by which all art is judged, or rather, understood—its fidelity to life and its truth-telling about that life. It is not cleverness or entertainment or enjoyment, but this intrinsic reflection of reality that is most deeply expressed for Christians in the experience of the triune God.

If worship is the artistic work of God's people seeking to express by the media at their disposal the reality they have known through Jesus Christ, then worship will, as an artistic medium, have its own integrity to live up to. It is not some arbitrary external notion imposed upon it—there is something of the structure of being itself in all genuine worship. Conversely, all fraudulent worship, superficial worship, or trivial worship, like all artistic failure, is likely to be the subversion of the artistic reality to something less than its true being.

By asking whether art conveys the truth, we also mean that there are indeed internal criteria by which to distinguish good and bad worship. Art comes in all forms and social levels, from primitive to deeply sophisticated. Worship is not merely music and words and institutional effectiveness. The true measure of good worship is immeasurable but discernable. It lives on in human lives that have touched the depths of human existence, and it reflects honorably the deepest truths about God.

If our worship is not "true," this can be defective in many directions. It may be unscriptural or theologically suspect, and this is where our lamentations usually take us. But the quest for artistic theological integrity takes us in the other direction as well—does what we present accurately and truthfully convey human existence as God made it? Do we tell the truth about life, or merely seek to impose temporary escape from it? Do we soften the harshness of death with our sugary and sometimes premature need to reassure? Sayers's reflections hold us accountable to being "true to life" as well as true to our theological positions.

False worship can occur in any style and with any music. Sayers's Trinitarian criteria help us to remember that all forms and styles of worship are prone to the loss of one of the three dimensions of being.

Good art opens up the world. Bad art mocks it and mocks those who purport to enjoy good art. This is why entertainment is not worship and worship cannot merely entertain, even if those who participate have a good time or feel good. Like a bad movie, book, or piece of music, bad art or bad worship is forgotten before the observer gets home from the viewing. Great art haunts a life because it participates in reality even as it points beyond itself.

If this leaves us in a somewhat unresolved position about styles, musical choices, or correct structures and aesthetics, so be it. The creative work of the people of God is ongoing, and new combinations are inevitable. Those who want "rules" to guarantee effective worship are going to be disappointed. The desire of our culture to find principles, rules, and guaranteed shortcuts explains much of what is defective in our worship today.

It seems to me that the question that matters most is "How can we render most faithfully the truth about ourselves, the world, and, most of all, about the God who made us and saves us into the artistic experience that we call weekly worship?" Since worship is about crafting small pieces of this endeavor week by week, it will take genuine artists who are theologically astute to do this work.

It follows, then, that pastors as well as musicians need to be at least sensitized to the arts. Artists need to know some theology and church reality. This means more than "I like the arts" or having preferences about music and liturgy. The kind of contemplation about the nature of art can be helpful to us in thinking about how we facilitate the act of worship. If the lives of people are a medium, we need to become serious artists of that medium.

Even if we think evangelistically, the question is not necessarily "What will bring the most people into the church?" but rather "What elements of the Christian story and worship will facilitate and express the deepest longings of humanity for God and for God's search for people?"

Finally, we must ask, "How can this daunting weekly effort we call worship change from a performance into a truer reflection of life, God, and ultimate reality as revealed to us in the remarkable story?" It seems to me that to anchor our reflections and efforts here, in the being of the Triune God as expressed in the artistic form, might lead us in some enduring and creative new directions in our task of planning.

This may also invite us to be less critical of our halting efforts to worship God and less prone to be always evaluating it by secular standards. We should resist the attempt to quantify the results of worship and instead see it as an opportunity for us to surrender our lives. The "meaning" of worship is not finally about human ingenuity or cleverness but about being true to our deepest truths so we know who we are and why we are here. The most damning judgment that can fall upon us is not whether people liked our worship or whether we felt better when it was done, but whether, at the end, we involved ourselves more deeply in the mystery that is God with us.

Into All the World: The Missionary God Who Calls and Sends

WANDA S. LEE

Introduction

For the casual observer of today's church who knows little of the history of Christianity, or world religions for that matter, the vast missionary movement of this generation must be a puzzling thing. Some may see it as a response to strategic planning of denominational missions boards, or to innovative leadership in churches. Others might think it is a phenomenon of our modern-day search for peace and an understanding of God. Even those of us immersed within the life of the church may find all the talk about missions and the foundational motivation behind missionary activity quite confusing.

Fisher Humphreys has spent most of his adult life helping students understand God's Word and how it applies to the life of today's church. Fisher's convictions about the missionary nature of God and how the church is to respond to Jesus' call to "go and tell" are well-known by those he has taught and those who have read his writings. His concept of Jesus as a personal Savior and Lord is the foundation of all he believes. In the opening pages of his book, *I Have Called You Friends*, Fisher writes, "Christians are people who have heard the story of Jesus Christ and who have responded by trusting in him as savior and Lord. All Christians are called to be followers of Christ."[1] He goes on to describe various images found in the New Testament that guide Jesus' followers about how to lead their lives; these images also describe how to relate to the body of believers called the church. As followers of Christ, we are called to live as missions people who freely share the same story of Christ with those we meet.

[1] Fisher Humphreys, *I Have Called You Friends* (Birmingham AL: New Hope Publishers, 2005) 21.

The word "missions" has been defined in many different terms, but at its root understanding lies the concept that missions is not man-made, nor does it happen at the initiative of man; it is what God does through his church to spread the truth of the gospel to all people everywhere.

Paul Borthwick wrote in his book, *A Mind for Missions*, "The message of missions is woven throughout the Bible, and the sending of God's people into all the earth was not an appendix to the story of redemption. Missions were in God's heart all along. Our God is a missionary God!"[2]

For some, the idea of looking for a thread of missions from Genesis to Revelation is a new thought, especially since the word "missions" is not found in the Bible. What if we look at the Bible as one book, rather than sixty-six separate ones; as one book with a singular theme—God redeeming his people from every tongue, tribe, and nation? If we look at Scripture with this view of missions in the forefront of our minds, how we view God's purpose in the world is radically altered.

In the Beginning

With only a brief look into Scripture, support can be found for this idea of a missionary thread being woven from Genesis to Revelation. From the very beginning, God's heart for the nations of the world and for all of his creation can be clearly seen.

From the first chapter of Genesis through chapter 11, God was at work creating the world and those who would live in it. He had a plan for peace and harmony, for fellowship, for a people who would love and obey his commands, demonstrating respect for him as Father God. But as people created with a free spirit, they chose a different path over obedience. The fellowship between God and humankind was broken.

And yet, God demonstrated his deep love for his creation. In the familiar story of Noah and the flood, we see how, in the midst of God's grief over the sins of humans, the faithfulness of one emerged. Because Noah was faithful, God saved a remnant of his creation and promised never to destroy them again. Unfortunately, when the people believed once again they could be like God and began to build a tower that would

---

[2] Paul Borthwick, *A Mind for Missions* (Colorado Springs: NavPress, 1987) 23.

take them to heaven, God had to intervene. This time he stopped their plan without destroying them. But what had been a world of one people with a common language now became a world of many languages, causing great confusion. The people building the tower could not continue to build because they could not communicate with one another.

In one moment, God moved the world from one language and one culture to many languages and distinct groups of people. God demonstrated that he was God. He wanted the people to know Yahweh, the one true and loving God of creation and all of life. His desire was for all people to know him and worship only him. He began again calling his creation back to himself.

The Thread of Missions Begins

Genesis 12 provides the backdrop of how a missionary God began to redeem his lost relationship. It is the account of God's call to Abraham and Sarah. "The Lord said to Abram, 'Leave your country, your people and your father's household and go to the land I will show you. I will make you into a great nation and I will bless you; I will make your name great and you will be a blessing'" (Gen 12:1–2 NIV).[3] God created a covenant, a promise, with Abraham that would one day lead to reuniting God's people into one family with one purpose, worshiping one God—Yahweh. With the call of Abraham, the story of a missionary God who calls and sends his people began.

God promised Abraham that he would bless him and make him the leader of a great nation. But God's blessing brought with it an important responsibility. God chose Abraham because he loved him and through him wanted to extend his blessing to all the people he had created. God entered into a covenant with Abraham in order to bless others through him and lead them back into fellowship with him.

God continued to affirm Abraham's call throughout the book of Genesis. In Genesis 22:18 we read, "Through your offspring all nations on earth will be blessed." God repeated the promise to "bless the nations" through the descendants of Abraham through Isaac in Genesis

---

[3] All Scripture quotations are taken from the Holy Bible, New International Version (NIV).

26:3–4 and through those of Jacob in Genesis 28:13–15. The covenant was repeated again in Genesis 35: 9–12.

Throughout the Old Testament a recurring phrase begins to surface. God's desire to be "made known among the nations" becomes a clearly stated purpose for many of his actions, reinforcing the missional character of God. For instance, David's conquest of Goliath provided an opportunity for God to be made known among the nations. In 1 Samuel 17:46 we find that David killed Goliath so "the whole world will know that there is a God in Israel." In 1 Chronicles 16:8, David himself acknowledged how the people were to make God "known among the nations, what he has done." Isaiah, Jeremiah, and the other prophets repeat over and over how God leads his people to "make him known among the nations."

A missionary thread is also found in the Psalms. In worship, the people were reminded that the desire of God was to be known among the nations. "May the nations be glad and sing for joy" is decreed in Psalm 67:4. And in Psalm 96:3 Israel is called to "declare his glory among the nations, his marvelous deeds among all people." God chose to live among a special group of people. He chose to bless them so he could become known among all people and restore the broken fellowship caused by sin.

From Old Testament to New Testament

The missions thread of the Bible stretches beyond the Old Testament into the New Testament: "For God so loved the world that he gave his one and only Son, that whoever believes in him shall not perish but have eternal life. For God did not send his Son into the world to condemn the world, but to save the world through him" (John 3:16–17). God's ultimate demonstration of his missionary purpose was in sending Jesus, his only Son, to live and walk among the people just as he had proclaimed through the prophet Isaiah long before (see Isa 7:14; 53:1–12). Jesus' ministry on earth demonstrated, from beginning to end, the heart of a missionary God as he touched the lives of the untouchable, called the least likely to follow, and prepared them to carry on the task of making God known among all people. Even though Jesus' beginnings were among the Jews, God's love for the nations of the entire world was always deeply embedded in the mind and heart of Christ. The missionary purpose of God was evident as Jesus taught the disciples during their three years together, and even in his final instructions.

To connect the missionary messages of the Old Testament and the New Testament, it is important that we believe that the Bible is truly a missionary book. An example of this is found in one of the most quoted passages in the Bible, Matthew 28:18–20. Jesus actually reissues the Great Commission that was first stated in Genesis 12:1–3. Abraham was commissioned to reach all nations. Jesus' instructions to the disciples to "go and make disciples of all nations" reaffirmed God's missionary nature and gave the disciples their purpose for the days ahead. The calling of Abraham as the beginning point for the Great Commission was so much a part of the lives of the early disciples that they quoted Genesis 12:3 when they were preaching. Peter references it in Acts 3:25–26; Paul uses it in Galatians 3:8, as does the writer of Hebrews in 6:13–17.

When Jesus spoke in Matthew 28:19–20 and in Acts 1:8 to the disciples he told them to return to Jerusalem where they were to wait for power, for the coming of the Holy Spirit. On the Day of Pentecost, the sound of many languages was heard. How could a group of Galileans communicate what they had experienced in the resurrection? In Acts 2:5 we read that Peter's message to the many groups present on the Day of Pentecost was miraculously understood by all in their own language. About 3,000 people came to faith that day. For the message to reach the world, it had to be preached in a way that people from various nations of the world could hear it. As they heard the stories of those who had encountered Yahweh in Abraham's day, they understood that God is a powerful God. Upon hearing Peter's message, they left the city repeating stories of a risen savior who performed miracles and who could change their lives.

The missionary movement began with the call of Abraham and continued with the fervor of those early disciples who, because of their relationship with Jesus Christ, had seen and heard the power of God, who was restoring his people into a right relationship with God, a people who worshiped only him. God was being "made known among the nations" because he is a missionary God who calls and sends his people.

Missions and the Church

The book of Acts relates how God would continue to call and send his people following the resurrection of Christ. Christ gave himself for the church, and it would be through the church that God would continue to pour out his Spirit and call out his people. The church exists to worship God and to serve him. Fisher Humphreys wrote, in the first edition of *Thinking about God*, "The mission of the church is part of the church's privilege. God has honored his church by calling her to share in his great work in the world. A society, like an individual, can suffer from a sense of uselessness when there is no important task it feels called upon to perform. God has blessed the church by commissioning her to do his work in the world. The church is the body through which Christ acts today."[4] While the call to missions has remained constant since the call of Abraham, the response to God's call by individuals and the church has found its way through a process of maturing and change across time.

The earliest missions movement was led by common men and women committed to telling the story that they had experienced themselves, and later it was led by those who had heard it firsthand from the disciples and the apostles. Paul's missionary journeys provide an example of the intentional plan of the early church to spread the gospel to all nations. These early missionaries were not professional missionaries as we think of today, but they were deeply committed to their faith. Some, like Paul, shared what they knew with others while continuing to work at their trades to provide for their needs. They often housed visiting "missionaries" while they assisted with discipling new believers. Churches were planted and the gospel spread.

In an early Christian document known as *The Letter to Diognetus* written around A.D. 200 the early Christians were described as follows:

> Christians are not distinguished from the rest of humankind either in locality or in speech or in customs. For they dwell not somewhere in cities of their own, neither do they use some different language, nor practice an extraordinary kind of

[4] Fisher Humphreys, *Thinking about God* (New Orleans: Insight Press, 1974) 181.

> life...while they dwell in cities of Greeks and barbarians...and follow the native custom in dress and food and the other arrangements of life, yet the constitution of their own citizenship which they set forth, is marvelous, and confessedly contradicts expectation.... They dwell in their own countries, but only as sojourners.... Their existence is on earth, but their citizenship is in heaven.... In a word, what the soul is in a body, this the Christians are in the world.[5]

The church in the book of Acts and the church of today share this common *dynamic* of being people who see the world differently because of the difference Christ makes in our lives. We share a common humanity where imperfections are the norm, but we also carry the same responsibility to be salt and light in the world. How we live, how we speak, and how we love one another have always spoken volumes to those around us from the beginning of the church to today.

A Historical View of Missions

In the history of the early church, the church that was scattered endured persecution and grew at a rapid rate in the world beyond Jerusalem because of the notably different lifestyle of the early believers. They had gone into all the world as transforming agents with a dynamic commitment to live as Christ taught them. Unfortunately this visible nature of the church waned. History reveals that in time the people lost touch with God and his purposes for the early believers. By A.D. 312, when the Roman emperor Constantine publicly embraced the Christian faith, Christianity as a religion was becoming an accepted part of the culture. While this transition brought benefits to many Christians, such as the lessening of persecution, there was a down side as well. Christianity became routinized and lost much of its early rigor. A growing distance between the missionary purpose of God and his people developed and continued for many centuries.[6]

---

[5] *The Letter to Diognetus* 5f, cited in David J. Bosch, *Transforming Mission* (Maryknoll NY: Orbis Books, 1991) 211.

[6] Kenneth Scott Latourette, *A History of Christianity*, rev. ed, (New York: Harper & Row 1975) 1:9–93, 187–188.

God was not asleep, nor was he indifferent as to what was taking place during the ensuing years. As has always been the case, God was raising up new leaders and calling his chosen people to stand firm for his purposes. With the fall of Rome in 410 and the Christian church's stability threatened, God's voice was heard through a variety of people. One of those people, with spoken and written words, was Augustine. He repeatedly called God's people to a renewed faith. He reminded them of Paul's teaching on justification through faith, of the sinless nature of Christ, what Christ's death on the cross meant for all people, and of the perils of sin and the need for forgiveness.

Augustine's thought continued to guide the church during the medieval era, although some of his evangelical emphases were lost in the institutional constraints faced by the church during the Middle Ages. Communication channels took a quantum leap forward with the invention of the printing press in 1455. In addition to the low literacy level, the painstaking task of hand copying manuscripts made Scripture and other religious writings unavailable to the average person before the printing press. When Martin Luther was born in 1483, the beginning stages of a reformation were in the works. As he studied the Greek New Testament and grew in his understanding of the nature of the gospel, Luther began to protest the excesses and inaccurate teachings of the established church. In 1517, through speaking out against the contemporary Catholic Church, Martin Luther launched the Reformation. Before long, the Word of God was translated into the vernacular languages of the people and God's work of the church became clearer as well. Little missionary outreach occurred for the first two centuries following the Reformation despite the strong teachings of Luther on how God had entrusted the church with his Word—the gospel for *all* people. The debate was taken to a renewed level in 1590 when a Dutch theologian named Adrian Saravia published a tract espousing the responsibility of the church under the leadership of clergy in accepting the binding nature of the Great Commission on the role of the church.[7]

---

[7] Bosch, *Transforming Mission*, 247.

From Reformation to Enlightenment

As the period of the Reformation was subsiding, the era known as the Enlightenment, or the "age of reason," was rising. With it, a renewal and a redirected focus on missions emerged as well. David Bosch wrote, "It was inevitable that the Enlightenment would profoundly influence mission thinking and practice, the more so since the entire modern missionary enterprise is, to a very real extent, a child of the Enlightenment. It was, after all, the new expansionist worldview which pushed Europe's horizons beyond the Mediterranean Sea and the Atlantic Ocean and thus paved the way for a worldwide Christian missionary outreach."[8]

God began calling out those who would respond to the new opportunities and challenges. In his famous published work, *An Enquiry into the Obligations of Christians to Use Means for the Conversion of the Heathens*, William Carey, a poor shoemaker in England, challenged the belief of his day that said if God wanted to save the heathen, he would do it without their help. As a result, his passion for personal involvement in missions caused him to spend forty-one years of his life sharing the gospel with the people of India. Carey's most famous words of missions challenge to the people of his day continue to inspire us today: "Expect great things. Attempt great things."[9]

Early Years of Missions in America

By the 1800s a passion for missions in American churches was growing. In 1812 the first American woman, Ann Hassletine Judson, was appointed as a missionary under the Congregational Church. She became, for many women, a symbol of courage and endearment as she and her husband, Adoniram, served in Burma under the harshest of conditions, including a time of war. Little girls grew up reading Ann's story of sacrifice, her early death as well as the loss of several children, all for the sake of spreading the gospel among the Burmese people. Ann's example paved the way for many to follow. Charlotte Diggs "Lottie"

---

[8] Ibid., 274.

[9] Timothy George, *Faithful Witness: The Life and Mission of William Carey* (Birmingham AL: New Hope Publishers, 1991) 32.

Moon was one of the little girls who read Ann's story. Lottie grew up in a family with means that afforded her access to many books and to adult conversations where events of the day were discussed. As one of the most educated women of her era, Lottie was well-read on many subjects. She became a teacher and was the headmistress of a girls' school in Georgia. But the pull to missions grew stronger and stronger. In 1873 Lottie went to China. According to some reports, Lottie understood mission strategy like few other missionaries in her time. Through her letters home, she pleaded for more workers and the funds to do greater work. The women at home took up the challenge. They organized missionary societies and raised money for missions. A Christmas offering named for Lottie Moon continues to provide over half the financial support for missionaries appointed through the Southern Baptist International Mission Board.

On the wave of so many people committing themselves to give their lives for service in a foreign land, not every missionary was as prepared and wise as Lottie in how to adapt to new cultures. Instead of embracing the new way of life, some missionaries found it difficult and ended up transporting Western culture, idealism, and economics in ways that were inappropriate. Christianity at times became associated with Western styles of worship and churches. The health of missionaries became a concern as they died from foreign diseases. In some cases, the missionaries brought their own diseases to the people they sought to reach. History reveals that in some fields of work paternalistic relationships developed instead of partnerships. This led to financial dependency later on, making it difficult for the nationals to assume leadership for some of the schools and hospitals. God used this period of missionary advance to further his kingdom despite the missteps of some and the effects of colonialism on others.

As missionaries were appointed, it became increasingly important to educate the church people about the needs of the missionaries as well as the need for financial support. To encourage members' informed participation, mission agencies of many denominations developed and began to prepare a full line of programs with written information for the church. In 1888, for example, the Woman's Missionary Union (WMU) was organized by women representatives from thirteen states to fulfill a desire and a calling to organize support for Southern Baptist missionaries.[10] In 1904 WMU produced their first printed curriculum, and an organizational structure for missions education in the church emerged. Christians in other denominations followed suit. Consequently, a new generation found a way to be involved in missions alongside those who served on the front line. The twentieth-century missions movement grew in the number of appointed missionaries and in financial support needed to send increasing numbers. With a developing system of travel that grew easier and more affordable for the average person to use, the world began to shrink. The church began to develop a broader view of the world and a deeper understanding of the needs of so many living in a world without Christ—limited in access to the gospel and Scripture in their own languages.

As has always been the case, regardless of the challenges of the times, through the scattering of God's church, people have been drawn to him and souls have been saved. As a missionary God who calls and sends, all that has happened through the course of history has been within his sight and his knowledge. God alone can see the final result as described by John in Revelation 7:9, "After this I looked and there before me was a great multitude that no one could count, from every nation, tribe, people and language, standing before the throne."

Today's Challenges

God has always been a faithful missionary God calling and sending his people into all the world, and continues to do so today. But the face of missions is changing once again. Just as past generations of Christians have faced challenges culturally, economically, spiritually, and in many other ways, today's generation is no exception. We live in a world of constant, unprecedented change. The thrust of Christianity that at one time was so prevalent in the Western world, namely Europe and the United States, has now shifted to the Southern hemisphere and other places in our world. Author Philip Jenkins in *The Next Christendom* states, "We are currently living through one of the transforming moments in the history of religion worldwide.... Over the past century...the center of gravity in the Christian world has shifted

[10] Catherine B. Allen, *A Century to Celebrate* (Birmingham AL: Woman's Missionary Union 1987) 45–47.

inexorably southward to Africa, Asia, and Latin America. Already today, the largest Christian communities on the planet are found in Africa and Latin America."[11]

Mission agencies of all denominations and regions have found themselves moving into new realms of missions methodology as they shift their focus from more established mission regions or countries to a focus on people groups. This is especially true in areas referred to as the 10/40 window, or the un-evangelized areas of the world.[12] Many Western agencies have divested themselves of institutions and financial commitments in an effort to free up resources to allow greater flexibility and mobility as they adapt to change. With these changes, and all the good that has come as a result, instability has also resulted among some Christian groups left to support the work without this assistance. At times of change of this nature, in the absence of trust and clear communication, of broken relationships are brought about within the Christian community.

Here again, a new opportunity exists for those willing to engage in significant partnerships. As larger missions agencies move into new strategies, churches and individuals are entering into partnerships to provide nationals with new avenues of support. The benefit to the church is personal involvement. People who experience missions firsthand, through volunteer projects and extended reciprocal partnerships between cities, countries, or people groups, have their view of the world broadened. They begin to see the world around them differently, even the world just outside the door of their church. As the world becomes smaller because of easier access to one another, the influence of Christians who take seriously their Great Commission responsibility becomes ever more critical to sharing Christ with "all the nations" of the world.

God is at work among his people, especially among the laity. A movement is underway today that is more closely aligned with the New Testament than we have seen in centuries. Also, Christians are obtaining

---

[11] Philip Jenkins, *The Next Christendom, The Coming of Global Christianity* (New York: Oxford University Press, 2002) 1–2.

[12] Patrick Johnstone and Jason Mandryk, *Operation World*, 6th ed. (Waynesboro GA: Paternoster 2001) 6.

education, developing marketable skills that many countries need, and are moving themselves to live immersed in new cultures. Professionals taking their skills and planting their lives in new places, simply to be the body of Christ in the world, constitutes perhaps the next wave of missions activity to be seen in our coming generation.

William Tinsley, in *Finding God's Vision: Mission and The New Realties*, says, "The global economy of the twenty-first century is re-creating a similar context in which the first-century disciples carried the gospel to the ends of their known world.... The church of the twenty-first century needs to recognize that these successful business people can create the greatest opportunities for missions the world has seen."[13]

Imagine the impact of business leaders who take their responsibility to be the missional people of God seriously and see their businesses as entry points for sharing their faith around the world. Someone recently noted how many fast-food chains or soft drink companies are found in every country. Just think of what might happen if the workers who start up these enterprises are Christians who believe they can change the world wherever they are. Imagine what could happen if a Christian young adult asked for a transfer from a Starbucks in the United States to one in China to live and work as a vessel of Christ. Imagine the impact of a Christian teacher who became certified to teach English in Japan to businessmen coming to America to invest. God is doing something new in our generation, something new in how he calls and sends his people into the whole world. Missionaries sent by traditional methods will continue, but this new wave of self-starters, business leaders, professionals, and the laity who understand the possibility of living missionally as they travel and work will be the future agents of change for Christ.

So what is our responsibility as the church? I believe God desires that we embrace the new while continuing to value and support the more established missions ways of sending, so long as the message of Christ is being presented to those who have never heard it. God calls us to be alert to the ways he is working during these in-between times and to open our ears, our hearts, and our minds to his call for our personal

---

[13] William Tinsley, *Finding God's Vision: Mission and The New Realties* (Rockwall TX: Veritas Publishing, 2005) 38.

response as well as the response of our churches. Os Guinness reminds us that "calling is the truth that God calls us to Himself so decisively that everything we are, everything we do, and everything we have is invested with a special devotion and dynamism lived out as a response to His summons and service."[14]

We serve a missionary God who continues to call and send his people into all parts of the world today. The church bears a tremendous responsibility to hold high the missionary nature of God who has one desire: to be known among the nations and peoples of the world as a God who forgives and desires to have an intimate relationship with his creation: "For God so loved the world he gave his one and only Son" (John 3:16).

---

[14] Os Guinness, *The Call: Finding and Fulfilling the Central Purpose of Your Life* (Nashville: W Publishing Group, 1998) 4.

That They May All Be One:
The Unity That Is Ours and Not Ours

STEPHEN J. DUFFY

I first met Fisher Humphreys when he was teaching at the New Orleans Baptist Theological Seminary. Over the years Fisher, his wife Caroline, and I have become friends, and we have broken bread together when our paths crossed in New Orleans and Birmingham. When I became involved in the Southern Baptist/Roman Catholic conversations of the late 1990s, I recalled Fisher's participation in an earlier round of conversations and I read what I could find of it. When I was asked to prepare a paper presenting a comparative study of Southern Baptist and Roman Catholic soteriologies that would serve as a basis for discussion, I turned to Fisher to steer me on to the Southern Baptist sources that I would need. I find in Fisher a friend and a colleague, a theologian concerned (as I am) with the problematic issue of the unity of those who count themselves Christians.

To a world of discord the Christian churches persistently proclaim a message of unity and reconciliation. Yet Christians themselves inhabit a house divided and are less than credible ambassadors of reconciliation unless they pursue reconciliation among their own fragmented communities (2 Cor 5:18–20). The need for unity is linked to the mission imperative (John 17:21). Painful awareness of the scandal of division among Christians gave rise to an ecumenical movement among the churches, an effort to achieve reconciliation and full visible unity. A beginning was made at the World Missionary Conference in Edinburgh in 1910. An explosion of "foreign mission" work brought home to Christians the puzzlement of indigenous peoples at the denominational differences among those proclaiming to them the Christian message. While conference organizers decided to avoid divisive doctrinal issues and to discuss instead missionary cooperation, participants to their surprise found more doctrinal agreement than they had anticipated. The seeds of ecumenism were sown. Despite the disruptions of the Great War (1914–1918) and of the Second World War (1939–1945), ecumenism grew among Protestants. In 1948 representatives from 147 churches met in Amsterdam for the founding assembly of the World Council of Churches (WCC) along with the incorporation of two important commissions: Faith and Order, committed to discussion of questions of doctrine and church organization, and Life and Work, devoted to shared service projects despite doctrinal divergences. Meanwhile Pius XI (1921–1939), who feared religious indifferentism, committed Catholics to an "ecumenism of return": if Protestants seek unity, let them come home to Rome and accept the teaching of Trent and Vatican Council I.[1] Rome wanted nothing to do with the ecumenical movement.

But however slowly, Catholicism can and does change. In 1961, under John XXIII (1953–1963), the first official Roman Catholic observers attended the third assembly of the WCC in New Delhi. And the Second Vatican Council (1962–1965) with its *Decree on Ecumenism* (1964) steered Catholicism into the currents that had begun to shift with Edinburgh at century's turn. The council's call for "restoration of unity" signaled abandonment of the "ecumenism of return." Nowhere does the decree use the word "*reditus*" (return). The council stated: "Division among Christians openly contradicts the will of Christ, scandalizes the world, and damages that most holy cause, the preaching of the gospel to every creature."[2] In speaking of faults committed against unity, the decree admits that Catholics must shoulder their share of the blame. Twice the decree calls for reform: personal reform of individual Christians, and, for the first time in a conciliar document since Basel (1431–1434), continual reform (*perennem reformationem)* of the Church. This needed saying. Ecclesiology must be in accord with our anthropology. The Church is people, not a Platonic abstraction. As individual Christians we are, as Luther said, *simul iustus et peccator*, but

---

[1] Pius XI, "Mortalium Animos," in *Selected Papal Encyclicals and Letters*, (London: Catholic Truth Society, 1939) 1:20–21.

[2] *Decree on Ecumenism (Unitatis Redintegratio)* 1. For translation of Vatican II documents, see Walter Abbott, ed. *Documents of Vatican II* (New York: Herder and Herder, 1966).

also *as Church* we are exposed to the ambiguity of human history and sinful, hence in need of continual reform. What is needed and what Vatican II called for is not the return of Protestants to Rome, but the return of all Christians to Christ to find their unity in him. Ecumenism is now integral to Catholicism, for, like it or not, want it or not, no Christian can go his or her own way indifferent to other Christians, for across denominational lines Christians bond together in shared belief in the one triune God who is Creator and Redeemer, one Lord and Mediator, Jesus Christ, one Scripture, the necessity of the grace of forgiveness and justification, and the life of the world to come.

At a deep level, therefore, the churches are not apart. There is no ecclesial vacuum beyond the borders of Catholicism. Vatican II declared that the church of Christ "subsists in (*subsistit in*) the Catholic Church... nevertheless many elements of sanctification and truth can be found outside her visible structure."[3] Attempts to uncover technical philosophical meanings for "subsists" are misguided. Vatican II affirmed that while the church of Christ is found in the Roman Catholic Church, it is not found there exclusively.[4] It is illusory to think that any one tradition monopolizes God's gifts. The other Christian communities are not just associations of people of good will, nor merely sites where elements of sanctification and truth are randomly scattered. There is a cohesion and configuration of those elements in service of an ecclesial mediation of the gospel and of new life in Christ. These elements are not held by Christians individually, but ecclesially. For the first time, Catholicism recognized the post-Reformation churches as "ecclesial communities," where before, it saw only heretics and schismatics separated from Rome. Vatican II, therefore, marks a shift in emphasis from the institutional to the spiritual or mystical elements of the Church. One result is a focus less on membership and more on communion (*koinonia*), a gift of the Spirit, who brings about a shared

---

[3] *Constitution on the Church (Lumen GentiumI)* 8.

[4] *Decree on Ecumenism*, nos. 19–23; *Constitution on the Church*, n. 15. See Francis Sullivan, "The Significance of the Vatican II Declaration that the Church of Christ 'Subsists in' the Roman Catholic Church," in *Vatican II: Assessment and Perspectives*, ed. Rene Latourelle (New York: Paulist Press, 1989) 2:284–85. John Paul II in "*Ut Unum Sint*" (Vatican City: Libreria Editrice Vaticana, 1995) nos. 11–14, recently reaffirmed all this.

relationship among believers: vertically, a bond with Christ and the Father; horizontally, a fellowship among believers. First effected in baptism (1 Cor 12–13), the shared life of believers and their shared life with God is manifested and deepened in the Eucharistic sharing of one bread and cup (1 Cor 10:16–17). *Koinonia* also entails the bond of unity among the local churches within the whole body of Christ—a helpful antidote to any universalist ecclesiology that swallows up the local churches into the universal church (pre-conciliar Catholicism) and to any congregationalism that fragments the universal church into a loose confederation of autonomous local churches (evangelical Bible churches). Further, unlike the either/or of juridically defined institutional membership, communion with Christ and with one's fellow Christians admits of gradations. From the perspective of *koinonia* the church of Christ may be less, equally, or more realized in a church separated from Rome. *Per se*, there is no direct and necessary correlation between institutional and spiritual wholeness. Presently, communion among all Christians and among their churches is real, but remains fully to be realized as long as we remain estranged brothers and sisters of one family.

But all that said, a caveat. A focus on *koinonia* ought not lead to a neo-gnostic denigration of institutional elements that are crucial to fostering and sustaining *koinonia*, though it is the indispenible institutional dimensions that have proven most difficult to resolve in ecumenical dialogue. So divided we remain. And too many Christians are insensitive to the wounds of division and the need to heal our disunity. There are several reasons for this. To begin with, American society is marked by the individualism bequeathed us by the Enlightenment. Our atomized society has little sense of community and many Christians have even less a sense of belonging to a Christian tradition by which their lives are defined. Moreover, in many cases local churches do little to foster a sense of community and belonging, though this is no easy task given our mobile society and its myriad distractions. Second, there is an increasing number of self-styled "Christians" of a neo-gnostic, Manichaean stripe who are given to "spirituality" and are more interested in the gnostic gospels *á la* Elaine Pagels than in the canonical gospels and creed, more given to private perception than shared tradition, and certainly not belonging to any "organized religion," which can never be pure enough for them. They harbor distrust—even contempt—for the embodiedness of institutions, which they consider purely self-interested. Still others, who are church members, lack any strong identification with a religious tradition. These are generic Christians influenced by a liberal Protestant milieu that encouraged a common Christian identity and downplayed denominational profiles. Third, church authorities, occupied with in-house problems and denominational survival, often fail to raise the ecumenical consciousness of their people. The remarkable doctrinal convergences reached through dialogue, especially between Lutherans and Roman Catholics and between Anglicans and Roman Catholics—for example on baptism, the Eucharist, justification, and even the Petrine ministry—are not communicated or celebrated at the grassroots level. The work of specialists seldom meets with the reception it requires and deserves.[5] Ecumenical reception is a process whereby a church tradition appropriates a truth that has not arisen within that tradition but that it now recognizes and accepts as a formulation of faith in conformity with the life and message of Christ and the apostolic community witnessed to in Scripture and handed on in many communities of faith. This Spirit-led process is ongoing. Reception requires openness to the Spirit's guidance into Christ-willed unity but also to structures of authority that make reception of agreements reached in dialogue binding realities, structures most churches do not now have. Thus intellectuals grow impatient and prone to weary indifference.

There is, then, a general retreat from ecumenical urgency, a tendency not to take ecumenism seriously or to think it will lead to

---

[5] For texts deriving from bilateral and multilateral theological dialogues that show growing convergences and a reduction of the church-dividing issues of the past, see Harding Meyer and Lucas Vischer, eds., *Growth in Agreement Reports and Agreed Statements of Ecumenical Conversations on a World Level* (New York: Paulist Press, 1984); and Jeffrey Gros and Harding Meyer, *Growth in Agreement II: 1982–1998* (Grand Rapids: Wm. B. Eerdmans, 2000). On the theological notion "reception," see William G. Rusch, *Reception: An Ecumenical Opportunity* (Philadelphia: Fortress Press, 1988); and "The Journey to Reception: A Progress Report," *Ecumenical Trends* 32 (2003): 1–8; Harding Meyer, "Ecumenical Consensus: Our Quest for the Emerging Strains of Consensus," *Gregorianum* 77 (1996) 213–25.

anything, especially when concrete results are meager and we cannot envision what the finished product will look like. We grow accustomed to disunity and assume it normal that there be a Christian marketplace of churches meeting varied spiritual tastes. Unity is no longer a priority, just an academic topic or *eschatological telos*. As long as ecumenism is just "getting to know one another" and "getting along," it is acceptable. But once it is seen as leading somewhere, having results that call for change, it tends to be ignored. Often there is more concern with the fashionable new interest in interfaith explorations than with the more costly concern of visible church unity. Courage is lacking to live out the Lord's prayer that his followers be one. Herein resides a serious impediment to Christian proclamation. Churches could without compromise of identity accept the agreements and recommendations of the theological dialogues, and should do so, making them part of their faith and practice and engaging more often in prayer and worship together. And on a whole range of matters they could and should bear witness together. Yet some churches self-righteously go their own way in isolation from and studied avoidance of other churches. These are groups with no felt need or responsibility for the closer unity in Christ of all who claim to be Christians. Insofar as all who claim the name of Christ fail to participate in the movement toward unity among Christ's followers, the ecumenical movement falls short of its hope and our division contradicts the gift of God. Perhaps these unecumenical or anti-ecumenical churches will join in the quest for oneness only when they perceive the richness beyond their own borders and sense their own impoverishment owing to forfeiture of the exchange of gifts that interacting traditions bring to one another in ecumenical encounter.

Further, at this time in history the churches sorely need unity in face of the daunting phenomena of secularization and globalization, which affect all Christians and have already rendered Europe post-Christian and Americans religiously illiterate. Secularization brings with it pluralism, which, while not without benefit, easily degenerates into relativism and religious indifferentism. In pluralistic, secularized societies religion is privatized and religious convictions are locked within the inner lives of individuals and deprived of a voice in the public square. Globalization betrays the unity it might create by turning the global community into a market in which everything and everyone is commodified and persons are reduced to producers and consumers. In this context the churches need the unified voice they could have despite their differences. But disunity diminishes their voice in proclamation and witness. Christians as individuals can do only so much. There are challenges that only the full strength of churches at the institutional level can meet. This exposes the weakness and the "cheap grace" that is the lot of neo-gnostics who proclaim themselves "Christians" while disdaining religious communities and institutions. Traditionless and without community, the solitary individual becomes her own norm and the gospel's challenge wanes or is feebly addressed.

Full visible unity, then, is the goal of the ecumenical movement. This includes reception of agreements reached in official dialogues, as well as the growth and change this might entail. It is far more than collaborative fellowship. Full visible unity of the churches has been the stated goal of the movement ever since the New Delhi Assembly of the WCC in 1961, a quest for unity in the truth as found in Jesus Christ (Eph 4:21) and into which the Spirit leads us (John 16:13). New Delhi's vision was endorsed and refined at Uppsala in 1968 and at Nairobi in 1975. Unity does not imply creation of a meta-orthodoxy arrived at by compromise, indifferentism, or settlement on a lowest common denominator. Rather, the churches together must search the Scriptures, beliefs, and practices of the Christian traditions with the aim of arriving at "a common expression of the apostolic faith today."[6] Unity is one of the marks of Christ's church. Christians profess it in their creeds. Unity is not something contrived by us for our purposes. The New Testament, when it speaks of the church, speaks of its unity as well: "Let there be no factions...has Christ been divided into parts?" (1 Cor 1:10). Unity is

[6] Nicholas Lossky et al., eds. *Dictionary of the Ecumenical Movement*, 2nd ed. (Geneva: WCC, 2002) xvi. "Apostolic faith" refers to the faith passed on from the apostles as articulated in Scripture and the ecumenical councils. The discussion paper of the fifth World Conference on Faith and Order at Santiago de Compostela in 1993 challenged churches not using the ecumenical creed to acknowledge it and use it on occasion as an expression of the apostolic faith. Churches using the creed are challenged to recognize that the apostolic faith can be expressed by churches in other than creedal forms. See Thomas Best and Günther Gassman, eds., *On the Way to Fuller Koinonia; Official Report of the Fifth World Conference on Faith and Order* (Geneva: WCC, 1994) 263–95.

both gift and task. It is "already and not yet." Unity is a God-given gift, but it must be received, cherished, lived by Christians, and made visible and functional, which is the aim of the ecumenical movement. An imperative accompanies the indicative. Thus the phrase "visible unity" points to the distinction between God's graceful gift-giving and human reception and fostering of the gift of unity, which is no abstraction but intended to be a trait of the concrete, empirical reality of Christian life.

But what would full visible union involve? While the vision of unity has undergone several permutations, the WCC at New Delhi in 1961 issued a "Declaration of Unity" that laid down seven constitutive elements of full visible unity: mutual recognition of baptism; common confession and proclamation of the gospel and of apostolic faith; common celebration of the Lord's supper; common worship, intercession and thanksgiving; common witness and service in the world; mutual recognition of ministers and members; and willingness to speak and act together in face of particular tasks and challenges.[7] This goal can be met in varied models, as the full communion agreements recently achieved illustrate—for example those entered into by the Evangelical Lutheran Church in America with the churches of the Reformed tradition (Presbyterian Church USA, United Church of Christ, Reformed Church in America) in 1998, with the Moravian Church in 1999, and with the Episcopal Church in 2001. Though there remain theological differences in these three agreements, each is a remarkable achievement of full visible unity.[8] Still, one can question whether there is as yet a shared understanding of the language of "full visible communion" or of terms such as "restricted communion," "partial communion," and "impaired communion." "Communion" denotes a bond of unity resulting from sharing things together. Ecclesial communion implies sharing what belongs to the nature of Christ's church. Whether a union is full or

---

[7] *The New Delhi Report: the Third Assembly of the WCC* (London: SCM, 1961) 116–18. Michael Kinnamon and Brian Cope, eds., *The Ecumenical Movement: An Anthology of Key Texts and Voices* (Grand Rapids: Wm. B. Eerdmans, 1997) is a most useful documentary source. On the present drift to fellowship rather than visible unity see Thomas Ryan, "The Ecumenical Landscape," *America* 194 (19 June 2006) 14–17.

[8] For discussion of these agreements, see Mitzi Budde, "The Goal of the ELCA Full Communion Agreements," *Ecumenical Trends* 32 (2003) 33–40.

partial, therefore, depends on how much of what pertains to the nature of the church is held in common between churches. The problem, then, resides in determining what necessarily belongs to the nature of the church, hence what two churches must share if they are to be in full communion. *Koinonia* and full visible unity cannot be fully realized as long as Christians differ as to what pertains to the very nature of the church. Another and connected reason why Christians differ as to what constitutes full visible unity is their tendency to conceive the visible unity that is ecumenism's goal as very much like or even identical with the kind of visible unity manifest in their own church polity and structures. The unity sought by the ecumenical movement will probably have to differ from the structural unity of any existing church. Thus the need for change; thus, too, the fearful recalcitrance that calls for change beget and an unwillingness to let go. But all goodness and truth is not found in "my church." As Paul, the Jew who let go of circumcision, synagogue, and dietary laws, knew, it is all too easy for believers to make false gods of traditions that are but historically conditioned expressions of human understanding and devotion to the living God. The poet W. H. Auden catches us well: "We would rather be ruined than changed/ We would rather die in our own dread/ Than climb the cross of the moment/ And let our illusions die."[9]

In sum, several things impede churches from attaining full visible unity. First, many see the changes required as touching on the faith and polity, the very identity and survival of their church. Resolution of the difficulties involved—doctrinal, structural, and psychological—requires time and effort. But progress is afoot. Given two millennia of Christian history, the century since Edinburgh is not a long time. The participants at Edinburgh would probably be amazed at the extent of ecumenical cooperation today, the overcoming of caricature, the resolution of doctrinal differences reached in dialogue, and the full communion realized by some churches. Nor is it a small achievement that given a history of polemic and internecine hostility, the churches are now at peace with one another, though to no small extent this is a blessing of the pluralism that the Enlightenment and secularization brought.

---

[9] W. H. Auden, *Collected Longer Poems* (New York: Random House, Inc., 2002) 350.

Second, ecclesiological differences continue concerning the nature of the church, especially with regard to structures of authority and the character and requirements for ordained ministry. Third, differences over ethical issues such as abortion, homosexuality, stem cell research, and divorce have arisen and are potentially divisive for the churches. Fourth, there is no one model of visible unity accepted by all the churches. What visible unity should look like is not clearly seen by all the churches. This in turn stills any sense of urgency for the development of an ecumenical consciousness. Finally, within the churches themselves fault lines have developed. Seething tensions and divisions between progressives and conservatives make for internal disunity. These fissures often reflect cultural and political divisions in American society. Church and denominational borders, because of the divisions within, become porous, and new allegiances develop across denominational lines. Concerns about identity, survival, and the development of selling points for consumers then come to predominate. Thus the churches remain apart. Patience and persevering effort will be required to realize the Christ-willed unity that is ours and not yet ours.

Concerned that ecumenism has long been adrift and concerned over the polarization of the Life and Work and Faith and Order Commissions, sixteen theologians recently issued, after three years of reflection, an important document, *In One Body Through the Cross: The Princeton Proposal for Christian Unity.*[10] Produced by an independent group assembled by Carl Braaten and Robert Jenson, directors of the Princeton Center for Evangelical and Catholic Theology, and aiming to move the ecumenical movement beyond its present impasse. The document claims no official status but speaks to all churches and not for any one church. It calls for the ecumenical movement to awaken, change course, and return to pursuit of its principal aim: the worldwide unity of the Christian churches, of all whom are reconciled "in one body through

[10] Carl Braaten and Robert Jenson, eds., *In One Body Through the Cross: The Princeton Proposal for Christian Unity* (Grand Rapids: Wm. B. Eerdmans, 2003). Henceforth cited as *PP*. Numbers cited in the body of the text refer to paragraphs in *PP.* For the papers discussed in the group's meetings, see C. Braaten and R. Jenson, eds., *The Ecumenical Future: Background Papers for in One Body through the Cross: the Princeton Proposal for Christian Unity* (Grand Rapids: Wm. B. Eerdmans, 2004).

the cross." Based on the biblical vision put forth by New Delhi's declaration (1961), it warns against reducing unity to social harmony or shared service and calls the churches to a new life together that is sanctified by the Spirit and manifestly apostolic in form and content.

For the Princeton group, the priorities of the WCC have, in recent years, become problematic, for the council seems no longer focused on visible unity. Drift began with the Uppsala Assembly in 1968. Since then, Life and Work's concern with world unity has superseded Faith and Order's concern with church unity. The paradigm God-World-Church replaced the God-Church-World paradigm. The world sets the agenda.[11] Operating with a "new ecumenical paradigm," Life and Work's divisive sociopolitical agendas assume priority.[12] The *Princeton Proposal* sounds a clarion call for return to the vision of unity articulated at New Delhi, a visible unity of all those who have been baptized into Christ; confess him as Lord and Savior; and are led by the Spirit into one fellowship holding one apostolic faith, preaching the one gospel, breaking the one bread, joining in common prayer, and having a corporate life reaching out in witness and service to all while being united with the universal Christian fellowship in all places and ages and with ministry and members accepted by all and with all able to act and speak together as occasion demands for the tasks to which God calls (15). Viewing unity as divine gift and human task (2–10), the document states that "the unity which is already ours must appear more fully in our worship, mission, and structures of our religious life" (4). It adds bluntly that "to work against visible manifestation of the unity God has given us, or to accept its absence with resignation, is resistance to God's Spirit and exposes us to God's judgment" (6). Since it is the church's mission to be

---

[11] George Lindback, "The Unity We Seek: Setting the Agenda for Ecumenism," *Christian Century* 122 (2005) 28–31, claims the audience *PP* has in mind is chiefly evangelical, Pentecostal, Roman Catholic and Orthodox, among whom there is a measure of agreement—where the apostolic tradition is to be found and retrieved.

[12] The paradigm shift was announced by "a new general secretary of the World Council" (19). The reference is to Konrad Kaiser, *Ecumenism in Transition: A Paradigm Shift in the Ecumenical Movement* (Geneva: WCC, 1991). See also Kaiser's *For a Culture of Life: Transforming Globalization and Violence* (Geneva: WCC, 2002).

a sign of God's reconciling power in the world and the Trinitarian life of diversity in unity is our model, disunity among the churches is sinful. The link between unity and mission is drawn in Ephesians 4 and John 17:20–23, charter texts of ecumenism. Disunity undermines mission. But to seek unity means the churches must conform their teaching and practice to "the apostolic faith confessed in the ecumenical creeds" (40).

The *Princeton Proposal* contends that "normative teaching and authorized ways of ordering common life are necessary and essential elements of the church's apostolic existence" (37). Sadly, binding doctrine and practice, the *Princeton Proposal* contends, are no longer presented as normative but as always changing consumer options, and with them the identity of the church. Responsibility for this is laid at the doorstep of the Reformation churches, which have often shown less concern for truth than for the characteristics and "selling points" that render their identities distinct (38–42). The authority of normative teaching and practice will be lacking until churches unambiguously reach visible consensus "based upon common reception of the apostolic legacy" (43–45). Three basic requirements for visible consensus are, again echoing New Delhi, unity of faith and doctrine, a coordinated life of witness and service, and reciprocity of membership and ministry in continuity with the church through centuries past (46).

Achieving unity, the authors know, is no easy task; the road to unity is strewn with fundamental disagreements concerning doctrine, ordained ministry, the place of sacraments, and the role of bishops, especially the bishop of Rome. Progress will require a penitential spirit, conversation, willingness to loosen our hold on and leave behind elements and forms of our particular traditions, many of which are cultural accretions, whether Roman, Byzantine, or Enlightenment, that ought not be identified with the will of Christ. Citing New Delhi, the *Princeton Proposal* notes that achievement of unity will demand "the death and rebirth of many forms of Church life as we have known them" for the sake of the unity of the Church (15). Yet precisely because the journey requires far more than we humans can provide, here is hope that with divine grace the goal will be realized, and with it new life (72).

All this needs saying to redress the balance which, as the *Princeton Proposal* sees it, has been upset by the WCC and the National Council of Churches of Christ, U.S.A. Prioritizing Life and Work's social agendas, it is charged, pushed aside Faith and Order's quest for visible unity in confession of faith and in the sacraments (61). According to the *Princeton Proposal* the church must get its own act together if it is to bring reconciliation to the world. While some feel that the churches find their unity by participating in God's reconciling action in the world, for framers of the *Princeton Proposal*, Faith and Order has precedence over Life and Work, for faith takes precedence over works. Works are the fruit and sign of faith, not its cause; service in the name of justice is the fruit and sign of ecclesial unity, not its cause. Further, according to the *Princeton Proposal*, "The bishop of Rome is the only historically plausible candidate to exercise an effective worldwide ministry of unity." And the proposal adds, "The bishop of Rome and the magisterium of the Roman Catholic Church must teach in a fashion capable of shaping the minds of the faithful beyond those currently in communion with Rome" (65). In connection with this, it also urges that educational institutions with direct ties to specific denominations become teaching centers serving the whole church by hiring and encouraging scholars committed to teaching from an ecumenical perspective for the good of the whole church (49). As for the Petrine teaching office, it will need an ecumenical fine-tuning if it is to teach for all and to all the baptized, and it must be open to counsel regarding the faith and life of the entire Christian community (66). While bilateral and multilateral dialogues have been slow to embrace the necessity of a universal episcopacy, Anglicans and Lutherans, like the *Princeton Proposal*, have in dialogues with Catholics shown openness to a reformed universal primacy of the Bishop of Rome. In 1999 the Anglican-Roman Catholic International Committee (ARCIC) stated "that Anglicans are open to and desire a recovery and re-reception under certain clear conditions of the exercise of universal primacy by the Bishop of Rome." And this reception is considered achievable "even before our churches are in full communion," though only on condition that this ministry of unity "is exercised with collegiality and synodality."[13] The most recent US Lutheran Roman Catholic dialogue contends that "a specific ministry that serves universal

[13] *The Gift of Authority: Authority in the Church, III, An Agreed Statement by the Anglican-Roman Catholic International Committee (ARCIC)* (London: 1999) par. 45–48, 60–63.

unity is accepted by Catholics and not excluded by Lutherans. Lutherans and Catholics together need to discuss how such a ministry can be reformed so that it can be received by a greater range of the world's churches and thus better fulfill its own service to unity."[14] This marks a considerable advance in view of the fact that the papacy has been a bone that sticks in the throat of Reformation churches and, in its present modality, in the throats of not a few Catholics. These openings to a Petrine ministry should be received by Rome as welcome responses to John Paul II's invitation to the other churches in 1995 to reflect together on how the Bishop of Rome's ministry is to be exercised in an ecumenical era.[15] Whether they will be so received and acted upon remains to be seen.

It seems that neither Princeton, nor New Delhi before it, is calling for what has been termed "organic union." New Delhi appears open to a plurality of models for unity. Princeton appears to be calling for the church fellowship model (i.e., reconciled diversity) when it appeals to the markers of full visible unity that New Delhi established.[16] Organic union of autonomous churches in one body signals an end to church and denominational identities. It involves a common faith and practice, a common name, and common decision making and mission. This model was promoted in the early stages of the ecumenical movement. With Roman Catholicism's entrance into the ecumenical movement the organic union model receded. Catholicism's self-understanding and its privileging of bilateral over multilateral dialogues gave confessionality renewed vitality.

Unity in reconciled diversity incrementally achieved became the goal, not the melting down of confessional identities into a generic, but their reconciliation and the overcoming of their church-dividing toxicity. Unity was to rest on a reconciled diversity involving commitment to the

---

[14] *The Church as Koinonia of Salvation: Its Structures and Ministries. An Agreed Statement of the Tenth Round of the U.S. Lutheran Roman Catholic Dialogue* (2004) par. 70 (http://www.ecla.org/ecumenical/ecumenicaldialogue/romancatholic/index.html).

[15] John Paul II, *Ut Unum Sint.*

[16] For the following I am indebted to Peter DeMey, "A Call to Conversion: An Analysis of the Princeton Proposal (2003)" *Ecumenical Trends* 34 (2005) 50–58; Harding Meyer, "Reconciled Diversity," 960–61.

one apostolic faith, recognition of one another as churches in which the Church of Christ is visible, a differentiated consensus concerning the fundamental Christian doctrines and practices, mutual recognition of existing ministries, mutual sharing of liturgy and sacrament, and cooperation in mission and service. But churches would retain their own name and confessional identity, their own structures.

The diversity of church communities in their customs, spiritualities, liturgy, polity and doctrinal emphasis manifest complementary facets of the fathomless riches of the Christian tradition, and more profoundly, of the incomprehensible God revealed in Jesus Christ. The diversity of traditions manifests, too, the catholicity of the church and its vigor as a living community. Within the unity of communions diversity also displays the possibility of a reconciled and flourishing humanity.[17] Small wonder that Paul in 1 Corinthians 12 finds the variety of charisms in the one body of Christ a blessing, a diversity in the service of unity, and that Vatican II considers the church the poorer if diversity is lacking.[18]

The need to live out and interpret the one faith in varied and shifting contexts through diverse forms of expression is, rather than a threat to unity, the inevitable consequence of the incarnational character of Christianity, which finds a home in every soil. *Nil humanum alienum.* Two millennia of history bear this out. Yet, given the fallenness of believers, the riches of diversity are often squandered in fruitless conflict. Yet just as easily is the call for unity conscripted by forces seeking deadening uniformity. While New Delhi celebrates and encourages diversity, the *Princeton Proposal* seems wary of it (22–30). Unity trumps diversity, which must be questioned, judged, reconciled, and reconfigured within the unity of the body of Christ (Eph 4:14–17). In this light, one might view the *Princeton Proposal* as leaning toward organic union. In any case, visions of reconciled diversity are romantic illusions if they shelve the knotty questions of authority and structure. What kind of structures will be needed to preserve and foster the unity and identity of the churches at the local and universal levels? It does

---

[17] ARCIC, *The Gift of Authority*, par. 27.

[18] *Constitution on the Church*, n. 13; *Decree on Ecumenism*, n. 16–17, speaks positively of the diversity found among the Eastern churches. Why not of the diversity among churches of the Reformation?

seem that reconciled diversity would indeed require some realigning and unification of confessional polities.

Two models of unity, then, stand at the extremes. The first, which probably appeals to most Christians, is peaceful coexistence among the churches. This model is appealing because it demands nothing of us and lets us go our self-satisfied ways. The result is sheer diversity, scandalous division. The second model calls for the organic absorption of all confessions into one confessional community. The result is static unity without diversity, an unrealizable uniformity, given the God-created diversity of human beings.

Between the extremes lies the model of church fellowship or reconciled diversity in living, dynamic unity; or better, communion rooted in a shared life and interaction that gives coherence amid diversity, coherence in communion with God in Jesus Christ through the Spirit and therefore with one another. Such fellowship takes seriously the diverse riches each church tradition brings to the others in communion. But in such a fellowship there should be no place for a stark either/or: either the quest for visible church unity or the quest for social justice in the world. This false dichotomy must yield to a more complicated both/and: concern for both church unity and renewal of the human community. Maintaining the two in healthy tension rather than simple antagonism is an ongoing struggle to hold fast to the vision of John 17:21 ("that they may all be one...so that the world may believe") and Ephesians 1:10 ("to unite all things in him [Christ], things in heaven and things on earth," RSV). Ecumenical unity needs both its ecclesial and its social wings. They mutually reinforce each other. Without both it cannot be integrally Christian. If the church is not a social work agency, neither is it merely a liturgical assembly and herald of the gospel proclamation of the unity of the world in Christ.

The *Princeton Proposal* tilts toward the latter identification to bring the churches back on course. But the church/world dialectic should not be shorted. Grace presupposes nature. One finds God not on the threshold of another world but in the humdrum and ambiguity of this world and then turns to church and liturgy to celebrate and move more deeply into the gracious presence of this God, then to turn back into the world in witness to God through service of others, especially the weakest and "the least" of his brethren who are hungry or homeless, sick or imprisoned, strangers or unwanted (Matt 25:31–46). As the Jesuit priest and poet Gerald Manley Hopkins put it, "Christ plays in ten thousand places/ Lovely in limb and lovely in eyes not his/ To the Father through the features of men's faces."[19] Only so can the church be visible sacrament of Christ for the world and symbol of what life in the human community can be and is called to be.[20]

But if apostolic faith and service may unite us, what of the doctrinal differences that divide us? Since the mid-twentieth century, among those in the churches working to achieve unity, theologians came to the forefront as many churches began to engage in dialogue concerning doctrinal questions. This was a reversal. The Life and Work movement, under leadership of Nathan Soderblom (1866–1931), operated on the premise that "doctrine divides but working together unites Christians," a premise that the *Princeton Proposal* rightly opposes. Such a premise overlooks the fact that shared service presupposes shared vision; it also fails to realize that socio-economic issues can be as or more divisive of Christians than doctrinal issues. Early on, Faith and Order, under the leadership of Episcopal bishop Charles Brent (1862–1929), stressed discussion of doctrinal issues and of ecclesial governance, whose resolution, it was thought, could lead to visible unity of the churches. But the movement was over-optimistic in thinking such questions were readily resolvable and naïve in thinking doctrinal agreements would necessarily lead to visible unity.

Nonetheless, doctrines and doctrinal convergence remain crucial, especially in a day when the need for doctrines does not sit well with disparate modern tendencies toward anti-dogmatic rationalism, relativism, and scientism. Scholarly and non-scholarly moderns seek to go behind creed and gospel to find the "real Jesus," who often turns out to be one more kindly humanistic teacher of love. For many, being a "nice" person is more important than correct beliefs, if indeed there are

---

[19] Eugene H.Peterson, *Christ Plays in Ten Thousand Places: A Conversation in Spiritual Theology* (Grand Rapids: Wm. B. Eerdmans, 2005) An untitled sonnet by Gerald Manly Hopkins in the introduction.

[20] On the dialectical interrelation between the liturgical assembly and a Christian's life in the secular realm, see Karl Rahner, "Personal and Sacramental Piety," *Theological Investigations*, trans. Karl H. Kruger (Baltimore: Helicon, 1963) 2:109–34.

such. Even those Christians full of passionate intensity, the evangelicals, find the only orthodoxy they need in God's Word, the Bible, and see no need for concern with the babbling of humans in ever-changing doctrines, creeds, and confessions. Still others are given to an uncritical inclusivism dissolving all boundaries and differences; nice people, good music, and interesting activities outrank doctrinal niceties when church-shopping.

Perhaps, however, the most continuous challenge to the importance of doctrine and creeds is disjunction, real or perceived, between confessions of faith and the moral life of confessors. Thus the plea, "Deeds, not creeds!" Even Jesus condemned inconsistency between confession of faith and moral life (Mark 7:6–8). Always there are tares among the wheat. Living and believing are dialectically related. A basic human impulse underlies confession: "I believed, and so I spoke" (2 Cor 4:13 RSV). But to verify our confession, we should add, "and so I acted."

This modern doctrinal malaise notwithstanding, because faith seeks understanding, Christians through all ages have felt a need for doctrines, creeds, and confessions to establish their identity and self-understanding and to define boundaries as to what the biblical narrative (reflected in the creed) does and does not affirm concerning God, ourselves, and our world.[21] Doctrines are also important for integrating warmth of heart with clarity of judgment. Intimacy with Jesus, yes. But why with Jesus? What makes him worthy of commitment? And what does discipleship today demand? Without personal identification with Jesus, cognitive identification of who he is remains empty. But without cognitive identification of who he is and what discipleship requires, personal identification with him is blind enthusiasm. As Lionel Trilling observed, when a religion's doctrinal dimension is ignored, that religion may for a long time run on the fuel of emotion and good intention. But eventually it loses its staying power, indeed its very soul.[22] What we believe (*fides*

---

[21] See 1 Tim 1:3–7 and Titus 1:9. See Stephen J. Duffy, "Creeds and Confessions of Faith: From Ages of Belief to an Age of Creedal Malaise," *Religious Studies Review* 31 (2005): 37–45.

[22] Lionel Trilling, "Wordsworth and the Rabbis," in *The Moral Obligation to be Intelligent: Selected Essays*, ed. Louis Wieseltier (New York: Farrar, Straus, and Giroux, 2000) 178–202.

quae, believing that...) cannot be collapsed into simply believing (*fides qua*, believing in...). Both trust (*fiducia)* and adherence to doctrinal articulations of faith (*asssensus*) are necessary. A Christian community is not an amorphous crowd or a club that individuals enter on their own terms with beliefs and spiritualities of their own choosing cobbled together. Choice alone does not confer significance or value.

That said concerning the necessity of right doctrines and confessions of faith, qualifications are in order, and they are crucial for dialogue. First, God, transcendent and incomprehensible, forever eludes the formulations of finite minds. As the Catholic tradition holds, all God-talk, doctrines, and creeds employ analogical language. Words already decaying with imprecision strain, crack, and even break under the weight of an immensity and graciousness they cannot articulate. God escapes philosophy's rational pursuit and theology's broken discourse. Therefore, as necessary as they are, lest we be reduced to silence and agnosticism, theology and the doctrines it spawns always fall short and have about them a provisionality. Though they can point us in the right direction, we are unable to bridge the abyss between talk about ourselves and our world and talk about God. Hence no church can enter dialogue claiming its doctrinal formulations are the last or only word about God and God's relation to us and our world.

Second, dialogue occurs today in a new context, characterized well by Bernard Lonergan as the result of a shift from a classicist worldview to historical-mindedness.[23] In sum, the classicist mentality defines humanity abstractly with a definition that applies *omni et soli* and through properties verifiable of every human. Human being as such, because it is an abstraction, is unchanging. The classicist is no pluralist. The circumstances of life that change are accidental; behind them lies a fixed, stable, unchanging substance. Modernity, however, came to recognize the historicity of life and understanding. Our concepts are expressions of our understanding, and understanding develops over time and differently in different times and places. What meaning we find in reality is not fixed, static, and immutable, but developing; sometimes straying but

---

[23] Bernard Lonergan, "The Transition from a Classicist World-View to Historical-Mindedness," in *A Second Collection* (Philadelphia: Westminster Press, 1974) 1–11.

capable of correction and redemption. Inescapably subject to historicity, we need changing forms, structures, and methods. Into this arena of historicity and evolving understanding and meaning God's revelation has entered, and in the same arena the churches bear witness to that revelation.[24] Historical-mindedness does not mean relativism, but simply recognition that our understanding is historically conditioned, which affects the way we think about doctrines and knowledge of the truth.

Catholicism has been struggling to shift gears from classicism to historical-mindedness. Vatican I taught that the meaning of dogmas, once declared by the church, is to be perpetually retained, and it spoke of definitions that are "irreformable."[25] But Vatican II taught that the church's understanding of the realities and words handed down to us grows, that "the church constantly moves forward toward the fullness of truth."[26] The council also approved use of historical-critical tools in Scripture study. A 1973 document, *Mysterium Ecclesiae*, from the Congregation for the Doctrine of the Faith, noted that the meaning of a doctrine depends on the historically conditioned language that expresses it and that the truth can at a given time be expressed incompletely, not falsely, only later to receive a fuller expression.

The implication of all this is that the church, the whole church, must be a learner as well as a teacher.[27] It cannot simply be divided into teachers and learners. For all teachers—whether gospel writers, bishops, or theologians—are learners before becoming teachers. And learning entails coming to know that we don't know, and what we don't know.

---

[24] Bernard Lonergan, "Philosophy and Theology," in *A Second Collection*, 207–208; *Doctrinal Pluralism* (Milwaukee: Marquette University Press, 1971); *Insight: A Study of Human Understanding* (New York: Philosophical Library, 1957). See also Karl Rahner, "Basic Observations on the Subject of Changeable and Unchangeable Factors in the Church," *Theological Investigations*, trans. David Bourke (New York: Seabury, 1976) 14:3–32.

[25] Henricus Denzinger and Adolfus Schoenmetzer, *Enchiridion Symbolorum Definitionum et Declarationum de Rebus Fidei et Morum*, 36th ed. (Rome: Herder, 1976) no. 3020 and 3079.

[26] *Constitution on Divine Revelation (Dei Verbum)* n. 8.

[27] Frederick Crowe, "The Church as Learner: Two Crises, One Kairos," in *Appropriating the Lonergan Idea*, ed. Michael Vertin (Washington, DC: Catholic University of America Press, 1988) 370–84.

That necessitates asking questions, study, consultation, and prayer and then coming up with possible answers, weighing evidence for competing alternatives, and finally arriving at a judgment, or failing that, leaving the question open. Cases in point: Peter concerning Mosaic law and the church on the way to Nicaea. Too often teachers in the church are too quick to teach with too little learning. The Spirit's guidance is there, but again, grace presupposes nature. Because we are historical beings, we arrive at truth only by traveling the slow, difficult road of inquiry. Transposing the gospels' truth into new cultures and within shifting cultures and from one age to another requires inquiry, reflection, the give and take of debate, and even dissent, an ongoing learning process. Only so could the churches have changed their views on slavery, religious liberty, ecumenism, and the use of historical-critical methodology.

The ecclesial vocation of the theologian, then, is discernment of the gospel's truth in every time and place. Because the learning process leading to discernment is tedious, even divisive, the untrusting alternative, repressive authoritarianism, is a recurrent temptation. If the aim of dialogue is discernment of truth, without which unity is impossible, precisely the transition to historical-mindedness has enabled dialogue partners, if not always their communities, to recognize each other's doctrinal positions as possibly alternative articulations of a shared Christian vision, each with its valid emphases and nuances, strengths, and weaknesses. Where before we saw only heresy, we now often see complementarity and convergence.

Third, as Vatican II taught, there is a hierarchy among doctrines "since they vary in their relationship to the foundation of the Christian faith."[28] The Trinitarian and Christological doctrines lie closer to the foundations than do the virginal conception of Jesus and papal infallibility. This is important for dialogue. Yves Congar, who did much to arouse ecumenical consciousness in Catholicism, observed that Catholics sometimes emphasize the authority of the teacher more than the import of his teaching.[29] Conversely, a hierarchy of truths implies a

---

[28] *Decree on Ecumenism*, n. 11.

[29] Yves Congar, "On the Hierarchia Veritatum," in *The Heritage of the Early Church: Essays in Honor of Vasilievich Florovsky*, ed. David Neiman and Margaret

hierarchy of errors and divergences among dialogue partners, which leads us to ask which divergences are serious enough to be church dividing? What further complicates matters is the fact that while there is a theological hierarchy of truths, there is also a lived hierarchy in terms of how Christians over centuries have understood and embodied Christian truths in their theological emphases, spiritualities, and liturgies.

Finally, a corollary of our second qualification. A community's faithful repetition of its doctrines is inadequate to secure continuity at anything more than a formal level. As the long history of the churches shows, ongoing interpretation of doctrines is imperative because Christianity lives in shifting contexts of space and time. Doctrines require a hermeneutic, not merely reproduction, recitation, and subtle idolatry. This hermeneutic navigates between the shoals of naïve objectivism and sheer relativism. Doctrines require understanding. To understand is to interpret. And paradoxically, to understand the doctrines we have received from the "cloud of witnesses" before us is to understand them differently. Different musicians hear Mozart differently, and no one hears Mozart as Mozart heard Mozart. Nor can we today read or hear the Christological and Trinitarian doctrines that have been passed on to us since the fourth century exactly as Athanasius and the Cappadocians read and heard them. Too much has happened since then. The gap between then and now is filled with the continuities and discontinuities of a 1,700-year tradition, only in light of which can we now read and hear the doctrines and confessions handed down to us. Because of our historicity we approach the doctrines bequeathed us with our own pre-understanding, as did their authors. None of us can approach a confession of faith empty-headed, but only from within our own horizons and the horizons of our traditions with their historical and cultural baggage.

Tradition is our collective memory, a dynamic, extended to-and-fro conversation, something more than the *tradita*, a once-for-all deposit of beliefs and formulae passed on through centuries in the pristine purity of their origin. Words like "Creator" and "person" mean today something

---

Schatkin, trans. Uta Kriefall (Rome: Pontifical Institute of Oriental Studies, 1973) 411–19.

more and different than in previous centuries, even if not totally bereft of their previous understandings. Moreover, in endless oscillation between past and present, not only do we question our doctrines and confessions, they also question us and lay their claims on our lives today. They may break the spell of our pre-understanding and put before us new possibilities for living, a world we might find inhabitable, though not exactly the possibilities and worlds of their authors. We retrieve and recontextualize our doctrinal heritage in such a way that past and present fuse as doctrines are mediated, as they can only be, through our horizon and speak to the present. Doctrines come alive only insofar as they are drawn into our world of meaning where we see not only what they *meant* but what they *mean* for our understanding of God, ourselves, and our world.

Our Scriptures, classic doctrines, and confessions have withstood the centuries and remain forever contemporary, rife with meanings unforeseen by their framers, who built better than they knew. Their meaning stretches beyond the meaning and intent of their framers and their churches. Antiquarian interest in historical reconstruction of the past and of the intent of the framers is, therefore, not our sole or primary concern, but the truth here and now embodied in our texts, doctrines, and confessions related, as they can only be, to our pre-understanding. We can no more reduce doctrinal meanings to their framers' meaning and intent than we can an agent's action or an event to the agent's intention. Doctrines and confessions are not just reports about a long dead past but messages to the present. They made truth claims for their contemporaries and do so for succeeding generations as well. In the hermeneutical process, then, meanings neglected in a tradition's history of forgetting and/or remembering wrongly may be retrieved, established meanings may be extended, and valid meanings perhaps unintended by the framers of doctrines may through distanciation now occur to newly situated believers.

Yet the hermeneutical task is not completed with the work of understanding and interpretation. It demands a third step, application. The motive of interpretation is not antiquarian interest but existential concern. The historical-critical moment should never be silenced, but instead it should be integrated into a hermeneutical process that includes application to living. That doctrines and confessions be appropriated and lived is essential. Confessions and doctrines reproduced and parroted do not communicate faith. God communicates faith through Christians who bring to life in their lives the truth they confess. Doctrines spring from lived faith. Without performance, doctrines and confessions are lifeless. The score of the "Credo" of Bach's glorious *Mass in B Minor* lies lifeless on a shelf, but it bursts to life in orchestral and choral performance. Similarly, doctrinal confession comes alive only when played out in the existence of believers. In the Augustinian view, lived faith is required for understanding (*credo ut intelligam*), a view animating Pascal's wager and Ricoeur's hermeneutics of wager.

Today, in the post-confessional West the future of belief is questioned. This challenges all Christians and their churches. What future the churches will have and what unity will depend on those who translate into the rhythms of mundane existence the truth they find in the doctrines and confessions of their traditions, thereby creating a commonality greater than some are willing to recognize. Enactment, sometimes at great cost, is the lifeblood of transmission. In the end, dialogues concerning doctrines are not merely academic exercises. Their concern, finally, though not immediately, is the shape of our lives as Christians, individually and communally as church in our time and place.

The unity we seek is well expressed in the prayer of the *Didache* (c. 70–100): "Just as the bread broken was first scattered on the hills, then was gathered and became one, so let your church be gathered from the ends of the earth into your kingdom" (9.4).[30] The many becoming one, the transcendence of divisions in Christ (Gal 3:28) that we desire are eschatological realities, gifts not yet ours, yet seminally, already ours. Every Eucharist is anticipation of final oneness in Christ. For now, unity is a work in progress. Jeremiah's image of the potter at his wheel speaks to our situation: "The vessel he was making of clay was spoiled in the potter's hand," but rather than destroying it, "he reworked it into another vessel, as it seemed good to the potter to do" (Jer 18:4 RSV). As individuals and as churches we are flawed vessels. But Jeremiah's vision that despite the flaws, we can in our potter's hands be remolded into something other and better gives hope. But unlike the potter's clay, we

---

[30] *Early Christian Fathers*, trans. and ed. Cyril Charles Richardson (Philadelphia PA: Westminster Press, 1953).

have a responsibility to cooperate in the work of the maker who would refashion us.

Ecumenism is not painless. Insofar as the churches remain separated siblings due to willful or negligent disobedience to their Lord's command that they all be one so the world may believe, there is need for a spiritual ecumenism grounded in repentance and conversion. Repentance involves the recognition that we are flawed vessels and the confession of our individual and corporate failings, and conversion involves turning and moving in a new direction, in reliance on the Potter who remakes us and is the final Giver of unity.[31]

Our second challenge is the creation of an ecumenical consciousness in our churches through wider reception of the agreements that have been reached.[32] This will exact a price, for reception of the results of ecumenical engagement will demand the discomfort of implementing the agreements reached and new ways of thinking, acting, and being church. Agreements mean little unless incorporated into church faith and life.

Third, we will need to sustain our bilateral and multilateral dialogues slogging away at theological issues that divide us. Nowhere is this truer than in the area of ecclesiology. Issues of authority are critical since they concern the establishment and fostering of unity among the churches. Core differences perdure concerning a Petrine ministry, apostolic succession in the episcopate, and the character of ordained ministry. There is growing ecumenical openness to a Petrine ministry, but it cannot be imposed on any church in its present form. Refashioning is required. Questions arise concerning relations between primacy and collegiality and between local churches and the universal church. For future dialogues the differentiated consensus of the Lutheran-Roman Catholic *Joint Declaration on the Doctrine of Justification*

---

[31] John Paul II stresses repentance in *Ut Unum Sint*, 19–22.

[32] Roman Catholicism's Pontifical Council for Christian Unity urges "that all Christians be animated by the ecumenical spirit," that those in pastoral work "acquire an ecumenical disposition," that theology and history be taught "with due regard for the ecumenical point of view," indeed that ecumenical perspectives permeate all theological study and a course devoted specifically to ecumenism be required. See *Directory for the Application of Principles and Norms on Ecumenism* (Washington DC: U.S. Catholic Conference, 1993) 39 and 47.

provides a model for the differentiated agreement at which they should aim—on one level, fundamental commonality, in that we can recognize together substantial consensus on basic beliefs on which previously we thought ourselves divided; on a second level, residual differences that leave room for secondary belief statements that are different but do not contradict the core beliefs. The latter also allows for differences in language, emphasis, and nuance that may enrich the dialogue partner's theology or at least are deemed tolerable by dialogue partners and do not call into question consensus on a fundamental doctrine, hence are not church-dividing. Certainly Luther's *simul iustus et peccator* enriches Catholic theology.

Fourth, we will need to establish institutional structures at the national, international, and grassroots levels that foster ecumenical consciousness, provide forums for exchange, and make possible shared service. This will mean supporting the WCC and the NCC, but it also includes a concern to build structures that will bring evangelicals and Pentecostals to the table.

Finally, the ecumenical movement has been and will remain the impulse of the Spirit. Hence spiritual ecumenism holds pre-eminence. Ecumenism is more than an academic exercise for theologians or endless meetings that often seem the road to nowhere. There must be an internal ecumenism, which is reform and renewal of our own communion's life. The closer we draw to Christ, the closer we draw to our sister churches. We must also find ways to pray, worship, and work together on a regular basis. The unity in Christ we already share ought not remain at a theoretical level. It demands manifestation and deepening in shared worship and witness, rooted in recognition that no church can be fully church without the other churches. Ecumenism stands at the threshold of a new chapter in its history. The course ahead will be difficult. But who a century ago, a brief span in history's sweep, would have envisioned the progress made and the place where the churches stand today? Much remains to be done. In the end, however, unity is more than we can attain. Therein resides our hope. Spoiled vessels though we are, we may yet be reworked by the creative, gracious hands of the Potter.

Sadly, Rev. Stephen J. Duffy, a priest of the Archdiocese of New Orleans, Louisiana, and a Professor of Systematic Theology at Loyola University, died on 29 March 2007. He was ordained a priest on 2 February 1957. He received a Licentiate in Theology from the Pontificia Universita Gregoriana in Rome and a Doctorate in Theology from Catholic University of America in Washington, DC. He will be sorely missed by family, students, colleagues, and friends.

We want to recognize and say thank you to Father Duffy's friend and colleague, Dr. Denis Janz, Provost Distinguished Professor of the History of Christianity at Loyola University, who assisted us with Dr. Duffy's edits and queries.

Moving toward the Kingdom of Racial Reconciliation[1]

RICHARD LAND

During the time when our lives intersected and our friendship began at New Orleans Baptist Theological Seminary (1970–1972), Dr. Humphreys and I discussed no subject as often or with as much passion as we did the subject of racial reconciliation, as we lamented the lingering vestiges of racism manifested in our Southern Baptist Zion. His encouragement as I pursued this issue, including vigorously defending the inclusive integration policies of my student pastorate (Vieux Carre Baptist Church in the French Quarter), was deeply appreciated.

As I write these words, I must confess I am deeply disappointed, sometimes even depressed, that in the year of our Lord 2008 we have not come far enough as Americans in our quest for a racially reconciled society. I was a junior in high school when the Civil Rights Act of 1964 was passed. I do not think former President Jimmy Carter ever spoke truer words than when he said he was grateful to God for the 1964 and 1965 civil rights acts because they liberated us (and when he said "us" he meant white Southerners) from a situation in which we had manifestly shown we were unwilling, or unable, to extricate ourselves. The civil rights revolution allowed us to rejoin our country as fully participating citizens and to be liberated from the segregation that victimized us all.

---

[1] This article is a revision of a sermon preached by on 9 January 1999, in Atlanta, Georgia, during the International Summit against Racism sponsored by the Baptist World Alliance. It also incorporates parts of earlier messages delivered to the Christian Life Commission's special conference on "Southern Baptists and Race" (17 January 1989) in Nashville, Tennessee, and to the commission's 1997 annual seminar in Louisville, Kentucky (4 March 1997). (The Christian Life Commission is now known as the Ethics & Religious Liberty Commission of the Southern Baptist Convention.)

As a seminary student from 1969 to 1972, I believe I could be forgiven for having been optimistic about racial reconciliation. As I entered seminary in August 1969, I could look back at the revolutionary progress achieved between the US Supreme Court's 1954 *Brown vs. Board of Education* decision and the civil rights legislation of the mid- and late-1960s and confidently conclude that having made that much progress in a decade and a half, we would be much farther down the road toward true racial reconciliation than we have come in the last forty years.

In his second letter to the Corinthian church, the Apostle Paul wrote:

> Therefore if any man be in Christ, he is a new creature: old things are passed away; behold, all things are become new. And all things are of God, who hath reconciled us to himself by Jesus Christ, and hath given to us the ministry of reconciliation; To wit, that God was in Christ, reconciling the world unto himself, not imputing their trespasses unto them; and hath committed unto us the word of reconciliation. Now then we are ambassadors for Christ, as though God did beseech you by us: we pray you in Christ's stead, be ye reconciled to God. (2 Cor 5:17–20 KJV)

As men and women who have come to a saving knowledge of Jesus Christ, we have experienced that reconciliation. In 2 Corinthians 5:18, the word "reconciled" is in the aorist tense, which means that there was an action at a point in time and that has taken place. It took place at Calvary. It was confirmed on the first Easter morning when the resurrection took place. As a consequence, we are reconciled. In verse 19, the participle denotes "reconciling" past action with continuing consequences. In other words, in our past, present, and future, we have been reconciled in Christ Jesus to God Almighty as we are "twice-born" men and women.

The fact of that vertical reconciliation, which is symbolized by the universal symbol of our common faith, the cross of our Lord and Savior, Jesus Christ, gives us the hope of the horizontal reconciliation with brothers and sisters around the world, whatever their ethnic background or derivation, whatever their skin hue, whatever their sex, or their national origin. But we must understand that the true reconciliation we seek can only come when it is rooted in, and witnessed to, by that vertical reconciliation that we have in Christ.

We must understand the nature of the enemy we confront. It is an enemy within as well as without. Racial bigotry is woven into the very warp and woof of our society. I cannot speak with an expert's or a native's authority about other cultures, but I can speak about this one. American society has racism in its very nature as sin is an integral part of human nature. After the fall, the Bible tells us the "heart is deceitful above all things, and desperately wicked: who can know it?" (Jer 17:9). That verse is bad enough in English. It is worse in the original Hebrew because there the heart and its adjectives are inextricably connected, and it literally means that the heart of man is incurable because that is its nature. It produces what it is. It knows nothing else.

In this increasingly secularly-dominated age in which we live, we who are born again believers and who have experienced that vertical reconciliation in Christ have a unique responsibility to remind our society that racism, as well as many other problems, will not be fully solved without the spiritual dimension.

The last half century of our world has been an evil, and in many ways terrible, time in terms of what people have done to one another. At the end of the nineteenth and the early part of the twentieth century, there had been remarkable economical progress that resulted from the Industrial Revolution. Almost everyone was better off, in terms of standards of living, than they were before; better off materialistically than anyone could remember being; and the Christian faith had been taken virtually around the world through the great missionary expansion of Christianity. But that optimism, that increasingly misplaced faith in the perfectibility and the goodness of human nature, collapsed in the horror of World War I.

Barth has described how the optimism of the reigning liberalism of the age was drowned out by the guns that destroyed a generation of European youth. Then, before humanity had time to take a deep breath, we were visited by a monstrous evil that sprang forth in what was, by most accounts and measures, the most scientifically, educationally, medically, technologically advanced society in the world—Germany.

What happened in that society, the Third Reich, between 1933 and 1945 was something so evil that we have not been fully able to rid ourselves of the ghastly pall cast by its horrendously evil shadow. It shattered the optimism of modern man, or it should have, and it reminded us that education, science, and cultural sophistication and advancement do not inoculate us against the evil that lurks within. What happened in Germany could not have happened in the Germany of Martin Luther. It awaited a leadership that had taken away the German people's confidence in Luther and Luther's God so that there was only a minority of those blessed saints called "the Confessing Church." As early as 1934, those left saw evil, knew it when they saw it, and spoke unflinchingly against it.

In 1949 the Nobel laureate T. S. Eliot warned of the West's inevitable choice between a reassertion of Judeo-Christian values in culture or acquiescence to an emerging pagan humanistic culture that worshiped itself.[2] Aleksandr Solzhenitsyn, one of the twentieth century's greatest and bravest men, warned of the dangers of this humanistic thinking of ourselves more highly than we ought to think. In 1978 Solzhenitsyn delivered Harvard University's commencement address, in which he warned America of the grievous consequences of this fallacious, humanistic world view: "The humanistic way of thinking, which has proclaimed itself our guide, did not admit the existence of intrinsic evil in man, nor did it see any task higher than the attainment of happiness on earth. It started modern Western Civilization on the dangerous trend of worshipping man and his material needs as if human life did not have any higher meaning."[3]

Dr. Martin Luther King Jr., another Nobel recipient, understood the depth of evil, both without and within, which confronted him and he understood the insufficiency of mere human power and reason to

---

[2] T. S. Eliot, "The Idea of a Christian Society," in *Christianity and Culture* (New York: Harcourt, Brace and World, 1949).

[3] Ronald Berman, ed. *Solzhenitsyn at Harvard* (Washington, DC: Ethics and Public Policy Center, 1980) 16–17.

conquer it. He told his people in 1963, "The humanist hope is an illusion."[4]

In his book, *The Naked Public Square*, Richard John Neuhaus recounts an incident that illustrates the point I seek to make. Quite soon after Dr. King's assassination in April 1968, an ecumenical memorial service took place in Harlem. Neuhaus tells how television cameras covered the event: "The announcer...spoke in solemn tones: 'And so today there was a memorial service for the slain civil rights leader, Dr. Martin Luther King, Jr. It was a religious service for the slain civil rights leader, Martin Luther King, Jr. It was a religious service, and it is fitting that it should be, for, after all, Dr. King was the son of a minister.'"[5] How to explain this astonishing blindness to the religious motive and of Dr. King's ministry? The announcer was speaking out of a habit of mind that was no doubt quite unconscious. The habit of mind is that religion must be kept as once removed from the public square, that matters of public significance must be sanitized of all religious particularity. It regularly occurred that the klieg lights for the television cameras would be turned off during Dr. King's speeches when he dwelt on the religious and moral-philosophical basis of the movement for racial justice. They would be turned on again when the subject touched on confrontational politics. In a luncheon conversation Dr. King once remarked, "They aren't interested in the why of what we're doing, only in the what of what we're doing; and because they don't understand the why, they cannot really understand the what."[6]

Newscasters and social analysts like these are not part of any conscious conspiracy against the religious, but they are "victims of a secularizing mythology of which they are hardly aware."[7] And, as President Kennedy reminded us, "The great enemy of truth is very often

---

[4] Quoted in Taylor Branch, *Parting the Waters: America in the King Years, 1954–1963* (New York: Simon & Schuster, 1988) 700–701.

[5] Richard John, Neuhaus, *The Naked Public Square: Religion and Democracy in America* (Grand Rapids: Wm. B. Eerdmans, 1984) 97–98.

[6] Ibid. 97–98.

[7] Ibid. 98.

not a lie, deliberate, contrived and dishonest, but the myth, persistent, persuasive and unrealistic."[8]

The fact that racism is at its foundation a spiritual problem and will be vanquished ultimately only by spiritual means does not mean that legislative and judicial remedies should or must not be applied to racial discrimination and bigotry. Another myth that must be challenged is the belief that "you can't legislate morality." Actually, to a very significant degree, society can, and it must. As New Testament Christians, we believe the most sustained statement in the Bible concerning the role of the divinely appointed civil magistrate is the book of Romans; there Paul writes that it says God ordained civil magistrates to punish those who do evil and reward those who do what is right (Rom 13:1–7). If one takes away the government's authority and ability to do that, one has taken away from government the primary reason God gave us government.

Laws against murder, theft, rape, and racism are the legislation of morality. And when we pass laws making murder, theft, rape and racism illegal, we are not so much trying to impose our morality on murderers, thieves, rapists, and racists as much as we are trying to keep them from imposing their immorality on their victims. Murder, theft, rape, and racism are by definition not between consenting adults in private.

Racial discrimination furnishes an excellent example of this principle. Legislative and judicial remedies radically altered the status of *de jure* segregation and legally institutionalized racial discrimination in our society. Some of us, if we were in a particular time and place, are old enough to remember and to have experienced the dramatic differences between then and now. I am just old enough to have lived during the very end of legalized, institutional segregation. I can remember segregated buses as a young boy. I can remember segregated waiting rooms and water fountains. Born in 1946, the first year of the baby boom, I grew up in Houston, Texas, a city whose population was approximately 25 percent African American. And yet the racial segregation I grew up in was so rigid that I met and got to know the first African American my age when I was a freshman at Princeton University.

---

[8] President John F. Kennedy, "Commencement Address" (Yale University, New Haven CT, 11 June 1962).

I was always taught at home—and I thank God for this—that racism was wrong, and that not only was it wrong, it was sinful. It was against the teaching of Jesus to treat anyone as less than you yourself because of the color of his or her skin. Still, I went to a segregated school, lived in a segregated neighborhood, and worshiped in a segregated church.

So, I went off to Princeton in fall 1965 and learned that one of my suite mates was an African American from New Orleans. As we were the only Southerners in the dormitory, we soon discovered that we had more in common with each other than with anyone else in the dorm. First, we both nearly froze to death. Second, we could not figure out what they were feeding us in the dining hall. Third, we were the only two folks there who did not have an accent.

Yet, when the law changed as a result of the prophetic witness of Christians and ministers like Dr. King, black and white, Northern and Southern—the South changed. You do not think the law made a difference? In terms of housing and enrollment patterns, the census of 1970 showed the South was the most segregated region of America. Twenty years later, in the 1990 census, the South had become the most integrated part of the nation in terms of those same measurement patterns. One of the primary reasons was that those civil rights laws applied more directly to the South than to any other part of the country because Southern societal practices revealed massive evidence of widespread patterns of systemic discrimination.

What about when one moves beyond the law? What about *de facto* segregation and discrimination? Here one is dealing with attitudes, not actions. When one enters the realm of the mind and of the heart, one moves beyond the power of restraint. If elimination, not restraint, of racial prejudice and bigotry is the goal—and as Christians it must be—then we must move beyond legislative and judicial answers to spiritual ones. However, belief in the necessity of the latter does not eliminate the need for, or our obligation to support, the former.

It is instructive to note a particular sermon that was delivered 19 April 1961 in the chapel at the Southern Baptist Theological Seminary in Louisville, Kentucky. It was delivered by a thirty-two-year-old new Ph.D. graduate—Martin Luther King Jr.—the co-pastor, with his illustrious father, of the Ebenezer Baptist Church in Atlanta, Georgia. He spoke of the winds of change and of the church's opportunity and responsibility on the frontiers of racial tension. He said, "We are broken loose from the Egypt of slavery; we have moved through the wilderness of segregation; we stand on the border of the Promised Land of integration."[9] If with profound humility I could extend Dr. King's biblical progression, I would note with great sadness more than four decades later we still await the kingdom of racial reconciliation.

Dr. King said directly that racism was a moral issue and had to be confronted by the churches as such. He said somebody must have "sense enough to resist physical force with soul force, to resist hatred with love, and to do so non-violently."[10]

From chapel, he went to speak to students from all ethics classes at the seminary. So many other students wanted to hear him lecture that after several moves from a large hall to a still larger hall, they eventually returned to the chapel—the only building on campus large enough to house the many students who wanted to hear Dr. King. Over 500 students were in attendance at that noon hour luncheon. Dr. King spoke for an hour and received a standing ovation at the conclusion of his message. He was leaving the seminary campus and going directly to meeting with Louisville's mayor and civic leaders. Knowing this, the seminary students presented him with a previously prepared petition signed by approximately 250 students calling on the mayor to integrate all municipal facilities in Louisville. During his message, Dr. King spoke about the need for the church to confront its past, to confront the fact that the most segregated moment in American life is when we gather to worship God on Sunday morning.

That is still true, and one reason it is true is because worshiping is the most voluntary moment in American social life. We are free to go worship *where* we want and *with whom* we want. We segregate ourselves so that it is the most racially divided moment in any point in our week. The point Dr. King attempted to make and the one I am trying to make,

---

[9] Martin Luther King Jr., *Road to Freedom*, analog sound cassette of a sermon preached in the chapel to the ethics classes at Southern Baptist Theological Seminary (Louisville KY, 19 April 1961) MLKEC: ATR–18. 610419–014, http://www.stanford.edu/group/King/publications/inventory/inv_04.htm. accessed 7/31/2007.

[10] Ibid.

as well, is that the law changed a lot of things. Those things needed to be changed and they would not have changed without the law being on the right side. However, while the salt of the law can change actions, it is only the light of the gospel that can change attitudes. The salt of the law can change behaviors, but it is only the light of the gospel that can change hearts.

As Christians, we have the only answer to the sin nature that makes us think more highly of ourselves than we ought to think, which is the foundational core of racism. That sin nature entices us and seduces us into creating gaps to put distances between ourselves and those who are different from us.

One more myth must be addressed at this point. It is a prevalent myth in America, and it is one against which we ought to be able to give eloquent testimony. That is the myth that the people who are the objects of racial prejudice are the only victims. Many of us know from personal experience the fallacy of that myth. All of us, perpetrators and victims alike, are shackled by the chains of prejudice—it victimizes everyone. As a Princeton sophomore, I took a course on racism in American culture. As part of that course's assignment I read *Killers of the Dream* by Lillian Smith, a native Georgian who finally left the South in despair at mid-century. In *Killers of the Dream*, Smith writes with breathtaking and brokenhearted pathos of her Georgia girlhood experience of this joint victimization. Recognizing that she penned these words in 1949, I trust you will accept her heartfelt words and forgive her dated ethnic terminology:

> The mother who taught me what I know of tenderness and love and compassion taught me also the bleak rituals of keeping Negroes in their "place." The father who rebuked me for an air of superiority toward schoolmates from the mill and rounded out his rebuke by gravely reminding me that "all men are brothers," trained me in the steel-rigid decorums I must demand of every colored male.... So we learned the dance that cripples the human spirit, step by step by step, we who were white and we who were colored, day by day, hour by hour, year by year until the movements were reflexes and made for the rest of our lives without thinking.... Something was wrong with a world

> that tells you that love is good and people are important and then forces you to deny love and to humiliate people.... In trying to shut the Negro race away from us, we have shut ourselves away from so many good, creative, honest, deeply human things in life.... The warped, distorted form we have put around every Negro child from birth is around every white child also. Each is on a different side of the frame but each is pinioned there. What cruelly shapes and cripples the personality of one is as cruelly shaping and crippling the personality of the other.[11]

Everyone is victimized when bigotry and racism occur: the oppressor and the oppressed, perhaps the oppressor more than the oppressed, because the former has to deal with the guilt of what one intuitively knows from the law written on the conscience is wrong (Rom 2:15).

When I shared Lillian Smith's quote with my Christian Life Commission trustees of the a few years ago, a female Caucasian trustee approached me after the session with tears streaming down her face. She said, "When I was a little girl, about ten years old, I went downtown to have lunch with my father. When I got on the bus, the white section of the bus was full. An adult white male got up and told a black woman to get up so I could sit down. I can't tell you the anguish and shame I felt." She added, "I had always been taught to do what adults told me to do, but there was something inside me that knew how terribly, terribly wrong that was. The pain of that act has stayed with me to this day." How many millions of times did that happen? Every time it happened, it shriveled and shrunk the soul and the spirit of the oppressor, perhaps more even than the oppressed.

Lillian Smith despaired of the victims ever completely overcoming such a formative, or should we say "de-formative," experience. Even when they summoned the strength and knowledge to escape the frame, she viewed them, and herself, as "stunted and warped and in our lifetime cannot grow straight again."[12] Happily, Lillian Smith was wrong.

---

[11] Lillian Smith, *Killers of the Dream* (1949; repr., Garden City NY: Anchor Books, 1963) 17, 27–28, 81.

[12] Ibid., 28.

In Christ Jesus we can be made new. In Christ we can be healed and liberated from our past. In Christ we can start over with our past and we can start over with our dreams. Paul tells us that we "can do all things through him who strengthens me." (Phil 4:13 ESV). Victimizer and victim alike find liberation from their victimization in Jesus Christ. Many of us have seen this change with our own eyes. Some reading this chapter have experienced it personally. People who internalized racism in all of its spiritual virulence have, in Christ, overcome it and been truly changed.

I remember vividly the moment when the moral and theological insufficiency of mere passive belief in racial equality crystallized for me, a postwar baby boomer, raised in a rigidly segregated society. This was the moment when I understood my responsibility never to tolerate but to challenge racism whenever and wherever I encountered it. I was sixteen, sitting in my living room in Houston, Texas, watching the evening news on 28 August 1963. Suddenly, extraordinary television images flickered across the screen. People, tens of thousands of people, filled the expanse between the Lincoln and Washington memorials. Then a voice rolled across the scene with soaring, eloquent words of hope and conviction and Dr. King said:

> Even though we face the difficulties of today and tomorrow, I still have a dream. It is a dream deeply rooted in the American dream. I have a dream that one day this nation will rise up and live out the true meaning of its creed: "We hold these truths to be self-evident; that all men are created equal." I have a dream that one day on the red hills of Georgia the sons of former slaves and sons of former slave owners will be able to sit down together at the table of brotherhood.... I have a dream that my four little children will one day live in a nation where they will not be judged by the color of their skin but by the content of their character.[13]

---

[13] Dr. King's television address at Lincoln Memorial Civil Rights Rally, Washington, DC, 28 August 1963. (A transcription of Dr. King's "I Have a Dream" speech by Michael E. Eidenmuller may be viewed on the web at http://www.americanrhetoric.com.)

I must pause at this point to note that Dr. King's dream was not a secular dream, but a moral one that envisioned discernments and judgments made according to character not "color."[14] Dr. King continued his elegant oration: "This is our hope. This is the faith that I go back to the South with. With this faith we will be able to transform the jangling discords of our nation into a beautiful symphony of brotherhood… This will be the day when all of God's children will be able to sing with new meaning, 'My country, 'tis of thee, sweet land of liberty, of thee I sing: land where my fathers died, land of the pilgrims' pride, from every mountainside, let freedom ring.'"[15]

Those were words to confront and penetrate the Christian spirit and convict the American soul. Why should I not have been convinced, captivated, and convicted? And I was! For what was Dr. King doing but appealing to the truth I had imbibed in Sunday school? "Red and yellow, black and white, they are precious in His sight. Jesus loves the little children of the world."[16] What was Dr. King doing? He was focusing attention on the pledge that I took each school day in my segregated school: "I pledge allegiance to the flag of the United States of America and to the republic for which it stands, one Nation under God, indivisible, with liberty and justice for all."[17] What was Dr. King doing, but appealing to the fulfillment of the promise of our national documents such as the Declaration of Independence? "We hold these truths to be self-evident, that all men are created equal, that they are endowed by their Creator with certain unalienable Rights, that among these are Life, Liberty, and the pursuit of Happiness."[18]

---

[14] For a brilliant treatment of the background leading up to this speech, I recommend Taylor Branch's *Parting the Waters: America in the King Years 1954–1963.*

[15] *America: My Country 'tis of Thee.* Lyrics by Samuel F. Smith (1832), spoken by Martin Luther King, Jr. in his "I have a Dream" speech on 28 August 1963 at the Lincoln Memorial, Washington, DC.

[16] C. Herbert Woolston (words) and George F. Root (music), "Jesus Loves the Little Children of the World" (MIDI score, public domain).

[17] The Pledge of Allegiance to the Flag, (2007) in *Encyclopaedia Britannica*, http://search.eb.com/eb/article–9060389 (accessed 1 August 2007).

[18] Declaration of Independence. A copy may be viewed in *The Columbia Electronic Encyclopedia*, 6th ed. (New York: Columbia University Press, 2006).

The author of the Declaration of Independence, Thomas Jefferson, understood the principle's unfulfilled promise. Jefferson's troubled words regarding the glaring disparity between the nation's promise and the nation's practice, *his* promise and *his* practice, are chiseled into the wall of Jefferson's memorial in our nation's capital: "Can the Liberties of a nation be secure when we have removed a conviction that these liberties are the gifts of God! Indeed I tremble for my country when I reflect that God is just, that his justice cannot sleep forever. Commerce between master and slave is despotism. Nothing is more certainly written in the book of fate than that these people are to be free."[19]

In our resolve to go forward, to do more, we should pause to take inspiration from the progress that has been made. It has not been enough. It has been woefully inadequate, but there has been change. We need to draw courage from that change to move from standing on the border of the promised land of integration to moving forward to the kingdom of reconciliation. It will not happen without a faithful Christian witness. We have failed too often in the past in America. We have had two great religious awakenings and slavery survived both. This happened because we did not understand adequately the need to move from our personal lives to our prophetic commission to be salt and light in our society.

Jesus *commanded* us to be salt. He commanded us to be light. Salt has to touch what it would preserve and come into contact with what it would purify. Jesus commanded us to be salt and light! A Christianity that has lost its vertical vision has lost its salt. But a Christianity that forgets that its horizontal commission is to be ambassadors of reconciliation has forgotten the Incarnation, the Word made flesh that dwelt among us (John 1:14). Racism is a global problem and it has a global solution. That hope is found in the cross of our Savior. Now, I am not talking about a merely pietistic "Let's just change hearts." We have to call for racial justice, and we must live racial justice and racial

---

[19] Inscription taken from Thomas Jefferson Memorial, located at East Basin Drive, SW, Washington, DC. Words were originally written in a bill for Establishing Religion Freedom, 1777, before being inscribed on the memorial for the third president of the United States of America. http://www.nps.gov/archive/thje/memorial/memorial.htm (8/12/2007).

reconciliation. Those who have been identified as the oppressors have a special burden to reach out again, again, and again to those they have historically pushed away and shunted aside.

As one African-American Southern Baptist pastor said to me when we got to know each other well enough that we could be honest, "Richard, you've got to understand that you white people are a very complicated people. You don't always mean what you say, and you don't always say what you mean." That observation needed no explanation.

Some people see things the way they are and ask "why?" Others dream dreams that never were and ask "why not?"[20] Let's identify with men and women like Dr. King who see visions that never were, who dream dreams that never have been, of a society in which we are judged not by the color of our skin but by the content of our character.

An old African proverb says, "Tell me and I'll listen; show me and I'll believe." This is what we must do. We must allow God to change our minds and our hearts until our actions are transformed. We must show the world that we really believe what we say we believe and that God will really do what we say he will do.

We must pray that God will give us passion as well as compassion. We must call upon Baptists and other Christians to resolve to stand publicly and privately for racial reconciliation and justice and to speak out against racism whenever and wherever we encounter it.

We must—as individuals, families, and communities of worship—reach across racial boundaries and establish friendships through mealtimes, prayer times, and recreational times.

We must call upon Baptists and other Christians to apologize for past bigotry and to pray for and minister to those still within its deadly clutches, either as persecuted or as persecutor.

As a Southern Baptist, I call upon my fellow Southern Baptists, out of our incessant past experience and intermittent present experience with

---

[20] A popular quote by Robert Francis Kennedy (US Attorney general and adviser [1925–1968]) is "There are those who look at things the way they are, and ask why…I dream of things that never were, and ask why not?" The quote was originally by George Bernard Shaw (Irish literary critic, playwright and essayist, awarded the 1925 Nobel Prize for Literature, 1856–1950) in his play *Back to Methuselah* (1921): "You see things; and you say, "Why?" But I dream things that never were; and I say, 'Why not?'"

racism, to witness both near and far to racism's devastating and debilitating impact on all its victims, persecuted and persecutor. As Southern Baptists we have not always stood for these things, but God has, his Word has, and with his help, we do now, and we shall in the future.

"Jesus Thown Everything Off Balance": Emily Dickinson, William Faulkner, and Flannery O'Connor on the Necessity of Christian Radicalism in the Study of Literature

RALPH C. WOOD

When I first met Fisher Humphreys in 1997, it was by way of his invitation to attend, together with his wife Caroline and my wife Suzanne, a dramatic production at a small theater in the Five Points district of Birmingham, Alabama. The Humphreyses wanted to welcome the Woods to Samford University and Birmingham in an appropriate way. Already from the start, therefore, I knew that Fisher Humphreys was a theologian who cared about the arts, and of course this delighted me greatly since I have devoted my career to the study of Christianity and literature in their often complicated relation. And since this particular play also offered a delightfully irreverent spoof on certain forms of conservative faith, I discovered that Fisher did not revere the arts only as they might offer adventitious props and easy confirmations of Christianity. His eagerness to meet the secular world on its own terms rather than ensconcing the gospel within its own little ghetto was confirmed yet again by his serving as a theologian in residence at the University of Alabama in Birmingham—there to confront and engage tough-minded academics with tough-minded theology.

I soon learned as well that Fisher is not a hale-fellow-well-met when it comes to theological argument. He disagrees with Stanley Hauerwas's condemnation of niceness as a Christian virtue by contending that, for most Southern Baptists, niceness would be a huge advance over meanness! Even so, Fisher refuses to deal in smiles and nods when engaging his interlocutors about serious matters. I learned to appreciate this admirable feature when we sometimes tangled on fundamental matters, especially on the nature of divine grace in its relation to human freedom. I can recall one especially memorable occasion in Samford's Reid Chapel when we had a public debate on the subject. I fear that Fisher won this little dust-up since his eloquent defense of his Arminian position drew a large round of applause, whereas my case for a Barthian kind of Calvinism left most of the audience perplexed.

These fond personal remembrances are but ways of saying that all three sections of my essay address some particular aspect of my friendship with and admiration for Fisher Humphreys. The section on Emily Dickinson's poetry treats the problem of faith and doubt that has exercised Dr. Humphreys's work no less than mine. The section on William Faulkner deals with our greatest Southern writer in what is to me his most deeply convincing—but also his most deeply troubling—work: *Go Down, Moses*. There we encounter Faulkner's profoundly tragic vision in such arresting fictional terms that, as Fisher Humphreys rightly insists, no sentimental version of the gospel will suffice as answer. Then finally in my analysis of Flannery O'Connor's most famous and controversial story, "A Good Man Is Hard to Find," I seek to honor Dr. Humphreys's conviction that Christian faith is not one religious option among others—much less a humanistic attempt to speak of God by speaking of man in a loud voice—but rather the most radical and drastic and life-transforming news ever heard.

Christian tradition knows no sharp distinction between soul and mind. When our Lord commands us to love God with all our mind and soul, he is employing a Semitic doublet that admits of no real distinction: mind and soul are virtually the same thing. When St. Paul urges us in Romans 12:2 to be transformed by the renewing of our minds, he means nothing strictly mental or intellectual. The Hebrew *leb/lebam*, like the Greek *nous*, has little to do with mere intelligence or ratiocination, with abstract thinking or academic learning. These words *leb* and *nous* are often translated "soul" and "heart" as well as "intellect" and "mind." The two qualities are utterly inseparable, as the *Book of Common Prayer* makes evident in its Collect before Holy Communion: "Cleanse the thoughts of our hearts by the inspiration of thy Holy Spirit." Only when heart and mind, soul and intellect, are woven into a seamless web do we become fully human: creatures made in the image and likeness of God.

My Hebrew scholar-friend James Kennedy points out that the word commonly translated "heart"—as in Samuel's telling Saul that God has found a man "according to his own *leb*"—does not refer to David's extraordinary piety but to God's extraordinary action: He has decided on David and none other. Kennedy adds that only when God fashions him from dust (*apar*) and soil (*adamah*), breathing into him the breath of life (*neshamma*), does man become a living being, a vital *nephesh*. And when Yahweh withdraws his breath—his spirit—we are indeed dead. As creatures thus fashioned from the ground, we may comically be regarded as animated mud, as dirtballs with a conscience! Blaise Pascal put the matter more politely but with the still scandalous claim that we are "thinking reeds." "*Ni ange, ni bête*," said Pascal.[1] Walker Percy wittily adds, however, that male humans are also "walking genitals," the only creatures whose sexual drive does not depend upon the female's being in a state of estrus.

The upshot is that our biblical ancestors set the standard for the entire Christian tradition by insisting on the radically inseparable relation between the outward and the inward life, envisioning us always as embodied souls or ensouled bodies. Our conscience and character, our loves and desires—our essential identity before God and man—lies in the irreducible unity of our body and mind and soul and spirit. We should be redeeming our *bodies* since what we do with *them*—together with all of their extensions, especially our property and possessions—signals our integral and undivided nature.

I

It is surely a scandal that "a nation with the soul of a church," as G. K. Chesterton famously described our country, should have produced so few writers who are Christian in any substantive sense of the word. Emerson, Thoreau, Dickinson, Melville, Poe, Hawthorne, Twain, James, Frost, and Faulkner—nearly all of our eminent writers are

---

[1] Blaise Pascal, *Pensées*, VI: Les philosophes, 358. Translation: "Neither angel nor beast."

heterodox at best, atheist or even nihilist at worst. Only such major-minor writers as Flannery O'Connor and Walker Percy can be called distinctively Christian: writers whose artistic vision and work derive from the scandalous claims of God's own self-identification in the Jews and Jesus and the church. The perhaps obvious answer to this conundrum is that brilliant minds gifted with artistic imagination have seen biblical faith for the snare and delusion that it is and thus have refused to make its false claims essential to their work. My counter-case is that our major writers have little substantive regard for Christianity because our churches have made it virtually impossible for them to do so. Despite our nation's inveterate religiosity—exceeded perhaps only by that of India—I maintain that the church has become virtually invisible in America. It has so fully identified itself with the American project that our artists have had little cause to heed any unique and distinctively Christian witness in the churches.

Let us first consider Emily Dickinson as an example of a writer who was unable to embrace the faith of the church because it had become so closely identified with New England culture. She was the legatee of an evangelicalism that had made inward individual experience the crucial mark of authentic Christian faith. Not the church but the state had been entrusted with the most important outward affairs, most notably slavery and its military defense. Well before the Civil War and the frontier revivals, this arrangement had become established as the nation's unofficial religion. It left Dickinson unable to embrace Christian faith not, I believe, because she had encountered its authentic expression and found it wanting, but rather because she spurned its triumphalist moralism and pietist individualism. That she rejected such moralism may have caused her to take refuge in a religious individualism, retreating into a reclusive life in order to avoid being enlisted for an allegedly Christian cause that she knew to be dubious at best, spurious at worst.

During her single year of college life at the Mount Holyoke Female Seminary, the seventeen-year-old Dickinson was tutored by the school's founder, the redoubtable Mary Lyon. Like other Whig evangelicals of her day, Lyon envisioned Christianity as forming a powerful tandem with science and education for bringing about a moral revolution of the entire planet. The kingdom of heaven was soon to come on earth—if not in the nineteenth, then surely in the twentieth century, which would so certainly be the *Christian Century* that a still-existing journal was thus named. In an 1842 address setting forth this confident evangelicalism, Lyon envisioned a time rapidly approaching when all people would "act according to the principles of reason and religion," when "all that now goes into the war channel, will then be consecrated to the service of knowledge and benevolence."[2]

The key to such moral transformation lay in the idea of punctiliar salvation—the notion, namely, that one is defined as a Christian by way of a sudden emotional conversion experience. Such a dramatic inward rebirth was public proof that one had personally appropriated the gift of divine grace. A miraculous conversion was the spiritual equivalent of the physical "violations" of nature that were said to be miraculous evidences of God's existence. "In working toward the conversion of her students at Mount Holyoke," Roger Lundin writes, "Lyon divided them each year into three groups." The "Christians" were those who could testify to the certainty of their salvation experience. The "Hopers" believed themselves on the verge of conversion. The "No-Hopers," by contrast, could not attest to any drastic emotional reversal that proved their faith in Christ.[3] What had begun in the seventeenth century with the Puritan practice of the examined conscience, whereby one sought outward objective evidence of divine election, thus led in the nineteenth century to a radical spiritual subjectivism. Salvation was located not in the church's public and communal enactment of the gospel by living out the story of God's presence in the gathered community's practices and doctrines. Rather was it radically relocated in the solitary and inward self, and thus in a traumatic individual conversion experience that alone could attest to the efficacy of Christ's work.

Emily Dickinson was numbered on the short list of souls called the No-Hopers. They were the special targets of fervent evangelical attention at Mount Holyoke and Amherst alike. Dickinson remained one of the few holdouts. "How lonely this world is growing," she wrote in spring 1850. "Christ is calling everyone here...and I am standing alone

---

[2] Quoted in Roger Lundin, *Emily Dickinson and the Art of Belief* (Grand Rapids: Wm. B. Eerdmans, 1998) 37.

[3] Ibid., 40–41.

in rebellion, and growing very careless."[4] That Dickinson declined to make a public profession of a tempestuous conversion experience does not mean, as Lundin clearly shows, that she was an atheist scoffer at all things Christian. On the contrary, Dickinson admitted in a letter to her friend Abiah Root "that I shall never be happy without I love Christ."[5] Yet if the love of Christ were signified by an overwhelmingly subjective conversion, Dickinson knew that she lacked it. The outward doctrinal claims of Christian faith were not her chief, or at least her only, worry. What vexed Dickinson were her own uncontrollable and potentially delusory emotions. To her friend Abiah Root, she thus explained her refusal to attend the Amherst revival meetings of 1850: "I felt that I was so easily excited that I might again be deceived and I dared not trust myself."[6] And if the world's wonder—especially her own poetic talent—were understood as something to be repudiated, Dickinson could not. A culturally established Christianity seeking to force Emily Dickinson's conversion could not possibly win her permanent esteem. Better than her own ministers and teachers, Dickinson saw that the Jesus of the gospels—whom she never spurned but always honored—demands no such emotional effusions. Dickinson is to be commended rather than condemned, I believe, for daring not to trust herself to the vagaries of the subjective self.

Writing again to Abiah Root, Dickinson also confessed that "I have perfect confidence in God & his promises and yet I know not why, I feel that the world holds a predominant place in my affections. I do not feel that I could give up all for Christ, were I called to die."[7] Surrendering all to Christ does not seem to have meant, for Dickinson, that she would be required to surrender her recalcitrant self-will. Dickinson was encouraged to believe, instead, that she would have to relinquish her poetic integrity if she became a professed Christian. Given this heretical dichotomy, Dickinson was surely right to refuse such a supposedly heroic act of abdication, such a gnostic denial of the good creation. In

---

[4] Ibid., 52.

[5] Ibid., 305.

[6] Ibid., 49.

[7] Quoted in D. Bruce Lockerbie, *Dismissing God: Modern Writers' Struggle Against Religion* (Grand Rapids: Baker, 1998) 41.

rejecting the deity of nineteenth-century Protestant piety, she did not minimize her soul's experience, as Bruce Lockerbie maintains, so much as she expanded it. Indeed, Dickinson became our most important poet of the spiritual life, not another one of the many dreary and virtually unreadable Victorian pietists.

A poem at once sprightly and memorable, precisely because it is at once troubling and edifying, is number 501. Here, I believe, Dickinson sets forth an arresting and perceptive understanding of the relation between faith and doubt:

This World is not Conclusion.
A Species stands beyond—
Invisible, as Music—
But positive, as Sound—
It beckons, and it baffles—
Philosophy—don't know—
And through a Riddle, at the last—
Sagacity, must go—
To guess it, puzzles scholars—
To gain it, Men have borne
Contempt of Generations
And Crucifixion, shown—
Faith slips—and laughs, and rallies—
Blushes, if any see—
Plucks at a twig of Evidence—
And asks a Vane, the way—
Much Gesture, from the Pulpit—
Strong Hallelujahs roll—
Narcotics cannot still the Tooth
That nibbles at the soul—[8]

It is noteworthy that Dickinson does not deny the finality of *all* worlds, but only of *this* outward and visible world. There is another species of the same genus called "worlds" that is indeed transcendent and

---

[8] Thomas H. Johnson, ed., *Complete Poems* (Boston: Little, Brown, 1960). This work is the source cited for all Emily Dickinson poetry in this chapter.

unbounded—namely, the heavenly and unseen world whose finality she does not doubt. Karl Barth observes that this mysterious heavenly realm is no less created than the earthly sphere, and thus that it is neither to be feared nor worshiped as divine, though it does indeed terrify and delight with preternatural wonder. In relation to his earthly environment, man is meant to see, hear, understand, and rightly have dominion over it. But with regard to the inconceivable celestial world, man remains at once unknowing and completely dependent:

> At this inner boundary of creation stands man as though even as a creature he had to represent this above and below, and thus, as a creature, to signify his place in a relationship which penetrates into the heights and depths in a quite different way from that of heaven and earth [i.e., the way of the angels and the beasts]. Man is the place within creation where the creature in its fullness is concentrated, and at the same time stretches beyond itself; the place where God wishes to be praised within creation, and may be praised.[9]

We must not claim too much for Dickinson, baptizing her as an anonymous Christian.[10] Thus would we violate the integrity both of her poetry and our own faith. Yet we must mark the failure of pietistic

---

[9] Karl Barth, *Dogmatics in Outline*, trans. G. T. Thomson (New York: Harper Torchbooks, 1959) 63.

[10] Johnson, *Complete Poems*, 1960. "I'm ceded—I've stopped being Theirs" is the poem in which Dickinson most clearly elevates her poetic vocation over the dubious demand of the church that she repudiate the world. Like Virgil crowning and mitering Dante at the end of the *Purgatorio*, Dickinson enthrones herself with the diadem of Artemis, virgin goddess of the new moon, baptizing herself not in the name of the Father, Son, and Holy Ghost, but with the honorific of the highest art, poetry:

> Baptized, before, without the choice,
> But this time, consciously, of Grace—
> Unto supremest name—
> Called to my Full—The Crescent dropped–
> Existence's whole Arc, filled up,
> With one small Diadem.

Christianity to honor the mystery of the invisible realm. It attempted to make outward and visible conversion experience serve as a surrogate for—rather than a sign of—our engagement with the inward and invisible world. Insofar as we can call Dickinson a believer at all, it must be in Williams James's and Rudolf Otto's sense of the term: she venerated what Otto called the *mysterium tremendum et fascinans*, the Holy Otherness that at once frightens and attracts, both alarming and alluring, repelling and captivating us. That her pietist community wanted to bypass this mysterious middle realm between earth and God was utterly unacceptable to Dickinson. If we are to honor the true God, we must praise him (as Barth suggests) from *within* the creation, glorifying him in gratitude for this created realm that remains as unseen as melody and harmony yet as real as resounding chords. Philosophical inquiry can fathom nearly everything under the sun but this most important thing: the mystery of the Infinite. The dry speculations of airy academics thus prompt Dickinson to an agnostic "don't know." Worldly wisdom, even at best, is but riddles and conundrums. Heavenly wisdom—the engagement with this unknown world that issues in real sagacity—requires a constant grappling with the unobvious, a daily martyrdom to easy nostrums, even the contempt of both the cultured and uncultured despisers of doubt-filled faith.

Dickinson's mystical kind of faith in the unseen world also entails radical risk. It is never something as clear and certain as a proposition. It is an affair of slipping and advancing, of losing and rallying, of weeping and rejoicing. So shy of self-confidence is such faith that it blushes when asked to expound its own piety.[11] Dickinson also joins Christians in acknowledging the limits of mere experiential evidence since it carries no more weight than a twig might bear, fruitful though it may be. She also calls us to remember that, as sinful citizens of the sinful church—the tattered Bride of Christ—we receive dubious direction from the wind-blown cock atop our cruciphobic churches. Though meant to announce

---

[11] The same holds with conversion to Christian faith properly understood. When someone asked Karl Barth to recount his salvation experience, he replied that it occurred on a Friday afternoon in the year A.D. 34, when Christ was crucified. Our great and small and necessarily on-going conversion experiences are but distant appropriations of this one saving act.

the miracle of the resurrection, it often blows with every wind of doctrine, even as it sometimes crows with undisciplined erotic energy. Despite the flailing of perfervid preachers and easy believers, true faith—whether in the unseen heavenly realm or in the incarnate God—is never free from the toothache of doubt. The feel-good pharmacists of the No-God offer vain narcotics to ease the agony entailed by authentic belief. The Lord of heaven and earth will not anesthetize shallow souls with worldly finalities, even of the most "spiritual" sort. So does the lesser lord of the celestial sphere implant the molar of diffidence no less than the tusk of certainty, and they both nibble at the soul like a mouse at cheese. Emily Dickinson's deity thus bears more than a distant resemblance to the true God. For they are both utterly unlike Blake's "Old Nobodaddy," Hemingway's "Our Nada Who Art in Nada," and thus the Big Guy in the Sky whose death we ought to celebrate. Her God resembles the one who abandoned his doubt-wracked Son in Gethsemane as he prepared to mount the bloody tree from which he would rule the world by reconciled lives rather than coerced conversions.[12]

I contend that we Christian scholars are obliged to honor such faithful Dickinsonian doubt by teaching our students not to dismiss it, but to absorb it. A "god" who cannot be doubted is also a "god" who cannot be believed in true biblical fashion. It is noteworthy, for example, that there are many more psalms of lament than psalms of praise, and yet we have not yet sung a single "lament chorus." Nor does Yahweh

---

[12] Dickinson understood, with Ivan Karamazov, that without faith in God, ethics hover over an abyss. Hence her willingness to embrace the moral equivalent of false fire than to rob the moral life of its transcendent basis:

> Those–dying then,
> Knew where they went–
> They went to God's Right Hand–
> That Hand is amputated now
> And God cannot be found–
>
> The abdication of Belief
> Makes the Behavior small–
> Better an ignis fatuus
> Than no illume at all. (#1551)

vindicate Job's alleged "comforters" for insisting that Job cease crying out his protest against divine injustice. On the contrary, they are punished while Job is rewarded. Why? Not in spite of his wrestling hard with the Lord God but rather because, like Jacob, he would not turn Yahweh loose until he received something far more important than a mere theodicy—namely, a theophany, a frightening and saving appearance of God. There Job learns that God has many other concerns than man alone, and thus that man should not read the disasters of nature as being directed willfully and divinely at him.

Here, I believe we should also follow the example of evangelical philosopher Merold Westphal.[13] He has taught us to regard Marx and Nietzsche and Freud, not as demonic enemies but as unintended friends of the gospel. The "god" whom they deny, Westphal rightly argues, is the "god" whom we should never have worshiped in the first place. Marx is right when he declares much of Christianity to be an opiate, a massive dose of morphine for people who want to give a comforting divine sanction to their privileged position in society.[14] Nietzsche is right when he accuses many Christians of what he calls *ressentiment*—a fundamental animosity against life, a deep discontentment with the rough-and-tumble character of a world where the rain falls on the just and unjust alike.[15] Freud is right when he declares that Jews and Christians often worship a nice and cuddly and friendly "god" whom they have projected onto a universe devoid of such deity.[16]

Karl Barth is altogether right in saluting these naysayers of the "no-God." He regards the pseudo-divinity of popular Christian belief as the most pernicious of all human inventions. Belief in this merely civil deity stanches any radical transformation of either persons or communities. "The cry of revolt against such a god," says Barth, "is nearer the truth than is the sophistry with which men attempt to justify him." Yet it is

---

[13] Harold Westphal, *Suspicion and Faith: The Religious Uses of Modern Atheism* (Grand Rapids: Wm. B. Eerdmans, 1993).

[14] Karl Marx, *A Contribution to the Critique of Hegel's Philosophy of Right. Deutsch-Französische Jahrbücher* (Feb. 1844).

[15] Friedrich Nietzsche, *On the Genealogy of Morality*, trans. and ed. Maudemarie Clark and Alan J. Swensen (Indianapolis: Hackett, 1998).

[16] Sigmund Freud, Cf., *The Future of an Illusion* (New York: W. W. Norton and Co., 1989).

ever so difficult to surrender belief in this comforting and consoling no-God who merely confirms "the course of the world and of men as it is":

> We suppose that we know what we are saying when we say "God." We assign to him the highest place in our world: and in so doing we place Him on fundamentally one line with ourselves and with things. We assume that He needs something: and so we assume that we are able to arrange our relation to Him as we arrange other relationships. We press ourselves into proximity with Him: and so, all unthinking, we make Him nigh unto ourselves. We allow ourselves an ordinary communication with Him, we permit ourselves to reckon with Him as though this were not extraordinary behaviour on our part. We dare to deck ourselves out as his companions, patrons, advisers, and commissioners. We confound time with eternity.... And so, when we set God upon the throne of the world, we mean by God ourselves.[17]

II

Emily Dickinson is but one of the many writers whom we should esteem for taking Christianity more seriously than the church itself often regards it. Melville and Hawthorne are two other figures who are especially discerning in their analysis of our terribly twisted condition. So is Emerson to be saluted for making a wholesale rejection of Christian faith, refusing even to celebrate Holy Communion in its non-sacramental Unitarian form. But for me, the non-Christian writer whose work retains overwhelming, even transformative, power is William Faulkner. Faulkner remains, in my opinion, our finest if also our fiercest literary assailant against acculturated Christianity in its Southern expression. That the church under-girded a savage system of chattel slavery was, for him, its chief failing. In disclosing the sinister quality of this institution that was so deeply linked to white Christianity, Faulkner

---

[17] Karl Barth, *The Epistle to the Romans*, 6th ed., trans. Edwyn C. Hoskyns (New York: Oxford University Press, 1968) 40, 44.

unwittingly enables the church to repent of its sin. Yet Faulkner makes no easy moralistic judgment of so obvious an evil.

The Old South was, in many ways, a wondrous place. That it produced Robert Penn Warren and Eudora Welty, Flannery O'Connor and Walker Percy, Allen Tate and Faulkner himself is sufficient testimony to its cultural excellence. Though Percy loathed "the monstrous mythologizing" of the so-called Southern Way of Life, he lauded the region's authentic virtues: "The conservative tradition of a predominantly agrarian society, a tradition which at its best enshrined the human aspects of living for rich and poor, black and white. It gave first place to a stable family life, sensitivity and good manners between men, chivalry toward women, an honor code, and individual integrity."[18] Even so, it was a culture that rested on human bondage, and nowhere more tellingly than in "The Bear" does Faulkner lay bare its fiendish cruelty.

Rather than offering a tract against slavery and the segregated society built on it, Faulkner enables his readers vicariously to experience a shock of recognition alongside his sixteen-year-old protagonist, Ike McCaslin. The boy finds himself examining an early-nineteenth-century ledger kept by two of his great-uncles, Buck and Buddy. The two brothers had entered half-literate jokes in the record book as they bantered back and forth about the McCaslin family's various dealings with their slaves. The crucial entry involves a black woman named Eunice: "*Bought by Father in New Orleans 1807 $650. dolars. Marid to Thucydus 1809 Drownd in Crick Cristmas Day 1832.*" A second entry almost six months thence reads as follows: "*June 21th 1833 Drownd herself.*" Writing two days later, the second brother adds: "*Who in hell ever heard of a niger drownding him self.*"[19] What young Ike McCaslin has discovered—to his staggering horror, though it had been caused only vague puzzlement to his uncles—is the cause for Eunice's suicide on the Feast of the Nativity. The day of the world's divine rebirth, we learn, had been the day of Eunice's deliberate death. What should have been

---

[18] Walker Percy, *Signposts in a Strange Land*, ed. Patrick Samway (New York: Farrar, Straus & Giroux, 1991) 51.

[19] William Faulkner, *Go Down, Moses* (New York: Modern Library, 1955) 267. Hereafter cited as *GDM.*

an occasion for great merriment and rejoicing was, instead, the time for final despair. Eunice had found out on that day a truth that was beyond her bearing: her daughter Tomasina was three months pregnant. This daughter, we also learn from the ledgers, had been fathered not by Eunice's slave husband, Thucydus, but by Carothers McCaslin, the plantation owner himself. Now, twenty-two years later, this same "Tomy" had been impregnated by this same Carothers McCaslin—by her own father.

Like their forbears, Buck and Buddy McCaslin could not conceive of Negro slaves as fully human beings, as having their own moral integrity, as capable of suicidal rage against this most fundamental violation, and thus of killing themselves. Blacks to them were dumb chattel—objects to be sold in markets and traded in card games—having little more dignity and worth than an ox or a mule. Yet the brothers' mention of Eunice's self-murder, six months later when her daughter Tomy died in childbirth, reveals that Buck and Buddy were not totally opaque to the truth. They were haunted with a dim and inchoate sense of guilt, with a moral burden that would become a deadly weight only a generation later in young Ike McCaslin. For in discovering that Eunice had taken her own life in an act of sheer metaphysical renunciation—repudiating a system so evil that it could allow the father of a slave child to summon this same slave daughter to his bed of carnal lust and to father yet another child on her—young Ike also repudiated his plantation legacy. Rather than becoming a wealthy cotton farmer, he elected to live as a landless itinerant carpenter—not unlike the son of the Nazarene carpenter who declared that his kingdom was not of this world.

I encountered "The Bear" as a young man who had grown up in the piney woods of eastern Texas, where my church had taught me to sing "Red and yellow, black and white, they are precious in His sight; Jesus loves the little children of the world." It was also a world where blacks were consigned to inferior schools, confined to "colored only" drinking fountains and restrooms, and excluded entirely from restaurants and hotels, but most especially from the white churches. My ministers and teachers had failed badly in the educational task shared, albeit in different ways, by church and school alike: the task that Aristotle described as "training in virtue." Ideally, the academy makes citizens by way of the classical virtues. So does the church make saints by way of the transformed and infused virtues. Both should seek the right ordering of our moral and religious lives.

In my own case, it was a secular college professor teaching a racist Baptist youth how to read Faulkner who enabled me to be struck with the moral force of lightning when I read the ledgers passage from "The Bear." I was knocked flat in the belated recognition that I had been a contributor to such an evil system, even if it had taken the form of segregation rather than outright slavery. Faulkner the non-Christian was thus making a witness to me that my church had not made, and thus did he serve as one of God's unacknowledged prophets. So did Mark Twain have a similar effect on me when I read Huckleberry Finn's feigned story about a shipwreck on the Mississippi to account for his lateness in returning to Aunt Sally's place. So well had Huck been inculturated into the Southern way of life that he didn't need to think about an appropriate response when his aunt asks him if anyone were injured. "No'm," replies Huck. "Killed a nigger." "Well, it's lucky," Aunt Sally rejoins, "because sometimes people do get hurt."[20]

That black slaves were regarded not as human beings but as dispensable animals is also the shocking recognition that strikes Ike McCaslin. When he comes of age five years after the last of the annual hunts that have given him profound reverence for both the beauteous mystery and feral fierceness of the natural world, he decides to repudiate his patrimony. Thus will he preserve, if only in his own undefiled conscience, the virtues of the primitive hunt over against the vices of so-called civilization. Rather than perpetuate the evils that he has inherited from his McCaslin ancestors, he will break the chain of violence, exploitation, and greed. He will make atonement for the sins of his fathers. Ike cites Genesis as giving humanity its original summons to become stewards and communicants with the land, not its domineering owners and arrogant proprietors. Man was created, Ike argues, "not to hold for himself and his descendants inviolable title forever, generation after generation, to the oblongs and squares of the earth, but to hold the

---

[20] Mark Twain, *The Adventures of Huckleberry Finn* (New York: Holt, Rinehart, and Winston, 1948).

earth mutual and intact in the communal anonymity of brotherhood."[21] Despite Cass Edmonds's utter incredulity at Ike's decision, the youth renounces his plantation inheritance for the sake of the universal human verities that Keats voices in his "Ode on a Grecian Urn": "*He was talking about truth. Truth is one. It doesn't change. It covers all things which touch the heart—honor and pride and pity and justice and courage and love. Do you see now?*"[22]

Cynical Cass will never discern the metaphysics and thus the morals of the hunt. Yet Faulkner seems also to have had his own doubts about the efficacy of Ike's act, even though Ike repeats the ringing rhetoric of Faulkner's Nobel Prize address more than two decades in advance.[23] For it cannot be denied that Faulkner parodies nearly every aspect of Ike's sterling act of moral repudiation. For example, Hubert ("Uncle Buck") Beauchamp had left the young Ike a legacy of thirty gold pieces in a silver cup. Quite apart from the demeaning allusion to Judas's similarly sized guilt-money, Buck had rapidly reduced the value of the legacy by borrowing against it even before Ike was born. Finally, he took the silver cup itself, leaving in its place only a tin coffee pot filled with copper coins and worthless IOU's.

Ike's noble moral protest—his attempt to preserve the virtues of the hunt, if only in the inner sanctum of his own solitary self—proves increasingly bootless. When his wife learns, for example, that Ike has refused his inheritance, she refuses all further sexual intercourse with him. Without property, Ike can never become a responsible father of their children. Thus does McCaslin becomes a fatherless and ne'er do

---

[21] Faulkner, *GDM*, 257.

[22] Ibid., 297.

[23] "I decline to accept the end of man. It is easy enough to say that man is immortal simply because he will endure: that when the last ding-dong of doom has clanged and faded from the last worthless rock hanging tideless in the last red and dying of evening, that even then there will be one more sound: that of his puny inexhaustible voice, still talking. I refuse to accept this. I believe that man will not merely endure: he will prevail. He is immortal, not because he alone among creatures has an inexhaustible voice, but because he has a soul, a spirit capable of compassion and sacrifice and endurance." (*The Faulkner Reader: Selections from the Works of William Faulkner* [New York: Modern Library, 1959] 4).

well carpenter—"not in mere static and hopeless imitation of the Nazarene," but rather as a new kind of racist himself.[24] We learn in "Delta Autumn" that because Ike had repudiated the plantation that had rightfully fallen to him, it has been taken over by Cass Edmonds' son Roth, a ruthless *roué* who treats its black inhabitants far less humanely than Ike might have done. In fact, Roth has formed a liaison with the octoroon great-granddaughter of Tomy's son Turl, in fact fathering a son on her. Roth tries to silence the mother of his child with a monetary payment that he makes Ike himself deliver. But Ike, who was once the defender of Negroes and the courageous critic of their exploitation, is scandalized to discover that this nameless woman is racially tainted and that she wants Roth not to pay her off but to marry her. In a burst of racist fury, Ike urges the young Negress to wed a fellow black and to move back to the North: "Maybe in a thousand or two thousand years in America, he thought. But not now! Not now! He cried, not loud, in a voice of amazement, pity, and outrage: 'You're a nigger.'"[25] The woman of such negligible importance as to have no name responds with a critique of Ike that brings his supposed moral revolution to less than naught—indeed, to shame and ignominy: "'Old man,' she said, 'have you lived so long and forgotten so much that you don't remember anything you ever knew or even felt about love?'"[26]

This dour conclusion to the Ike McCaslin stories may seem to indicate that Faulkner is a profound moral realist and that he shares something of Reinhold Niebuhr's suspicion of an ethical idealism that naïvely and self-righteously refuses to make necessary compromises with fallen human nature. Yet there is something far darker animating Faulkner's vision. What Nietzsche called the will-to-power is intrinsic to human existence, Faulkner suggests, and it operates in the woods no less than the town. For if the hunters did not kill their prey, they could not live. If blacks are not made slaves, some other race or group will just as surely be subjected to human bondage, whether legal or cultural. The institution of property merely systematizes this urge that the hunt spontaneously expresses. Unless we assert ourselves against nature,

---

[24] Faulkner, *GDM*, 309.
[25] Ibid., 361.
[26] Ibid., 363.

mastering it to our own will and use, we cannot survive even as animals, much less as humans. To be human is thus to own and to control and to kill. To have an ego is to be an egotist; it is to subdue others to our own interest. It is not ennobling tragedy that Faulkner displays in his fiction but the brazen will to power in a Hobbesian-cum-Darwinian world wherein all make war against all.

It follows that communion with the mysterious spirit that animates both the heavenly and earthly realms, the invisible and the visible worlds, filling human consciousness with longing for truth and beauty and goodness, cannot serve as the basis for human existence. For Faulkner, there is neither a God nor a community able to liberate human life from the endless internecine struggle of wills. We are left with an indeed bleak and withering solace. It is to be found only in an irrevocable sense of loss and guilt—in the bootless pangs of conscience—to which we are doomed as alienated and isolated creatures. "Knowledge of one's estrangement, and the unwillingness to make one's peace with it," writes John Sykes, "is in Faulkner's world the highest achievement of moral man."[27] Ike McCaslin is a noble and admirable failure, we must conclude, but also the inevitable failure that—in ultimate terms, and apart from the gospel—every human creature is destined to be. In no way does this dour fact lessen the worth of Faulkner's work. On the contrary, we owe him an unpayable debt for posing the sharpest possible critique of Christianity by offering the keenest and most drastic alternative to it—a vision of human life as having a history entirely of our own making, a history at whose core there is furious and resounding clash of wills signifying nothing.

III

"When you can assume that your audience holds the same beliefs you do," Flannery O'Connor declared in one of her most celebrated pronouncements, "you can relax a little and use more normal means of talking to it; when you have to assume that it does not, then you have to

---

[27]John Daniel Sykes Jr., "The Romance of Innocence and the Myth of History: Faulkner's Religious Critique of Southern Culture" (Ph.D. diss., University of Virginia, 1986) 201–202.

make your vision apparent by shock—to the hard of hearing you shout, and for the almost-blind you draw large and startling figures."[28] O'Connor was not referring to her secular audience alone as needing to be startled into attention; she was no less worried about her Christian readers. "If you live today," she wrote to Elizabeth Hester, "you breathe in nihilism. In or out of the Church, it's the gas you breathe."[29] Though she had no desire whatever to compete with Faulkner—knowing well that his talent was immeasurably greater than hers—she discerned that her fiction would need to embody a radical answer to the implicit nihilism of his work if it were worth any credence at all. The nothingness that Faulkner willingly and consciously embraced, as she saw with uncanny prescience, infects almost the whole of modern American culture, ecclesial no less than secular.

O'Connor was especially impatient with the glib sophistication of the elite who, without wrestling with the doubt that vexed Emily Dickinson and William Faulkner, sought refuge in a complacent humanism. At a New York dinner party hosted by the poet Robert Lowell and his then-wife Elizabeth Hardwick, the novelist Mary McCarthy was present along with O'Connor and others. McCarthy would later proclaim her emancipation from the church in *Memories of a Catholic Girlhood*.[30] Here she was content to opine that she still found the symbolism of the Eucharist to be useful for her fiction, though of course she didn't believe a word of its hocus-pocus. The ordinarily quiet and unassertive O'Connor—who rarely spoke to strangers unless first addressed, and then only with a shy hesitance—made a notoriously acid reply: "Well, if it's a symbol, to hell with it."[31] The shocked response

---

[28] Flannery O'Connor, *Mystery and Manners: Occasional Prose*, sel. and ed. Robert and Sally Fitzgerald (New York: Farrar Straus & Giroux, 1970) 34. Hereafter cited as *MM*.

[29] Flannery O'Connor, *The Habit of Being: The Letters of Flannery O'Connor*, ed. Sally Fitzgerald (New York: Farrar Straus & Giroux, 1979) 97. Hereafter cited as *HB*.

[30] Mary McCarthy, *Memories of a Catholic Girl* (New York: Quality Paperback Book Club, 1993).

[31] Flannery O'Connor, *The Collected Works of Flannery O'Connor*, Sally Fitzgerald, ed. (New York: The Library of America, 1988) 977. Hereafter cited as *CW*.

recorded by the other dinner guests must have been similar to the pattern described by William Buckley: if you mention God at a New York dinner party, you will be stared at; if you mention God twice, you will not be invited again.[32]

From the very beginning, O'Connor set her work against the grain of her culture and time. Not at all for the sake of any kind of Christian obscurantism was O'Connor a contrarian. Quite the opposite, she discerned that something far more radical and drastic would be required if both the church and the world were to be rescued from the abyss of nothingness. Unlike advocates of the civil religion that was aborning in the 1950s, that would triumph by the end of the millennium, and that continues to rule much of evangelical America in the early twenty-first century, O'Connor regarded *dogma* as a salutary rather than a pejorative term. Thus did she make her upper-case confession: "My stories have been watered and fed by Dogma."[33] She rejected the common view that dogmas divide while ethics unite ("deeds, not creeds") since doctrines are supposedly focused on esoteric matters, and thus are not amenable to practical use. O'Connor declared, quite to the contrary, that the creeds are precisely what unite Christians, however much we may remain divided about moral matters. The creeds are compressed narrative summaries of God's self-identification in Israel and Christ, and as such they are vehicles "of freedom and not of restriction."[34] "Dogma is an instrument for penetrating reality," O'Connor insisted. On another occasion she added that "Christian dogma is about the only thing left in the world that surely guards and respects mystery."[35]

O'Connor does not make mystery a synonym for puzzle, riddle, or conundrum—those things that balk the mind and stifle understanding. Nor was it a convenient locution for vaguely spiritual concerns. Here she is close to Dickinson, while delving much deeper—not merely into the invisible world but into the divine realm itself. To Claude Tresmontant, one of her favorite Old Testament scholars, mystery is, "To St. Paul and

---

[32] James M. Wall, "God as a Hobby: Public Language, Private Belief," *Christian Century* (6 October 1993).

[33] O'Connor, *CW*, 930.

[34] Ibid., 943.

[35] O'Connor, *MM*, 178.

to the early Christian thinkers...on the contrary the particular object of intelligence, its fullest nourishment. The *mysterion* is something so rich in intelligible content, so inexhaustibly full of delectation for the mind that no contemplation can ever reach its end. It is an eternal delectation of the mind."[36] The more deeply we penetrate mystery, the greater our ignorance grows. "Mystery isn't something that is gradually evaporating," O'Connor wrote to the skeptical Emory student (and future prize-winning poet) Alfred Corn. "It grows along with knowledge."[37]

It also develops only with fierce struggle, for O'Connor was quick to recognize that Christian faith can never be instrumental to any other good, no matter how noble. The gospel can never be employed as a mere means to some allegedly greater end—not even for such noble causes as economic justice, the recovery of family life, or peace between warring tribes and nations. This explains why, though she supported Martin Luther King Jr., she could never be fervent enthusiast for the civil rights movement. She rightly saw that, once the races were integrated, we would still be bedeviled by the crookedness of the human heart. Hence her unshakeable conviction that the gospel is not a mechanism or vehicle for anything else, especially the culture wars. It is, instead, the very basis for the drastically alternative community that God is seeking to create for the salvation of the whole world—the maculate and whoring Bride of Christ called the church.

O'Connor is not naïve about the church. She had little patience with "mass" Catholics who receive the weekly sacrament without its making any discernible difference in their lives. "The Church for them," she wrote, "is not the body of Christ but the poor man's insurance system."[38] When once asked what kind of Christian she would become if she were not a Roman Catholic, she replied, far from jestingly, that she would join a Pentecostal Holiness church. Belief for Flannery O'Connor

---

[36] Claude Tresmontant, *The Origins of Christian Philosophy* (New York: Hawthorn Books, 1963).

[37] O'Connor, *HB*, 489.

[38] Quoted by Williams Sessions, "'Then I discovered the Germans': O'Connor's Encounter with Guardini and German Thinkers" (unpublished essay.

must be radical or it is not belief at all. Faith is not another item in the laundry list of one's loyalties: it is all or nothing at all. Thus did she confess that she was "a Catholic (not because it's advantageous to my writing but because I was born and brought up one) and at some point in my life I realized that not only was I a Catholic but that this was all I was, that I was a Catholic not like someone else would be a Baptist or a Methodist but like someone else would be an atheist."[39] O'Connor had no patience for a merely polite piety. She admired Camus and Sartre and Faulkner because they took God seriously enough to deny his reality.[40] O'Connor's God-botherers resemble an atheist in a Peter De Vries novel who cannot forgive God for not existing. Yet O'Connor's atheists, whether Christian or secular, are usually unable to elude the divine Pursuer.

One of O'Connor's most memorable characters, The Misfit from "A Good Man is Hard to Find," is another of her God-botherers who

---

[39] O'Connor, *CW*, 930. Here, as in so many other things, O'Connor stands near to Walker Percy. Anyone living in an age as morally and religiously intolerable as ours, said Percy, has the right to demand "a gift commensurate with the offense":

> This life is much too much trouble, far too strange, to arrive at the end of it and then be asked what you make of it and have to answer, "Scientific humanism." That won't do. A poor show. Life is a mystery, love is a delight. Therefore, I take it as axiomatic that one should settle for nothing less than the infinite mystery and the infinite delight; i.e., God. In fact, I demand it. I refuse to settle for anything less. I don't see why anyone should settle for anything less than Jacob, who actually grabbed aholt of God and wouldn't let go until God identified himself and blessed him ("Questions They Never Asked Me," *Signposts in a Strange Land*, ed. Patrick Samway [New York: Farrar, Straus and Giroux, 1991] 417).

[40] The only reference to Emily Dickinson in O'Connor's letters comes in a second-hand report that her mentor Caroline Gordon had "discovered a streak of diabolism in Emily" (*CW*, 1172). I suspect that Gordon had read Dickinson's mockery of the no-God of New England pietism as secretly demonic, when in fact it was quite justified. As we have seen, Dickinson's esteem for the invisible and unknowable world (but not for the God who is its maker and finisher) makes her work sub-Christian but hardly diabolical.

sees that the real issue is not humanism or civil religion or any of the other substitutes for radical Christianity. He is an ex-Christian who, having felt the Abrahamic knife at his own throat, has embraced the nihilistic life of mass murder. He is a serial killer before they became the vogue. And so he is appalled that Jesus raised the dead. This bringer of death is profoundly offended that the Giver of Life cannot be dismissed as a mere holy man or eminent ethical figure, but must be adjudged as either the incarnate God or else a wholesale fraud. Unlike the psychopathic Misfit, the Grandmother is a proper lady who would gladly reduce Christian faith to sociology or culture or personality development if, in so doing, she could save her own life. She proves to be a good Christian atheist in the sense memorably specified by John Wesley when he said that we are practical atheists whenever we live as if God does not matter.[41] The Grandmother's self-assurance is so complete that she believes she can manage not only her own life but her family's as well. She also believes that she can convince even this serial killer to spare them all. In a crescendo of desperate defenses, she assures The Misfit that he is a good man, that he is not mediocre, that he should pray for Jesus to help him. In a last maniacal attempt to save herself, even at the cost of her own soul, the Grandmother denies her own Laodicean faith, declaring that perhaps Jesus did not raise the dead. Undeterred by these frenetic acts of self-protection, The Misfit kills her in cold blood and with cynical clarity: "She would of been a good woman," he observes with perfect redneck grammatical truthfulness, "if it had been somebody there to shoot her every minute of her life."[42]

O'Connor offered a witty clue to the comedy implicit in this seemingly gruesome story, which also entails the heartless execution of the Grandmother's son and daughter-in-law and three grandchildren, one of them an infant, when she observed that, while a lot of folks get killed in her work, nobody gets hurt. No one is made to cringe while anticipating a horrible death or to suffer abominable tortures. Instead, the Grandmother's otherwise nondescript son and daughter-in-law muster a surprising dignity as they face their own and their children's

---

[41] John Wesley, "Sermon 125," 1872. http://new.gbgm-umc.org/umhistory/wesley/sermons/125/ (accessed 23 July 2007).

[42] O'Connor, *CW*, 153.

deaths. And the Grandmother herself, though brutally slaughtered, is not spiritually injured. The Misfit murders her, instead, as he recoils in horror from her confession of their deep kinship. He pumps bullets into her chest only when she touches him on the shoulder in an outrageous act of mutual identification: "Why you're one of my babies," she cries. "You're one of my own children."[43] In this single saving gesture that costs the Grandmother her life, she at last drops all of her fearful self-justifications, all of her vain attempts to stay alive at whatever price. Finally she tells the truth: she is not a good woman, he is not a good man, they both are in terrible trouble, and they both need radical help.

It is a perfect climax first anticipated when The Misfit initially confronts the Grandmother. For she confesses her essential kinship with this calloused killer: "His face was as familiar to her as if she had known him all her life but she could not recall who he was."[44] The Misfit is her *Doppelgänger*, her shadow, her second and secret self. This is not to say that the Grandmother is a monster of malevolence. Like nearly everyone else, she is a well-meaning but self-serving person—an ordinary Christian atheist. Her life rests on nothing more solid than her desire for respectability. She wears a hat and gloves when traveling so that, if found dead beside the road, she will be recognized as a lady. She fantasizes about taking her family to see a plantation mansion with white columns and a secret panel. She sees a naked Negro child standing in the door of a shack, not as a child living in abject poverty, but as "a cute little pickaninny." Convinced that her own way is always best, she manages to prevail in all family disputes.

Yet her conscience is sufficiently pained at having lied about the antebellum mansion that, in a sudden upsurge of emotional guilt, she indirectly causes their car wreck. The problem is that Grandmother has no deeply ingrained moral and religious character; she is a genteel and unacknowledged nihilist. When faced with the threat of death, therefore, she is willing to deny her faith in the hope of saving her life. The Grandmother is a woman who lives by her own lights, though they provide little illumination of her sinful condition. She is Flannery O'Connor's portrait, not of *l'homme moyen sensuel*, but of the average

[43] Ibid., 152.

[44] Ibid., 146.

Christian soul living amidst the compromises and deceits of ordinary life with a blithe obliviousness to the nothingness opening beneath her. Hence her capitalized generic name: she is not one of our grandmothers; she is one of *us*.

The Misfit perhaps once found himself in her place: a man seeking the easiest path, avoiding all trouble, staying out of harm's way. But at some indiscernible point, his good intentions ceased to suffice. He began to cut corners and to trim edges until he gradually came to commit and to justify evil deeds. The Misfit is thus a mirror of the Grandmother, a man who might well have the face of her own child. Seeing at last the desperate place to which he has come, she can also see how much it is like her own. Such shared sinfulness is what The Misfit dares not confess, and so he guns the old lady down with three quick shots.

Though the Grandmother enunciates no overt faith, she seems to make what ancient Christian tradition called "a good death." She dissolves a lifetime of complacency and conceit in a brief acknowledgment of her Adamic solidarity with her killer. Her divinely happy ending is perhaps figured in her final posture. Sinking down to death in her puddling blood, she is not wrought with anguish or regret; instead, her legs are "crossed under her like a child's and her face [is] smiling up at the cloudless sky."[45] O'Connor leaves her ending open to conflicting interpretations: the Grandmother can also be construed as having remained as spiritually childish in death as in life. Yet the cruciform legs and the beatific expression and the inviting heavens suggest that she has died in a state of grace.

It must be confessed that few readers have discerned the Grandmother's saving gesture of grace without O'Connor's later explanation: "Her head clears for an instant and she realizes, even in her limited way, that she is responsible for the man before her and joined to him by ties of kinship which have their roots deep in the mystery she has been merely prattling about so far. And at this point, she does the right thing, she makes the right gesture."[46] As a still maturing writer,

---

[45] Ibid., 152.

[46] O'Connor, *MM*, 111–12. O'Connor explains in a letter why The Misfit shrinks from the old lady's touch: "Grace is never received warmly. Always a recoil...." (*CW*, 1150).

O'Connor would not again make the moment of self-awakening so obscure, even though her endings would remain no less disturbing. They leave us with a chilling sense of our own complicity in the evils that her characters often commit.

If the Grandmother's final state is ambiguous, The Misfit's is not. He is a confessed nihilist who, unlike her, has wrestled hard with the God of the gospel. His unbelief is as thoughtful as her piety is unreflective. We learn, from his reported confession to a prison psychiatrist, that he has been reared as a Bible-believing Baptist. Having never heard of Sigmund Freud, The Misfit responded with a wondrous literalism to the psychiatrist's suggestion that his homicidal acts were products of an unconfessed Oedipal desire to slay his father. The Misfit will have nothing of such reductionist psychology. In his brilliantly cornpone way, he denies that he is a victim of his unconscious drives: he is, instead, the proud agent of his own will-to-power: "It was a head-doctor at the penitentiary said what I done was kill my daddy but I known that for a lie. My daddy died in nineteen ought nineteen [an unusual year, to say the least] of the epidemic flu and I never had a thing to do with it. He was buried in the Mount Hopewell Baptist churchyard and you can go there and see for yourself."[47]

The Misfit rejects the faith of his fathers because he's a good materialist, though he's far from knowing it: he will not credit ancient events that he cannot empirically verify. Since he was not present to witness Jesus' miraculous acts, he will not believe them. Yet his literalism also has its merits: it will not permit him to make the typical modernist disjunction between Jesus' message and his miracles—as if one could keep the former as moral truth while discarding the latter as crass superstition. The Misfit refuses this convenient dichotomy between the human and the divine. Jesus' power over physical death, he knows, is the mark of his power over spiritual death. Christ's raising of the dead constitutes a command for The Misfit also to be transformed: to surrender his proud sufficiency and to embrace the love of God and neighbor. From the fundamentalist sermons of his Baptist boyhood, The Misfit knows that he must either gladly seize or bitterly reject Jesus' invitation. There is no safe middle way, no accommodating alternative to

---

[47] Ibid., 150.

the drastic extremes of belief and unbelief, no bland neutrality between Jesus Christ and absolute nothingness.

> "Jesus was the only One that ever raised the dead," The Misfit continued, "and He shouldn't have done it. He thown everything off balance. If He did what He said, then it's nothing for you to do but thow away everything and follow Him, and if He didn't, then it's nothing for you to do but enjoy the few minutes you got left the best way you can—by killing somebody or burning down his house or doing some other meanness to him. No pleasure but meanness," he said, and his voice had become almost a snarl.[48,]

The Misfit has pushed the logic of his unbelief to its dreadful conclusion. He sees, as O'Connor often observed, that ours is not a culture of moral progress and evolutionary development but the culture of death. The final alternatives, The Misfit discerns, are not religion and science but the gospel and nihilism. Like Ivan Karamazov, he wants to return his ticket to the arena of life. But unlike Ivan, The Misfit has chosen nothingness as the substance of his being rather than a mere theoretical possibility. He is determined to offer scandalous signs of his spiritual offenses. In practicing his nihilism, The Misfit is not tempted by anything so small as theft. He is a murderer rather than a robber because, as he confesses, "Nobody had nothing I wanted."[49] To have stolen desirable objects would have been to acknowledge the goodness of things other than his own sovereign self-will. The Misfit relishes, instead, the deeds of annihilation: murder and arson and cruelty. They alone are able to display his naked *Wille zur Macht*.

Yet The Misfit is a civilized Nietzschean, a courteous killer whose manners match those of the Grandmother. He is embarrassed, for example, that he has no shirt to wear in the presence of women, having shed his prison uniform in making his escape. The Misfit always addresses the Grandmother as "Lady," and he always uses a proper

---

[48] Ibid., 152. The many corrected versions of "thown" betray a fundamental deafness to Southern peckerwood speech.

[49] OConnor, *CW*, 150.

"Yes'm" and "Nome" in responding to her. O'Connor was a stout defender of such outward politeness, but not when it serves to obscure the canker of soft-centered sentimentality. The Misfit's misery lies, he believes, in his failure to meet the expectations of society. He has failed to conform to the world's standards and thus to "fit in," to live the balanced and well-adjusted life that perhaps the prison psychiatrist had urged upon him.

For all the brilliance of his fundamentalist nihilism, The Misfit fails to see that it is not Nietzschean nonconformity but Christian eccentricity that he needs: to acquire another Center than the world's hub, to become a fool for Christ's sake, to be re-formed in the image of the cross. Gradually, therefore, he slides into whining self-justification. At first he admits that he is not a good man but a guilty convict, but finally alleges that he cannot even remember his evil acts and thus that he does not deserve to be punished for them. "I call myself The Misfit," he said, "because I can't make what all I done wrong fit what all I gone through in punishment."[50] Brave Nietzschean will to power thus ends in solipsistic victimology. If only he had been present at Jesus' miracles, The Misfit explains, "I would have known and I wouldn't be like I am now."[51] The Misfit is a closet Platonist in his belief that knowledge equals virtue and ignorance equals sin: he wants merely to *know* the truth, not to *do* it. Thus is the Misfit's voice choking with self-pity when the Grandmother extends him her surprising gesture of solidarity. And as soon as he kills her, the red-eyed homicide wipes his glasses, fogged as they are with a terrible tenderness toward himself. O'Connor discerns what our churches and culture have both failed to mark: the alternative to the hard realism of the Gospel is not an equally hard nihilism but a squishy self-pity. Sentimentality, she said, is to Christianity as obscenity is to art—it is a kind of pornography, an unearned feeling of either sweet solace or bitter.

If our teaching is to have any real trenchancy and purchase, it will have to be rooted in a Christian radicalism such as O'Connor so memorably enfleshes in her fiction. On the one hand, we will need to confess that we Christians often have ourselves to blame when the world

[50] Ibid., 151.
[51] Ibid., 152.

turns away from the gospel either by neglect or rejection. So poorly have our churches provided the world a drastically alternative way of life that our best writers have had cause to refuse any privileging of Christianity in their work. On the other hand, we will also praise them for having shown us what is right and good about a skepticism, which, in the case of Emily Dickinson, refuses all false versions of the Gospel. Her poetry also enfleshes a mystical faith in the unknowable, which, as Christians, we have due cause to embrace, even its spiritual incompleteness. So do we owe to William Faulkner unbounded gratitude for revealing the horrors of a culture built on the subjection of an entire race to their allegedly Christian masters, even if he remains despairing about any permanent remedy to the perpetual domination of the weak by the strong.

Only a non-defensive kind of Christian radicalism is sufficiently confident to affirm the work of the Spirit in these worthy interlocutors and antagonists. For there must not be a whit of smugness in our appropriation of the great canonical non-Christian texts of our literary tradition. There is no such smugness to be found anywhere in Flannery O'Connor's work. Yet neither is there a whiff of apology. She dedicated her life to the singular proposition that must also be ours as Christian teachers and scholars: If we are faithful to the God of Jesus Christ and his church, we will always be honored: whether in being persecuted and resented for having maintained our integrity or else in being welcomed with joy by our students and colleagues.

University, Seminary, and Congregation: Contexts for Theology

SAMUEL J. MIKOLASKI

During the early 1960s at the New Orleans Baptist Theological Seminary, a young student named Fisher Humphreys came into the first term of my systematic theology class for his introduction to theology. In that first hour he caught the vision that systematic theology should be the subject matter of his life. Later I recommended him to friends at Oxford University for graduate studies. Subsequently he completed his doctorate at New Orleans, and when my wife Jessie and I returned to Canada for ministry, Fisher succeeded me as theology professor at the New Orleans Seminary. He has had a distinguished career as professor, counselor to students and ministers, and theological leader among Southern Baptists. It is an honor to contribute to this dedicatory volume.

In this essay I address the loss of Christianity as a hermeneutic in America and propose some elements of a remedy within the academy, especially among Christian colleges, universities, and seminaries. From Augustine until the mid-twentieth century the Christian worldview was dominant culturally not only in Britain, Europe, North America, and the former European colonies overseas, but also within the academy as the prime metaphysical paradigm.

For example, with what can only be called religious fervor, Richard Rorty promotes an anti-Christian-religion agendum in the American academic community advocating a completely naturalistic perspective of life in the universe. This is strikingly ironic in view of his familial origins as the heir of his maternal grandfather Walter Rauschenbusch, the New York German Baptist pastor who created the Social Gospel of Liberal Christianity seventy years ago.

For Rorty, pragmatism displaces religion, though perhaps I should say it embraces all religions provided that they are secularized. In *Contingency, Irony, and Solidarity* he argues that no single cohering vision of the nature of reality and of human life in the universe is possible.[1] Instead, he opts for a practical, romantic polytheism within a liberal democracy.[2] This is a new religion created in America. Secular, social democracy displaces the fellowship of the saints of his local Baptist church ancestors, though the latter remains, I think, a haunting ideal for him.

Let us consider the metaphysical base of Rorty's developing social construct. How can the prevailing secular need-satisfaction behavioral model transcend its fundamental ego-centrism in the romantic polytheism he envisions?

What can be built on a non-binding moral footing (in his language, a non-creedal footing)? How is one to judge between diverse, often rival, polytheistic claims? Along the lines of what ethical principles will the social solidarity for which he pleads be fashioned? It appears that for Rorty, traditional Christian values of love as self-giving and other-regarding, not the self-interest of behavioral need-satisfaction responses, are key feature elements of his utopia, but absent their author and sustainer, God. That such utopias have failed miserably in the past, as in the case of the genocidal Marxist social experiment of the past century in the Soviet Union, escapes his analysis and criticism.[3]

Evangelistic secularism now extends to American politics in the popularly circulated allegation that religion, particularly committed Christian faith, is a menace to the formation of equitable public policy in America. To buttress this allegation, President George W. Bush's conversion and personal commitment to Christian faith and ideals are cited disparagingly.[4]

---

[1] Richard Rorty, *Contingency, Irony, and Solidarity* (Cambridge MA: Cambridge University Press, 1989).

[2] See Richard Rorty, *Achieving Our Country* (Cambridge MA: Harvard University Press, 1998).

[3] Note the trenchant critique in Richard Grossman, ed., *The God that Failed* (New York: Harper and Row, 1949) first published in 1944 in the midst of the World War II devastations. In this book former Marxists such as Arthur Koestler, Louis Fisher, and Stephen Spender mourn their previous obsession (Augustine's "fantasies of the mind") with Marxist materialist dogma.

[4] An example is the strident article by Garry Wills, "A Country Ruled by Faith," *New York Review of Books*, 16 November 2006.

Can we return to a more balanced view of confessional Christianity's contribution to the formation of the American political system and social ideals and to what Christians, including evangelicals, can continue to contribute to American life?

Christianity came into a world richly furnished with ideas. How did it come about that, as a result of the life and teachings of Jesus of Nazareth and the activities of a group of undistinguished and largely ethnically and culturally insulated followers in Galilee and Jerusalem, ancient political and social institutions, the cults, and the schools were displaced by Christianity?

The Christian doctrine of creation and grace is supremely anti-reductionist and is person-preserving. The choices before us are: do we choose theoretical models that increase freedom or those that limit freedom? The higher the spirituality of personal life, the less causally predictable are its choices because, as the spirituality of life increases, its choices refer less to the antecedents of action and more to moral goals in light of which the action is taken.

At first the early Christians had little time to contemplate philosophical and public policy implications of their heritage and faith because of their intense missionary work on the one hand and the persecution they had to endure on the other. But gradually they discerned the differences between their own firmly held views and the prevailing ethos created chiefly by the idealist and materialist schools of the ancient world alongside the popular polytheistic cults.

The philosophical idealism of ancient Greece and Rome was essentially mystical. In it the visible world is unreal, as Plato suggested in his Myth of the Cave.[5] Absolute being transcends this transient physical order and is adumbrated in beauty, goodness, and truth. The idealist heritage is traceable through gnosticism, Manicheanism, and Neoplatonism to modern forms of idealism. Systems of idealism have tended to denigrate the empirical world, and their views have been inimical to discrete full-blown personhood.

On the other hand, ancient materialism has remained remarkably consistent to modern times, with the addition of biological and

---

[5] Plato, *The Republic* (Book 7), trans. Paul Shorey (Cambridge MA: Harvard University Press, 1935) par. 514–16.

psychological characteristics. Leucippas, Democritus, and Epicurus said that all of reality is comprised of atoms in the void, denying the independent reality of the mind and the existence of the soul. Modern atomism is indistinguishable except for the dynamic rather than "hard bits of stuff" concept of the atom; modern hedonism, its ethical derivative, is indistinguishable from its ancient Epicurean counterpart. Mind is simply the physical functioning of the brain cells; there is no inner spirit, mind, or person. Freedom, as B. F. Skinner and Pavlov argued, is an illusion.

For their part, Christians declared that the world was created by God and that persons as spiritual beings were created to enjoy loving relationships with one another and fellowship with God. Human life is the art of the Creator and discrete personhood is not only the goal of redemption but is, as well, the highest level of reality. Christianity became an attractive alternative. In an age of brutality and high inflation, Christians cared about people. The Christian conventicles had a powerful sense of community and were radically egalitarian; each was a drastic social experiment, a cave of Adullum. Their ethical standards were high, their religious devotion to the one true God was intense, and their discipleship life-encompassing. The power and vigor of such dedication must be seen in relation to their view of God, the world, morality, and man. The existential appeal of the faith was joined inextricably to the defense of essential humanity within the terms of the creationist-personhood perspective.

Thus the Christian perspective may be more important to the future of humanity than has been assumed by many moderns. Ancient and modern forms of idealism have been substantially displaced by varieties of contemporary transcendentalism, and ancient atomism has developed into naturalism and behaviorism. The pursuit of personal identity in our time reflects deep concern about the future of humanity. In a unique way the Bible trumpets the call to arms for the defense of humanity. As fashioned in the image of God, each human soul is of infinite value. What we are and how we treat one another fall under a moral standard that is not purely behavioral.

One of my favorite writers is Camille Paglia, atheist, classicist, social critic, author, and professor of Humanities and Media Studies at the University of the Arts in Philadelphia. She was interviewed in *Salon* as one of its founding columnists.[6] She observed that though she is an atheist and secular Democrat politically, she believes that "without religion we'd have anarchy." She went on to comment that religion is a metaphysical system that honors the largeness of the universe that is absent from the cynical ideologies currently promoted by the elite universities. She added that the more (ideologically) liberal parents are, the less contact children have with religious ideas.

Fear of the political aspirations of certain Christian triumphalist fundamentalists has led to a misleading version of the doctrine of the separation of church and state, the point of which is, in fact, that the US "simply has no official state religion," she says.[7] Nevertheless, the formative influence in our intellectual heritage came from Puritan descendants in New England. Many universities, like Harvard and Yale, were founded on religious principles. Secular liberalism, she said, has become bourgeois and materialistic, offering no passionate engagement in life to appeal to young people. It has become "snide, elitist and politically marginalized."[8]

How can Christians in America recapture a place in the dialogue that leavens the formation of ideas, ideals, and the cultural ethos? I attribute the loss of evangelical intellectual influence in America to modern American evangelical rootlessness and the impression many in America have that the evangelical representation of Christianity is sectarian.

During the past century a significant and regrettable change has occurred in evangelical seminary education, the effects of which have been heightened by the extensive development of university and college departments of religion, some of which offer doctoral research programs. The aspect of this change that most concerns me is the eclipse of patristics (and medieval) studies and the wholesale transfer of serious patristics studies to universities and colleges.

---

[6] Camille Paglia, "Salon Interview" 27 October 2006, *Salon*, http://www.salon.com/opinion/feature/2006/10/27/paglia/print.html (accessed 9 July 2007) 7.

[7] Ibid., 8.

[8] Ibid., 8.

More than forty years ago I introduced courses in the Ante-Nicene, Nicene, and Post-Nicene Fathers at the New Orleans Baptist Theological Seminary, which, following a "taste-and-see" attitude of a few students who were prepared to test the novelty, rapidly became popular courses. Nevertheless, in most seminaries such courses are "introductions"—surveys of a period, the writers, and their texts. Rarely is time allowed and effort made to understand and evaluate critically the texts themselves.

A supporting anecdote: For the past forty years, almost without fail, every four years I have attended the International Patristics Conference at Oxford University (my *alma mater*). As well, for a great deal of that time I have been a member of the North American Patristics Society. Although I have rarely been able to attend the annual meetings of the latter, I regard their *Journal of Early Christian Studies* a must read.[9] Bear in mind that I am not a patristics scholar, though I have diligently read the writings of many of the early church fathers.

Patristics studies have burgeoned in universities and colleges during the past half-century, partly synchronized with the development of religious studies programs and programs of research in comparative religion and the intellectual roots of the major world religions.

In seminary curricula this shift is due in large measure to the alleged greater relevance of "practical courses"—leave the theological, philosophical, historical and comparative courses to the departments of religion. A quick overview of the ancient periods will suffice. I have heard this said in not a few faculty committee meetings. In many evangelical schools intensive courses are offered in Reformation and post-Reformation theology. As welcome as these are, the trend has created the impression that evangelical Christianity and its key confessional statements begin with the Reformation, with the concurrent impression formed within the Christian community and in society generally that evangelicals are a historical novelty somewhat disconnected from the roots of the Christian heritage, except for their Bible-thumping. The Roman Catholic, Anglican, and Eastern Orthodox

[9] *Journal of Early Christian Studies*, published quarterly for the North American Patristics Society by the John Hopkins University Press.

traditions have the field clear to themselves to claim continuity with the apostolic heritage.

The American media have picked up on this. Most current commentators on religious and theological questions on radio and television talk-shows are of the Roman Catholic or other Episcopal traditions. Evangelical commentary on religious topics is now rarely sought by the major media except to illustrate what is regarded as quaint or extreme. Most serious Christian commentary is sought from Roman Catholics who now dominate the voicing of opinion in the public square. The following well-known media figures are all Roman Catholic: Peggy Noonan, Bill O'Reilly, Sean Hannity, Larry Kudlow. Exceptions are few: John Kasich and Cal Thomas.

In the best interests of the churches I suggest renewed emphasis on foundational patristics studies in seminary curricula and the curricula of Christian college departments of religion. I suggest, first, Clement of Rome, Athenagoras, and Irenaeus; second, the Nicene Era; and third, Augustine.

Clement of Rome

As the earliest of the post-canonical Christian writings, from the church at Rome to the church at Corinth, *1 Clement* is a fraternal, not Episcopal, letter that speaks of the consent of the church in its election of leaders and deals with the quality of life within a congregation.

Clement, probably an elder of the church at Rome who was responsible for communicating with sister congregations elsewhere, stresses the importance of tradition of a very particular kind: the norms of Scripture buttressed by common sense. His array of Scripture references from both the Old and the New Testaments is striking, but his fundamental appeal is to the Scripture-informed conscience of the Corinthian Christians that he calls "the hidden depths of the heart" (21:2). This informing is shaped by the "rule of our tradition" (7:2), commonly called "The Rule of Faith," which is the truth of the Gospel anticipated in the Old Testament, fulfilled in Christ, and transmitted by Christ through the apostles to us. Clement urges, "We should give up empty and futile concerns, and turn to the glorious and holy rule of our tradition." (7:2)[10] This is not an appeal to the dead hand of tradition; rather it contends that the living word of truth conserved in the Scriptures has been transmitted to them and is continually being transmitted from one generation to another (note also 2:1; 13:1–2; 22:1; 42:1). Additionally he cites many items of folk wisdom to show that the force of truth to any rational mind is inescapable, from whatever source. If one is looking for that which is practical from the church fathers, here it is.

Athenagoras

Athenagoras was a converted philosopher who lived in Athens and addressed his *Plea* to the Emperor Marcus Aurelius and his son on behalf of persecuted Christians on the occasion of the emperor's visit to Athens in the latter part of the second century A.D. Methodologically it differs markedly from *1 Clement*. Clement writes an "in house" letter to Christians and cites Scripture copiously, while Athenagoras writes to a non-Christian from the standpoint of the logic of the Christian faith and the place of Christians as good citizens in society.[11] It is an excellent example of ancient apologetics that exhibits core concepts of Christianity without using the Scriptures as a club.

Athenagoras (knowing that Marcus Aurelius was a Stoic philosopher of note) pleads for toleration for Christians on grounds of the Stoic concept of Natural Justice. Further, he argues that it is more rational to believe in one God than in many gods. Monotheism is superior to polytheism, which many pagan poets and philosophers had already abandoned, and the Christian doctrine of divine providence is superior to (Stoic) determinism. He points out that Marcus Aurelius' own Stoicism predicates the non-material, singular reality of the divine causal Spirit that pervades the universe. He emphasizes the rationality of biblical teaching. He ends by satirizing endless philosophical babble about behavior by ethicists of the day while they fail to restrain their own

---

[10] *The Letter of the Church of Rome to the Church of Corinth*, commonly called First Clement in *Early Christian Fathers*, ed. Cyril C. Richardson (Philadelphia: Westminster Press 1953) 43–73.

[11] Ibid., 1, 37, 330–340.

impulses and commit egregious acts, such as the sexual abuse of children.[12]

Irenaeus

Irenaeus illustrates how one can be a defender of core elements of the Christian faith—he was indeed a vigorous polemicist against the gnostics of his time—while at the same time not be side-tracked from the primary task of preaching and extending the gospel. The conversion of many in Gaul, which is an example of a very significant church growth movement, was due to Irenaeus' intense missionary work.

Ancient gnostics believed that redeeming knowledge is insight into our true spiritual self, that redemption comes about by illumination, and that to bring this illumination was the task of the earthly Jesus. The later *Gospel of Philip* and the more recent release of the *Gospel of Judas* reflect parallel sentiments: we create gods of our own self-definition, not unlike Carl Jung's archetypes as images of the instincts. These take personality-like form, whether as alter-egos or, like the ancients, as gods and goddesses that stereotype values and emotions.

Not only are Irenaeus' writings important as polemics against both ancient and modern efforts to create God in human likeness, but also as a striking instance of the role of "The Rule of Faith," the content and truth of the Scriptures, which are based upon factual data and information attested to by witnesses, not illumination conveyed by secret initiation.

The Nicene Era

Second, I believe that intensive study of the Nicene era, including the formation in A.D. 325 of the Creed of Nicaea, the Constantinopolitan Creed of A.D. 381 (commonly known as the Nicene Creed), and the Creed of Chalcedon (A.D. 451) should be mandatory in the theological education of ministers for the churches.

These readings will lead students into the formation of early Christology, including Christ's deity, the two natures of Christ as divine

---

[12] Ibid., 34.

and human, the doctrine of the Trinity, and the formation and mission of the early Christians in the ancient world.

Third, in the transition from the patristic period to medieval times, including the rapid decline of the Roman Empire as an international force, the writings of Augustine should be a standard academic requirement.

Augustine on Reason and Faith

Augustine's theology was created in light of his conversion that entailed repentance and faith in Christ but also a dramatic metaphysical paradigmatic shift. The need of a paradigmatic shift in modern Western thinking applies particularly to today's church and its place in society as a hermeneutical witness.

How do we move beyond Augustine's personal conversion cry ("Thou hast made us for thyself and our hearts are restless till they may have found their rest in thee" [*Confessions* 1.1]) to the metaphysic of a world view—Camille Paglia's "largeness of the universe" that modern cynicism dismisses?

Augustine's theory of knowledge is that reason connects the data of the senses into a coherent continuum. It distinguishes and connects things that are learned (*De Ordine* 2.3). "By reason all those other things and also reason itself become known and are held together in knowledge" (*De Libero Arbitrio* 2.4).[13] The prime function of reason is to serve as the vehicle of faith, not faith as credulity, but faith issuing in understanding.

Nevertheless, in our condition we humans don't know enough (due to our finitude) and we distort what we do know (due to our sinning). The consequences are two-fold: first, we become enamored of "phantasies" (*Confessions* 3.6), by which Augustine means erroneous paradigms (in his case his absorption with Manichaeanism, Platonism, Skepticism) that, second, become ingrained as habits of thought in the way we see things. We end up neither willing the good perfectly, nor nilling the bad entirely (*Confessions* 8.9–10). This is what Augustine calls "imperfect piety"—our failure to commit unreservedly to truth and the

---

[13] Augustine, *Confessions*, *The Basic Writings of Saint Augustine*, 2 vols., ed. Whitney J. Oates (New York: Random House, 1948).

pursuit of truth perfectly. The failure becomes a self-fulfilling sequence: "because of a perverse will was lust made; and lust indulged in became custom; and custom not resisted became necessity" (*Confessions* 8.5).

This is a splendid backdrop to modern attitudes regarding nature, science, and the meaning of human existence. The dominant secular paradigm (for Augustine, the dominant phantasm) of our generation is American naturalism, which is ancient Democritean and Epicurean Materialism dressed up in modern hedonist garb as the, often cynical, pursuit of the good life.

One of my favorite philosophy professors was an ardent advocate of naturalism in its classical Epicurean and contemporary American hedonist form. He argued that the behavior of all organisms is conditioned solely by the biological and psychological urge to gratify the senses—the need-satisfaction cycle. This modern version of the ancient pleasure principle claims that what organisms in fact do is the true meaning of what they ought to do if those actions meet need or gratify the senses.

My professor insisted that altruism is intellectually and emotionally suicidal. The pursuit of any object of any interest defines the good. On this premise only self-gratification is the true motive for action. It remained a puzzle for me: if psychological hedonism is the root of action, why should intelligence lead any of us to care about anyone else except to conserve that person or that something for the sake of one's own gratification? Add to this ancient Epicurean and modern atomism and one arrives full circle at the concept that all of reality has come about by the chance concatenation of atoms and that to attribute mind or purpose or freedom of action to such a structure or within such a structure is sheer nonsense.

This was the question put to me: should I make pleasure the intrinsic motive of actions? Projecting such a thesis as the foundation of life was troubling. There was the unresolved ambivalence between egoism and altruism. Hedonists tended to minimize reason as the foundation of their premise but then went on to minimize motor-affective responses with regard to future actions when they advocated "highly refined," "permanent as against transient pleasures," and sought to distinguish between "negative" and "positive" motor-affective responses. As well, claims by behaviorists to being scientific mystified me. So much was said about behavioral responses when, as Richard Feynman the physicist argued, many of the most important things of life are not empirically discernible or manageable—not the least of which is an adequate accounting of freedom and the will.[14]

Is my willing (determining) to do something simply the last act in a behaviorally conditioned series? If so, when applied to human experience how can one account for the socially detaching power of religion in the lives of many martyrs? One may assign new uses to terms such as freedom, the good, or that which is right as against that which is wrong, but this does not and cannot preempt the realities for which the words stand. Reality entails something more intrinsic than mere behavior.

Paul deals with the popular hedonism of his day, which is virtually identical with our modern "pursuit of the good life" ethos. For Paul, the divinely motivating purpose principle trumped the naturalistic behavior principle.

Few students of Paul's writings grasp the distinctions he makes between a purposeful universe and one driven by the chance movements of atoms or the intensity with which he draws that contrast. In a satirical thrust he speaks of two ways in which "things that are not" (the *ta m_ onta* of ancient Greek metaphysics) are conceived: the atomism of Democritus and Epicurus as allegedly the only real things with the things that are not (i.e., despised spiritual realities). Paul says that atomism becomes a form of self-deception if it is thought capable of explaining all of reality. People, Paul says, become "slaves to the elements of the universe," where *elements* does not mean letters of the alphabet as some think, but the atoms of a mechanistically conceived universe.[15]

Paul agreed with the "pursuit of the good life" advocates of his day that our present life is an interim but not, as they said, between a past

---

[14] Richard Feynman, *The Meaning of It All* (London: Allan Lane, The Penguin Press 1998).

[15] 1 Cor 1:29 RSV. In classical Greek materialist metaphysics *on* identified what is real, while *me on* identified the not-real, as in Democritus. *Stocheion*, translated "element" identified the atom, that which is real in materialist metaphysics (N. D. DeWitt, *Epicurus and His Philosophy* [Westwood CT: Greenwood Press, 1954] 159). This is Paul's sense of the meaning of elements in Gal 4:3, 9 not "spirits." Note also 2 Pet 3:10–12 RSV.

black eternity and a future black eternity. There is more to the universe than matter and motion. While they construct theories about atoms that they cannot see and that theories they claim are not myths, the truth of the way things are beckons: the universe is not purposeless and its essential reality is spiritual in nature. The key to living is not avoidance of envy, ambition, and competition on the one side and the pursuit of pleasure on the other (all based on the principle of expedience). Neither is it a universe empty of over-arching morality nor is it a commitment, with only the scanning of advantage and disadvantage in any action or in any relationship.

What were the golden texts of the good life for those who pursued it so ardently, and should these become the tablets posted on the entrance foyer of my soul? Paul's scalpel (Phil 3:19) is sharp and discerning: First, fascination with food—"their God is their belly." Metrodorus had urged that "the pleasure of the stomach is the beginning and root of all good." Second, obsession with sex—"they glory in their shame."[16] Lanctantius said that all the dogs of philosophy were barking around Epicurus. Paul's warning "beware of the dogs" meant that humans should not flaunt sexuality publicly as dogs do. Third, "their mind is on earthly things," which means more than worldliness. Rather, it means a this-life-only attitude, a totally materialistic, purposeless view of reality. Hence Paul repeatedly contrasts flesh and spirit, by which he does not denigrate earthly existence nor the human body, but he disparages a mindset that views existence purely as a set of motor-affective responses.

What drives us must not be merely an external drive but an impelling inner suasion. This is, as A. N. Whitehead said, "the eternal urge of desire" for realization of the potentialities that inhere in life and that life's opportunities offer to us as spiritual beings.[17] This is never a matter of "whatever turns you on" or "makes you feel good." Rather, it is the decisiveness of an ideal, which, by the power of its attraction, draws

---

[16] N. W. DeWitt, *St. Paul and Epicurus* (Toronto: Ryerson Press, 1954) 23–25.

[17] A. N. Whitehead, *Process and Reality* (New York: Social Science Book Store, 1929) 522. Note also *Religion in the Making* (New York: MacMillan Co., 1930) 59–60, 157–159.

toward God-given, life-fulfilling purpose, not for self-gratification, but to grasp the truth of the way things are in order to more adequately contribute to what humanity may become.

The insights of Karl Popper, philosopher of science, reinforce the preceding discussion as to how our knowledge of the world is formed, whether by common sense knowledge or scientific knowledge, and try to correlate these insights with the limited knowledge about which Augustine and the Apostle Paul speak. Popper argues that the modern problem of knowledge is not the problem of our perceptions—epistemological—but the notion materialists entertain that knowledge is built up inductively from observations, that we observe and then inductively generalize as to what the world is and how it functions.[18]

Popper explores the mindset we bring to interpretation of data. He argues that an unquestioned perspective develops that pervades a particular field of enquiry and deforms its results. The results become normal science or current orthodoxy over long periods of time until support for their vested interests fades. The resulting paradigm—what Augustine called a fantasy of the mind—becomes politically or scientifically correct thought.

For Popper, truth is not merely a perspective immanent to a field of inquiry. Truth is objective. It is not contingent in relation to time, place, and paradigm. Popper strives to know the truth, that which is actually the case about the object of study, even though the ultimate truth may permanently elude us.

The scandal to modern practitioners of empiricism is that Popper denied the validity of induction and that scientific knowledge is certain. Claims for the inductive method of science, he adds, "had to be replaced by the method of (dogmatic) trial and (critical) error elimination."[19]

While we do test our understanding of the laws and processes we attribute to the natural order, such understanding is never certain or complete. It is and must continually be revised, but prior understanding of the way we think things work before observation, comes first.

---

[18] Paul Arthur Schilpp, ed., *The Philosophy of Karl Popper*, 2 vols. (La Salle IL: Open Court, 1974).

[19] Karl Popper, *Unended Quest: An Intellectual Biography* (La Salle IL: Open Court, 1976) 52.

Observations come later. Only at critical points of divergence (the falsification of previously held theory) does new insight occur. It is likely that in the present state of our scientific knowledge the true nature of reality—that which is actually the case—is probably not even imaginable.

Reversal, or a critical juncture of clarification, if not falsification, is what I take to be the meaning of Paul's use of the word knowledge as *epignosis*, which is transforming insight that overturns previous understanding. Progress occurs spiritually, as well as scientifically, only by the destruction of prior certitudes as these distorted our understanding of the nature of spiritual or material reality. This is, I think, what Paul meant when he said that "now we know in part" (1 Cor 13:12).

There remains a key metaphysical problem: how to account for the actualizing of life and form in nature. Is a completely naturalistic or completely idealistic answer credible in view of the displacement of former categories and the likelihood that some of today's categories will also be left behind? To believe that impersonal matter, which may have a limiting potency, and randomness by means of organic naturalism have produced a rational universe has become unpalatable to not a few scientists. The alternative to materialistic naturalism is some form of idealistic panpsychism or panentheism. Christians hold that creation of the world by a transcendent and personal Creator reaches to the heart of the matter.

Augustine on a Philosophy of History

Augustine is the first Christian father to formulate a philosophy of history: how Christians should view earthly kingdoms and the crucial role of hope in human experience.

Can human beings live without hope? There is a growing consensus in this post-modern cynical age that they cannot. It is striking that during its 1968 centennial year the University of California should have organized a conference on "The Future of Hope" featuring presentations by Ernst Bloch and Emil Fackenheim, among others.

Proponents of naturalistic, deterministic metaphysical systems argue that the universe is not and cannot be open-ended. But the failed modern attempt to blend economic and social utopianism with metaphysical determinism has forced revision to a possibility-oriented view of history, as in the case of the German Marxist Ernst Bloch.[20] He turns his back on a significant element of German cultural theory, namely, despair (*Weltangst*) about the human condition. In an earlier paper that he read at the 1968 University of California centennial year conference titled "Man as Possibility," Bloch prefigured the outlines of his later, major work. He begins with dreams. There is nothing in history, he says, that has not been sketched out in advance or planned in vision or dream. The only indestructible thing (a word-play against fixed determinism) is the "unconditionally indeterminate," namely freedom and hope: "I contend that the world is open, that objectively real possibility exists in it, and not simply determined necessity or mechanical determinism."[21]

At the same conference, Emil Fackenheim, in his paper titled "The Commandment to Hope: A Response to Contemporary Jewish Experience," says that the Hebrew prophets convey the message of hope as divine command. Israel is commanded not to despair but to live in hope. He adds that the tensions between particularity and universality in the Hebrew Bible, along with alienation and return, extend the paradigm of God's dealings to humanity in general beyond Israel. The key to the prophets is *God will do it*. Modern utopians have wrongly said *we will do it*. In the Hebrew Bible, says Fackenheim, the Jew is forbidden to despair of God; to exist as a Jew after Auschwiz is to be committed to hope.[22]

Philosophically, the Greeks saw history in mythological terms, as nature (*physis*) unfolding itself. The endless succession of events entails a dialectic of time—the cycle of rise and fall, of conflict, and of polarization of opposites as proposed by Empedocles. Epicurean theory was based on deterministic atomism and was thus behavioral and hedonist, without a sense of history. Stoic theory was more cosmology than historiography, as Cleanthes' *Hymn to Zeus* shows. The Stoic

---

[20] Ernst Bloch, *The Principle of Hope* (Boston: MIT Press, 1995).

[21] Ernst Bloch, "Man as Possibility," in *The Future of Hope*, Walter H. Capps (Philadelphia: Fortress Press, 1970) 51, 58, 62.

[22] Emil Fackenheim, "The Commandment to Hope: A Response to Contemporary Jewish Experience," in *The Future of Hope*, ed., Walter H. Capps (Philadelphia: Fortress Press, 1970) 90.

philosophers adopted the *Logos* concept as the inherent cosmic principle of intelligibility in the sense of inexorable destiny or fate, which they called justice (*dike*). The prudent man knows his place or role in the universe. The empire is a divinely inspired political and social manifestation that the emperor epitomizes, as Marcus Aurelius, the last of the great Stoic philosophers, declared.

Roman thought concentrated on the theory and functions of society, the *polis*, whether of an individual city or the empire as the expression of a divinely given and sanctioned order, an order that is reflected in the life cycle of nature annually. History shows how men succeed but also how within success lurks the inevitability of failure. A form of Platonic idealism legitimized the state. The state was regarded as a concrete manifestation of an ideal form. The ideal of justice, regarded as common to humanity, is embodied and implemented in the commitment to justice in the state.

What about early Christian understanding of history, the relation of Christians to the state, and divine providence in the affairs of humanity? Early Christian historians were chroniclers desiring to exhibit the historical authenticity of their faith. But during the fourth century, with the conversion of the Emperor Constantine and the growth of the church, they began heralding the arrival of the kingdom of God on earth. These included Eusebius of Caesarea (c. 260–c. 340), Sulpicius Severus (c. 363–c. 420/425), Socrates (c. 380–c. 450), Sozomen (early fifth century) and Theodoret (c. 395–c. 458). However, late in the fourth century Christian imperialist sentiment came under intense pressure when in A.D. 410 Alaric sacked Rome. The fall of Rome and worsening instability powerfully rejuvenated pagan sentiment and undermined the Christian view of God's providential favor toward the empire following Constantine's conversion. Dissolution of Roman power lent credence to the pagan charge that abandoning the gods for Christianity had brought disaster. The concept of the Christian divine *politea*—of the kingdom of God as arriving—was in jeopardy.

This is the issue that Augustine addresses in *The City of God*. His conclusion was fundamentally at variance with popular Christian opinion of the fourth century. Augustine turned chronicling into a Christian philosophy of history.

It is within the context of the late-fourth-century crisis that enveloped the Roman Empire that Augustine developed his concept of time. This concept has dominated all theories of time in Western thought ever since. Time, he said, is a function of creation. For Augustine, eternity is timelessness (*Confessions* 11.13) or immediacy: "in the eternal nothing is flitting, but all is at once present, *whereas* no time is all at once present (11.11); thy today is eternity (11.13);...but to be, now, for that is eternal: for to have been, and to be about to be, is not eternal" (9:10). Augustine declares that God is infinite and is absolute being, but he rejects the idea that absolute being excludes personhood and action.

Time came into being with the world. The first moment of creation is the first moment of time. God *creates* time. Time is the measure of motion: "we measure therefore, even whilst it passeth" (11.21). Three distinctions illuminate the nature of time (11.14): If nothing were passing, there would be no past time; if nothing were coming, there would be no time to come; and if nothing were, there would be no present time.

This conception of time is foundational to Augustine's view of history, God's providential working in history, and his concept of the kingdom. Creation and time are the contexts for ordered linear historical process that has divinely-given significance and ends. History reflects purpose. This is rationally and spiritually discernible in light of the biblical revelation. We discern the trends and their significance in history; we must not impose our notions upon history. Augustine complains that apocalypticism tends to magnify one's own problems, but viewed historically, the current troubles were not as bad as they could be, he said. God's mercy is still evident. The Christian lives in hope because a divinely-ordered end is in view. The present kingdom is not the final kingdom, nor is any earthly peace and prosperity the Christian final Sabbath rest. There is more to the divine ordering of history than the *Pax Romana*—the peace and stability that had been the hallmark of the empire.

Earthly kingdoms serve self-interest because human nature is flawed by pride and error. Rome itself was built on greed and conquest, he said, upon the myths of the gods and upon the political myth of the divine Caesar. Ultimately it is impossible to sanctify paganism. Like all human societies, the empire was founded on an illusion and continues to be an illusion. No earthly kingdom can be the City of God.[23] History does not disclose the anthropomorphic caprice of the gods, fortune and fate, or the inexorable movement of an inherent impersonal Logos principle. Fortune and fate are intellectually ridiculous and morally abhorrent (*City of God* 4.33; 5.1; 7.3; 12.13). History discloses the purposes of the personal Logos, the providential acts of God, not chance or blind force. The irrationalities of history are paradoxical, but they do not leave us in unreason and despair.

The inner power of the two cities is love, but of two different kinds. That of the earthly city is not really love but self-interest and egoism. That of the heavenly city is the love of God, who is the source and inspiration of all that is good. Redemption is not a trans-empirical connection between the soul and the Absolute (Plato), nor is it to be achieved by habituation (Aristotle), nor can it be founded upon a myth (the Imperium). Redemption is through regeneration, and regeneration is attended by and finally is based upon categories as to the nature of reality that are unique to the creationist view of the world. Redeemed men and women are part of societies that are mixtures of good and bad. The Christian must live pragmatically, with insight, and in hope of the final Sabbath of the soul.

Conclusion

While various forms of transcendentalism, whether modern revivals of gnosticism or the panentheism of Paul Tillich, absorb the interest of some Americans, the dominant ethos of our times is American naturalism, the modern descendent of ancient materialism.[24]

---

[23] Augustine, *The City of God*, 5.18–19, 21, 24.

[24] Idealism identifies various forms of ancient and modern transcendentalism, a much larger paradigm than the tendency of some moderns for whom idealism identifies reality as the content of our minds–associated with the view of George Berkeley, Baruch Spinoza, G. W. Leibniz, Emmanual Kant, and G. W. F. Hegel. Theological versions tend to embrace the concept of the absolute and transcendental values, as in the work of S. T. Coleridge, F. D. Maurice, John Caird, the process philosophy of A. N. Whitehead, and Paul Tillich. In its larger sense, idealism sees true reality to be other than the physical order; that the latter is merely appearance and that transcending the appearances of the senses is

This dominance is apparent in two crucial respects. First is the widely accepted metaphysical proposition that reality consists only of the material order—there is no spiritual world or soul. Thus, idealism and materialism in both their ancient and modern garb regard individual persons as epiphenomena, soon to be absorbed at death or erased by death. Second is the belief that values are simply behavioral responses of the human organism and therefore cannot be judged morally. Ultimately values are any object of any interest. No individual will survive the death of the body, and there can be no judgment about the private behavior of any individual.

In contrast to the foregoing, Christianity is essentially a hermeneutic of creation and redemption that ensures the recovery of humanity. In the Christian view, selfhood is a non-reducible reality that we know ourselves and other selves to be by immediate intuition. A person is not simply a unity of conscious experiences but the subject of that unity. Not only is this essential to our understanding of human beings as created in the image of God, but this truth cuts across the whole range of modern research, theory, behavioral techniques, and planning for humanity's future. The Christian outlook is predicated on the understanding that each person is a spiritual agent and that as spiritual agents we are called upon to spiritualize bodily life, to live in accordance with conscious, beneficent purposes in responsible fellowship with God our Creator and with one another.

---

the realm of the Absolute, for example, the Forms of Plato. Such views tend to depreciate the ultimate value of individual personhood.

Friendship as a Theological Virtue

PHILIP WISE

Dr. Liz Carmichael has written a groundbreaking book about the understanding of friendship in Christian theology.[1] When I met with Dr. Carmichael, who is the chaplain of St. John's College and a theology tutor at Oxford University, I began our conversation by mentioning the assigned topic of this chapter, "Friendship as a Theological Virtue." Her response was exactly the same one I made to myself when I first received the invitation to contribute to this *Festschrift*, "But friendship isn't one of the theological virtues."[2]

Were Dr. Carmichael and I right to respond in this way? Historically, the answer is "yes." Theologically, I think the answer is "no." In this chapter I want to make the case that friendship is a theological virtue. Also, I want to talk about how one theologian's friendships—those of Dr. Fisher Humphreys—have demonstrated what this virtue looks like.

If one looks up the phrase "theological virtue" in a dictionary of theology or a dictionary of ethics, one will discover that there are three theological virtues: faith, hope, and love. Sometimes the theological virtues are referred to as the "Christian graces."[3] These virtues when combined with the natural or cardinal virtues (justice, prudence, temperance, and fortitude) constitute the Christian virtues.[4] This does not mean that these are the only virtues that are

---

[1] E. D. H. (Liz) Carmichael, *Friendship: Interpreting Christian Love* (London: T & T Clark International, 2004).

[2] Personal conversation with the author at St. John's College, Oxford, England, 9 June 2006.

[3] J. I. H. McDonald, *Biblical Interpretation and Christian Ethics* (Cambridge: Cambridge University Press, 1993) 253.

[4] Robert H. Mounce, "Seven Cardinal Virtues," *Evangelical Dictionary of Theology*, ed. Walter A. Elwell (Grand Rapids: Baker Books, 1984) 193.

advocated by Christians. The New Testament writers, and Jesus himself, advocate many other virtues (such as honesty and humility) as worthy of pursuit. Some theologians refer to these as the amiable graces.[5] It does mean that the phrase "theological virtues" has come to have a set meaning for Christian theologians. The history of this development is fairly easy to trace.

Before tracing that history, we need to define "virtue." In the *Cambridge Companion to Christian Ethics*, Jean Porter defines it this way:

> A virtue is a trait of character or intellect which is in some way praiseworthy, admirable or desirable. When we refer to somebody's virtues, what we usually have in mind are relatively stable and effective dispositions to act in particular ways, as opposed to inclinations which are easily lost, or which do not consistently lead to corresponding kinds of actions. And so, for example, someone who has the virtue of generosity will consistently respond in generous ways in a variety of situations, including those in which generosity is difficult or costly, in contrast to someone who is moved by pity to one uncharacteristically generous act, or someone whose generous impulses are frequently overcome by desires for self-indulgence.[6]

There are, of course, other definitions, such as that of Charles Pinches, "The virtues are those qualities of character by which we become good."[7]

There is a long history of the use of "virtue" in philosophy and theology. However, this usage can be confusing since the word is used in two distinct ways. Although the word is used in English (and

---

[5] McDonald, *Biblical Interpretation*, 253.

[6] Jean Porter, "Virtue Ethics," in *The Cambridge Companion to Christian Ethics*, ed. Robin Gill (New York: Cambridge University, 2001) 96–116.

[7] Charles Pinches, "Virtue," in *The Oxford Companion to Christian Thought*, ed. Adrian Hastings, Alistair Mason, and Hugh Pyper (Oxford: Oxford University Press, 2000) 741.

its equivalent in most other languages) to "attribute some kind of value to conduct or action," this does not result in a singular meaning. The word may refer to morality or it may refer to effectiveness. Something is deemed a virtue if it is good or if it is effective. These two understandings can lead to very different sets of virtues.[8] Even in the New Testament and in the teachings of Jesus there is a distinction between those qualities that are virtuous regardless of their impact and those qualities that are deemed virtues because they enable one to build the kingdom of God. For example, Jesus commends childlikeness (whatever he may have meant by that word) as a prerequisite to entering the kingdom of God.[9] Also, he commends love as a virtue not because of a promised reward but because it is good to love others.[10] This tradition has continued in Christian theology. As Linda Hogan notes, "Virtue in the Christian tradition denotes both the orientation of a person's character towards the good and the application of knowledge of this good to concrete circumstances."[11] In this chapter the focus will be on the first of these, that is on those qualities that are good and, in the Christian tradition, point one toward God.

The "cardinal virtues" were first defined by Plato (427–347 B.C.E.) as temperance, courage, prudence, and justice. He understood these as checks on various types of human vices.[12] In delineating these virtues, Plato was responding to his teacher Socrates. Admittedly, it is difficult to distinguish which ideas belong to Socrates and which to Plato since our only record of Socrates' ideas come from Plato and the two did not always agree.

---

[8] Jerrold E. Seigel, "Virtue in and Since the Renaissance," vol. 4 of *Dictionary of the History of Ideas: Studies of Selected Pivotal Ideas*, ed. Philip P. Wiener (New York: Charles Scribner's Sons, 1973) 476–86.

[9] See Luke 18:17 ESV: "Truly I tell you, that anyone who will not receive the kingdom of God like a little child will never enter it."

[10] See John 13:34 TNIV: "I give you a new commandment, that you love one another; just as I have loved you, you also are to love one another."

[11] Linda Hogan, "Virtue," in *The New SCM Dictionary of Christian Spirituality*, ed. Philip Sheldrake (London: SCM Press, 2005) 636.

[12] J. Philip Wogaman, *Christian Ethics: A Historical Introduction* (London: SPCK, 1994) 18.

Nevertheless, according to Plato, Socrates (469–399 B.C.E.) challenged the Athenian society's prevailing understanding of virtues in order to develop a more adequate ideal. Socrates understood virtue as a kind of wisdom or knowledge concerning what is good. This knowledge, once acquired, leads to happiness. Thus all virtues are reflections of one quality: knowledge.[13]

Plato agreed with Socrates that the virtues could be distilled down to knowledge. However, he believed that this knowledge could only be gained by contemplation of eternal forms and, most especially, the forms of beauty and goodness.[14] The goal of human life is for the soul to ascend to the realm of pure being, where all these virtues would be fully realized.[15]

Sometimes Aristotle (384–322 B.C.E.) is mistakenly given credit for first delineating the four "cardinal virtues." Although it is true that Aristotle talks about them, he does so because his teacher Plato had identified these four as the basic or fundamental virtues. However, Aristotle did not limit the basic virtues to these four. He spoke positively about many other virtues including "pride."[16]

Aristotle did not accept Plato's ideas about the forms. He believed that virtues, like other subjects, could best be understood by studying what can be known by the natural senses. In this case he advocated a study of "the good." In this pursuit he taught that the emotions as well as the intellect should be taken into consideration. Both of these are influenced by "practical wisdom," which is wisdom that leads to good results. Since situations can affect the response (e.g., whether to tell a lie), he advocated looking for the appropriate (or "mean") response in a given situation. Only then can one determine what virtue entails.[17]

The Hellenistic Roman philosophers contributed significantly to early Christian thought. This is especially true of Cicero (106–43

---

[13] Porter, "Virtue Ethics," 97.

[14] Ibid.

[15] Carmichael, *Friendship*, 12.

[16] Stanley Hauerwas, "Virtue," in *A New Dictionary of Christian Ethics*, ed. James F. Childress and John Macquarrie (London: SCM Press, 1986) 649.

[17] Porter, "Virtue Ethics," 98.

B.C.E.). He was the most prominent Roman philosopher in the years leading up to the Christian era. Some scholars (e.g., Edward Clayton and Jean Porter) believe that he influenced Christian thinking more than any other pagan philosopher. Having acquired many ideas from the Stoic philosophers, Cicero did not introduce any significant new ideas about virtue, but he did systematize the ideas of his predecessors.[18] He accepted the Stoic and Aristotelian view that "virtue should be understood as a disposition to act in accordance with right reason."[19] In keeping with the Roman views on law and society, Cicero suggested that justice rather than practical wisdom should be considered the primary virtue.[20]

"Virtue" and "virtues" are not words used in the New Testament. In fact, as Archibald Alexander observed, "The language of 'virtue' is essentially foreign to the New Testament."[21] This does not mean that the biblical writers were not interested in ethical behavior. The Old Testament presents ideals of character. This is especially true in the wisdom literature and in the prophets. In the New Testament the authors list (and sometimes describe) character traits that are consistent with a Christian life.[22] The New Testament also has lists of vices.[23] Such lists are not found in the Old Testament; however some books in the Apocrypha (e.g. Wisdom of Solomon) do have such lists. This is a clear indication of the influence of Hellenistic philosophers on these writers and the New Testament writers. Making such lists was a well-established tradition in ethical thinking by the first century of the Christian Era. The Stoics, starting with Zeno (335–263 B.C.E.) three hundred years before Christ, were well known for developing such lists.[24] The

---

[18] Carmichael, *Friendship*, 25–27.

[19] Porter, "Virtue Ethics," 99.

[20] Ibid.

[21] McDonald, *Biblical Interpretation*, 42.

[22] Eph 4:2–3; Col 3:12–14; Heb 7:26; 2 Pet 1:5–7, Jas 3:13, 17–18; and 2 Tim 2:22–25 are examples.

[23] Some examples are Eph 4:25–32; Col 3:5–8; Titus 1:7.

[24] D. G. Reid, "Virtues and Vices," in *Dictionary of the Later New Testament & Its Developments*, ed. Ralph P. Martin and Peter H. Davids (Downers Grove IL: InterVarsity Press, 1997) 1191.

Apostolic Fathers also had lists of vices and virtues in *Didache*, *Barnabas*, Shepherd of Hermas, and Polycarp, *To the Philippians*.[25]

There were other non-Christian philosophers who influenced the Christian understanding of "virtue," but beginning with the New Testament period the influences were mainly scriptural.[26] The one formulation in the New Testament that broke new ground was Paul's short list in 1 Corinthians 13—faith, hope, and love. There are other places in the New Testament where faith, hope, and love are found together. Paul puts them together in 1 Thessalonians, Colossians, and Romans. They may also be found together in 1 Peter and Hebrews. However, they are not put together in the way Paul does in 1 Corinthians.[27] According to Porter, Paul's presentation of these three as "the guiding ideals of the Christian life has been more important for Christian ethics than his summary lists."[28] This does not mean that Paul's explanation in 1 Corinthians left no questions. As J. L. Houlden notes: "These terms are complex. Their reference is wider than the narrowly ethical sphere. They do not simply recommend lines of conduct. They are also ways of characterizing the Christian's response to God and his neighbor."[29] John Macquarrie adds that "strictly speaking the three are not virtues in the narrower sense, but may be thought of as introducing a new dimension into the moral life with its natural virtues—the dimension of grace, based on God's action on human life.[30]

---

[25] Ibid., 1192–93.

[26] I do not mean to imply that Christian theologians did not refer to non-Christian philosophers. They clearly did. For example, in *The Stomata* written by Clement of Alexandria in the second century C.E., he quotes freely from Plato, Philo, and the Stoics. See *Ante-Nicene Fathers*, ed. Rev. Alexander Roberts and James Donaldson (New York: Charles Scribner's Sons, 1925; repr., Peabody MA: Hendrickson Publishers, 1994) 2:369.

[27] Thomas B. Strong, *Christian Ethics* (London: Longmans, Green and Co., 1897) 79–80.

[28] Porter, "Virtue Ethics," 99.

[29] J. L. Houlden, *Ethics and the New Testament* (London: Mowbrays, 1975) 18.

[30] John Macquarrie, "The Theological Virtues," in *Dictionary of Christian Ethics* (Philadelphia: Westminster Press, 1967) 342.

The earliest theologian to call these three the "theological virtues" and to distinguish them from the "cardinal virtues" was William of Auxerre in his *Summa aurea*, written in Paris around 1215.[31] That does not mean that he was the first Christian theologian to reflect on Paul's three virtues. St. Augustine (354–430 C.E.) has extended discussions of the "cardinal virtues." Largely following Aristotle, Augustine interprets them in light of Christian love and clearly has 1 Corinthians 13 in mind.[32]

Although it had been used by theologians prior to his time, it was Thomas Aquinas (1224–1274 C.E.) in his *Summa Theologiae*, who limited the term "theological virtues" to St. Paul's fixed set for later theologians. He distinguished these virtues from the "cardinal virtues" by pointing to their origin. Aquinas rightly points out that the traditional definition of virtue is perfection and that only a divine being can achieve perfection. As he puts it, "Theological virtues are not the human virtues."[33] Even in English the original usage of the word virtue is reserved for the gods or God.[34] In Aquinas's mind, these virtues are God's virtues and can be ours only as we imitate God: "Faith, hope and charity (love) are virtues directing us to God, and are, then, theological virtues."[35] They are called "theological virtues," Aquinas says, "because God is their object, inasmuch as they direct us rightly to him, and because they are infused in us by God alone; and because they are made known to us by divine revelation in Sacred Scripture."[36]

---

[31] Carmichael, *Friendship*, 102.

[32] David Atwood, *Changing Values: How to Find Moral Truth in Modern Times* (Carlisle: Paternoster Press, 1998) 42–43.

[33] Saint Thomas Aquinas, The "Summa Theologiae" of St. Thomas Acquinas, translated by Fathers of the English Dominican province, (London: R & T. Washbourne, Ltd.: New York: Benziger) 1912–25. Also, see St. Thomas Aquinas, *Summa Theologiae* (London: Blackfrairs, 1969) 23:137.

[34] *Oxford English Dictionary*, 2nd ed. (Oxford: Oxford University Press, 1989) s.v. "virtue,"

[35] Aquinas, *Summa Theologiae*, 137.

[36] Ibid., 139.

After Aquinas there was a significant shift in Christian thinking about virtue. The shift was from internalizing appropriate virtues to acting in ways that show one is virtuous. This view, which is often called utilitarianism, stressed that what matters is whether one does virtuous deeds, not why one does them.[37]

The reformers—especially Martin Luther—turned away from the virtue ethics of Aquinas and toward this ethic of duty and laws. They justified this shift by appealing to natural reason or common sense. In America, Jonathan Edwards, following David Hume, defended the view of the reformers, but did so based on sentiment rather than reason. Edwards believed that it was the sense of being in the presence of the good or beautiful that makes one desire to be virtuous.[38]

In the twentieth century, Karl Barth disagreed with Aquinas about the "cardinal" and even the "theological" virtues. Barth contended that these virtues are not characteristics that are found in the basic nature of human beings and of God. Instead, he argued, these virtues are gifts from God to human beings and have no necessary correspondence in God's nature. We only know that we have been commanded by God to act according to these virtues.[39]

The value of virtue ethics reemerged at the end of the twentieth century, beginning with Alisdair MacIntyre's *After Virtue* in 1981.[40] MacIntyre was strongly supported by Stanley Hauerwas, who advocated a new communitarianism within the church in order to establish what virtues should be taught and practiced.[41] In a book written the same year as *After Virtue*, Hauerwas explains the rationale behind virtue ethics. He says, "The concept of character implies that moral goodness is primarily a prediction of persons and

---

[37] Pinches, "Virtue," 742.

[38] Porter, "Virtue Ethics," 103.

[39] Karl Barth, *Ethics*, trans. Geoffrey W. Bromiley (New York: Seabury Press, 1981) 30–33.

[40] Porter, "Vitue Ethics," 107. Also, Alasdair C. MacIntyre, *After Virtue: A Study in Moral Theory* (Notre Dame: University of Notre Dame Press, 1981).

[41] Frank G. Kirkpatrick. *A Moral Ontology for a Theistic Ethic* (Aldershot, England: Ashgate Publishing Limited, 2003) 153.

not automatic but must be acquired and cultivated."[42] In other words, what really matters "is not the act itself but the kind of person we will be."[43] What MacIntyre, Hauerwas, and other advocates of virtue ethics were suggesting was a return to the use of words like "character" and "virtue." They wanted to take seriously the Aristotelian and Thomist traditions in theology.[44] They wanted to disassociate themselves from what some call quandary ethics, which focuses on justifying one's actions by reference to rules, whereas virtue ethics focuses on the development of human character.[45] The new movement's relevance to modern thinking can be seen in the popularity of William Bennett's best seller, *The Book of Virtues*.[46]

The one thing that all these Christian theologians seem to agree on is that the three virtues mentioned by St. Paul in the Corinthian passage are normative virtues for Christians. What I would like to suggest is that these three virtues—faith, hope and love—are the very virtues that identify a Christian friend. In other words, when a person exhibits faith, hope, and love in a relationship, then it would be right to describe the friendship that is exhibited as a theological virtue. This kind of friendship, or so it seems to me, is the essence of what Paul was trying to describe in his felicitous passage in 1 Corinthians.

Before I try to make that case, we need to review the history of friendship in philosophy and theology and to see the relationship of friendship to the theological virtues. There is a relationship between "virtue" and "friendship." Frank Kirkpatrick explains the relationship this way: "Virtues are simply those dispositions,

---

[42] Stanley Hauerwas, *Vision and Virtue: Essays in Christian Ethical Reflection* (Notre Dame: University of Notre Dame Press, 1981) 49.

[43] Stanley Hauerwas, *Character and the Christian Life: A Study in Theological Ethics* (San Antonio: Trinity University Press, 1958) 8.

[44] James M. Gustafson, *Protestant and Roman Catholic Ethics* (London: SCM Press Ltd., 1978) 77.

[45] James L. Fredericks, "Interreligious Friendship: A Theological Virtue," *Journal of Ecumenical Studies* (Spring 1998): 160.

[46] William Bennett, *The Book of Virtues* (New York: Simon & Schuster, 1993).

tendencies, traits, and habits that enable the person to flourish, and in the process to express, as part of her deepest character, her capacity to love, trust, and be responsible for others as well as for herself."[47]

The classical philosophers of Greece and Rome often discuss friendship (*philia* in Greek) and usually in the context of their discussions of "virtue." For the Greeks the ideal of friendship was to be found in equality of age, sex, wealth, or position.[48] Homer, the Greek poet, defines friendship in terms of one's extended household. One is obligated to care for one's friends.[49] Socrates defines friendship in terms of "un-possessive love," by which he meant a desire for the beloved to be happy.[50] Plato describes friendship in the context of *eros*—the love of desire. Friendship is the desire for the good and the beautiful and leads one to pursue the eternal forms in heaven.[51]

Aristotle, more than any other Greek philosopher, gave special attention to the concept of friendship. He was "the first to investigate the nature and function of *philia* in the lives of individuals and the state."[52] According to Aristotle, there are three kinds of friendships. The first is based on affection—I like you. The second is based on usefulness—you are helpful to me. The third is based on character—I admire you.[53] Aristotle vacillates between saying that friendship is a virtue and that friendship is a relationship that implies or involves virtue.[54]

---

[47] Kirkpatrick, *A Moral Ontology*, 153.

[48] Craig S. Keener, "Friendship," in *Dictionary of New Testament Background*, ed. Craig A Evans and Stanley E. Porter (Downers Grove IL: InterVarsity Press, 2000) 382.

[49] Carmichael, *Friendship*, 8.

[50] Ibid., 11.

[51] Ibid., 12–13.

[52] Ibid., 15–17.

[53] Lewis Smedes, *Learning to Live the Love We Promise: For People Who Believe in Commitment...and Wonder Why* (Colorado Springs: Waterbrook Press, 2001) 76.

[54] Carmichael, *Friendship*, 19.

The Roman philosophers had a different understanding of friendship. Their ideal was closer to what we would call partisan politics—my friend is someone who thinks the way I do and helps me out. A friendship might also be a patron-client relationship.[55] In *De amicitia*, Cicero builds on the analysis that Aristotle has made of friendship. He "makes a useful distinction between an advantage to us that is the *result* of true friendship, and an advantage that is the source or motive of (a lesser) friendship."[56] This is a distinction that Aelred uses in the Middle Ages in his classic book on friendship.[57]

The Old Testament has a lot to say about friendship. It speaks of the "loyalty and honesty" of true friends (Prov 17:17), the pain of being betrayed by false friends (Ps 41), and the joy of friendly companionship (Ps 133). There are examples of good friends such as David and Jonathan (1 Sam 18:1 NSRV). Abraham is called "God's friend" (2 Chr 20:7 RSV) and Moses is designated the "friend of God" (Exod 33:1 RSV).[58]

The New Testament has even more to say about friends, if not much about friendship. The Greek word translated as "friendship" occurs only once in the New Testament (Jas 4:4) and then in an unfavorable light.[59] Nevertheless, Jürgen Moltmann says that friendship is at the very core of the Christian gospel: "Through Jesus' death the disciples become friends forever, and they remain in his friendship if they follow his commandment and become friends to others."[60] This view is supported by the many New Testament passages that allude to friendship. Jesus is called a "friend of tax collectors and sinners" (Luke 7:34 TNIV). Jesus addresses his disciples as friends (Luke 12:4). Jesus is a friend of Mary, Martha,

---

[55] Keener, "Friendship," 381.

[56] M. J. Langford, "Friendship," in *A Dictionary of Christian Spirituality*, ed. Gordon S. Wakefield (London: SCM Press, 1983) 165.

[57] Aelred of Rievaulx, *Spiritual Friendship*, tr. Mary Eugenia Laker (Kalamazoo: Cistercian Publications, 1977) 166.

[58] Mark Pryce, "Friendship," in *The New SCM Dictionary of Christian Spirituality*, ed. Philip Sheldrake (London: SCM Press, 2005) 316.

[59] Carmichael, *Friendship*, 37.

[60] Jürgen Moltmann, *The Open Church: Invitation to a Messianic Lifestyle* (London: SCM Press, 1978) 57.

and Lazarus (John 11:5). And in the passage that is perhaps most important for Christians, Jesus says, "Greater love has no one than this: to lay down one's his life for one's friends" (John 15:13 TNIV). He goes on in that passage to say to his disciples, "You are my friends, if you do what I command you. I no longer call you servants, because servants do not know their master's business. Instead, I have called you friends, for everything that I learned from my Father I have made known to you" (John 15:14–15). In addition, Paul repeatedly refers to his Christian readers as "friends" (Rom 7:4; Gal 5:11; 1 Cor 14:26). In both Luke and Acts, Luke includes numerous parables and stories that speak about friends or friendship.

When Christian theologians began to reflect on Christian virtues, one of the virtues on which they focused was friendship. They did so in part because Greek and Roman philosophers (especially Aristotle and Cicero) had done so, but also because of the biblical witness.[61] Augustine did more than any other Christian theologian to secure love's place at the heart of Christian theology. This emphasis helped develop a deeper understanding of love. Because Augustine had experienced great friendships, he was interested in integrating his experience into his theology. He did so by describing God's love for sinners as friendship. This relationship then leads Christians into similar relationships with others; that is, they could love others as God does. However, there is no mutuality here. Further, the idea of friendship carries some danger in that one can be hurt or distracted from more important (i.e., spiritual) things.[62]

The next major contribution in the study of friendship among Christian theologians was made by the twelfth century Cistercian abbot of Rievaulx, Aelred. In his book *Spiritual Friendship*, Aelred analyzes the origin of friendship, the fruits of friendship, and the characteristics required for unbroken friendship.[63] The book is in the form of a dialogue and borrows heavily from Cicero with Plato and

---

[61] Pryce, "Friendship," 316.

[62] Carmichael, *Friendship*, 55–68.

[63] Aelred of Rievaulx, *Spiritual Friendship*, 1.

Aristotle in the background.[64] His unique emphasis is the concept of "spiritual friendship," by which he referred to the kind of love that is godly and thereby prefigures the life to come.[65] This kind of friendship is spiritual rather than carnal. It exists in the nature of God. He concludes in a famous passage that "Deus amicitia est"—God is friendship.[66]

It was Thomas Aquinas who linked friendship and virtue. He does not call friendship a virtue, but he concludes that friendship is founded upon virtue. Friendship gathers the best virtues together into a relationship between persons. That is why true friendships result from our loving God: "To the extent we love God, we shall also show love to our neighbor just as we love a friend's children however unfriendly they may be to us."[67] Aquinas defined Christian love, which he understood to be the essential Christian virtue, as "a love of friendship." In other words, the true friendship that we experience in life with God and with others is the essence of Christian love.[68]

This emphasis on friendship began to diminish during the later Middle Ages and the Reformation. In fact, as D. A. Westberg observes, "Friendship with God became a mystical category, not a theological or moral one."[69] The contributions of theologians after Aquinas are very meager according to Carmichael. There is a new idea put forward here or there, but no new groundbreaking work has been done on friendship since Aquinas. Perhaps this is explained by the fact that friendship (*philia)* ceased to be closely connected with love (*caritas*).[70] This shift took place because Latin became the *lingua franca* of the western church, instead of Greek.

---

[64] Pryce, "Friendship," 316.

[65] Carmichael, *Friendship*, 79.

[66] Ibid., 85.

[67] Ibid., 121.

[68] Aquinas, *Summa Theologiae*, 219.

[69] D. A. Westberg, "Friendship," in *New Dictionary of Christian Ethics and Pastoral Theology*, ed. David J. Atkinson et al. (Downers Grove IL: InterVarsity Press, 1995) 399.

[70] Carmichael, *Friendship*, 4.

This should not be taken to imply that subsequent Christian theologians have not written about friendship or that they deny its importance. Recently, there has been a resurgence of interest in this topic. Some of this interest may be traced to the reemergence of virtue ethics in Christian theology. Frank Kirkpatrick expresses the feelings of the virtue ethicists, especially those who follow Hauerwas's communitarianism, when he writes, "Only in the context of community, especially one that is oriented toward the mutual development and flourishing of all its members, can an individual find the concrete embodiment, in both individual lives as well as in tradition and teachings, of what the virtuous, flourishing life looks like."[71] Peter Baelz echoes Kirkpatrick in stating the importance of relationships in spiritual development. In his book on prayer Baelz concludes, "Since the mystery into which we are being drawn is a mystery of boundless love, and since the way of God with his world as expressed and embodied in Jesus Christ is the way of love, the most fruitful analogies will be those drawn from the realm of loving human relationships."[72]

Moltmann has written extensively about friendship. Carmichael describes his views as "liberation oriented."[73] Sounding a lot like Aquinas, he reconnects love to friendship, explaining that "love is the friendship of man with God and all his creatures."[74] In giving his view of the teleological significance of friendship, Moltmann writes, "When in the field of human relationships, the parent-child relation comes to an end, when the master-servant connection is abolished and when privilege based on sexual position are [*sic*] removed, then what is truly human emerges and remains; and that is friendship."[75] In his book *The Open Church*, as in other works, he refers to this kind of extensive friendship as "open friendship," by which he means a

---

[71] Kirkpatrick, *A Moral Ontology*, 153.

[72] Peter Baelz, *Does God Answer Prayer?* (London: Darton, Longman & Todd, 1982) 34.

[73] Carmichael, *Friendship*, 178.

[74] Jürgen Moltmann, *The Church in the Power of the Spirit: A Contribution to Messianic Ecclesiology* (London: SCM Press, 1977) 121.

[75] Ibid., 116.

friendship that is open to all persons.[76] Moltmann did see a danger embedded in friendship. It was the same worry that Aristotle and Aquinas had. As Moltmann put it, "Friendship always stands in danger of becoming exclusive."[77]

In *I Have Called You Friends*, which describes various biblical metaphors for the Christian, Fisher Humphreys has written a chapter about friendship. In it he makes eight important points concerning friendship, which may be summarized in the following way:

> 1. It is easier to think of Jesus as our friend than it is to think of ourselves as Jesus' friend. However, we should learn to think this way.
>
> 2. We have an asymmetrical friendship with God, not as equals, but as with one who transcends us but condescends to us.
>
> 3. We have an asymmetrical friendship with Jesus as one who gives us commands, but has served us by sacrificing for us.
>
> 4. Friendship is a relationship that is chosen. Jesus chooses us as friends, but we must also choose him as our friend.
>
> 5. The paradox of friendship is that there is a part of us that still remains a mystery to our friends. (Fisher admits that Jesus remains a mystery to us, but does not argue that we remain a mystery to Jesus.)
>
> 6. Friends care for each other. God cares for us, and we care for God and the things that God cares about.
>
> 7. Friends are loyal, but that does not mean that friendship is without pain. Because we suffer, we sometimes feel that Jesus has not been good to us. This is a misunderstanding of Jesus and friendship.
>
> 8. Christians are meant to live in a community of friends, the church.[78]

As you may have noticed, none of the theologians surveyed makes the case that friendship is a theological virtue. There is this

---

[76] Ibid., 119.

[77] Moltmann, *The Open Church*, 60.

[78] Summarized from Fisher Humphreys, *I Have Called You Friends* (Birmingham AL: New Hope Publishers, 2005) 183–98.

accepted notion among theologians that the term "theological virtue" should be reserved for Paul's tripartite description of Christian virtue at its best—faith, hope and love. Admittedly Paul does elevate love above the other two, and some theologians, like Aquinas, have described this kind of unselfish love as "friendship." Aquinas put it this way, "Charity…means a love of friendship, to which, as we have said, we are led by hope."[79] This understanding is reaffirmed by other theologians. It is found in the great mystic theologians Julian of Norwich, Teresa of Avila, and John of the Cross.[80] In his Bampton Lectures published in 1897, Thomas Strong writes, "It is upon the basis of faith in the atoning love of God and hope in his promises that the true Christian love of God rests."[81] Perhaps Gilbert Meilander best explains the difficulty of this position. If one accepts that friendship is not a virtue, but a way of describing *caritas* or *agape*, then, "friendship stands in some tension with Christian love (*agape*) because *agape* is to be even more universal in scope and open even to the enemy, whereas friendship is preferential and reciprocal."[82]

What I am proposing is a different synthesis from the one proposed by Aquinas. I do so because, as Westberg has demonstrated, "the New Testament does not support a substantial difference between agape and friendship." The words *philia* and *agape* (both translated love) are used interchangeably.[83] This flies in the face of the argument by Anders Nygren in *Agape and Eros* and by C. S. Lewis in *The Four Loves* that *agape* is different from *philia*; however, Westberg's argument is irrefutable.[84] If this is true, and I

[79] Aquinas, *Summa Theologiae*, 219.

[80] Carmichael, *Friendship*, 122–23.

[81] Strong, *Christian Ethics*, 85.

[82] Gilbert Meilander, "Friendship," in *A New Dictionary of Christian Ethics* (London: SCM Press, 1986) 241.

[83] Westberg, "Friendship," 399.

[84] Anders Nygren, *Agape and Eros* (London: SPCK, 1982), which was first published in two volumes in Stockholm in 1930 and 1936; and C. S. Lewis, *The Four Loves* (New York: Harcourt, Brace, 1960). Westberg's contention is sustained by Peter Atkinson in his recent book *Friendship and the Body of Christ* (London: SPCK, 2004) 2.

believe it is, then friendship might not be just a description of love, but a synthesis of the theological virtues.

I believe that this proposal is a timely one. We live in a day when people are interested in rediscovering the meaning of friendship. With the isolation that can be achieved through the internet, television, and cocooning, friendships often seem a thing of the past. Researchers from Duke University recently reported that Americans are more isolated than they were thirty years ago. Nearly a quarter of people surveyed in the national study reported that they had no close friends with whom to discuss personal matters.[85] Despite this disturbing trend, there is a deep desire for friendship among moderns. This can be seen in a quote from Marc Anderssen in Thomas L. Friedman's best seller, *The World Is Flat.* Anderssen, who is one of the innovators who made internet connectivity possible, says, "When you give people a new way to connect with other people, they will punch through any technical barrier, they will learn new languages—people are wired to connect with other people and they find it objectionable not to be able to."[86]

As Anderssen suggests, there is enormous potential for good in finding ways for people to make connections with one another, especially if those connections lead to friendship. Feminist theologian Barbara Reid suggests that a Christian understanding of friendship can even make a difference in our war-torn world. In a recent article she writes, "The Gospel of John, with its theme of Jesus as friend who goes to a calamity's depths for his friends, offers an interpretation of Jesus' death that has the potential to interrupt cycles of violence and victimization."[87]

I can only sketch out what such a proposal would look like. It would take a very large book to demonstrate it. One of the difficulties, even in a sketch of this proposal, is the lack of

---

[85] Reuters Limited, Yahoo News, 26 June 2006, http://www.dukenews.edu/2006/06/socialisolation.html.

[86] Thomas L. Friedman, *The World Is Flat: A Brief History of the Twenty-first Century* (New York: Farrar, Strauss and Giroux, 2005) 63.

[87] Barbara E. Reid, "The Cross and Cycles of Violence," *Interpretation* 58/4 (2004) 376–85, esp. 384.

commonly-accepted definitions for faith, hope, and love. There have been many books written with the intent of explaining one or more of these.[88] None of these books has received uniform acceptance among theologians. What I propose is to take a simple theological definition of each of the three terms and then see how friendship synthesizes the three. In *A Dictionary of Christian Terms*, which Fisher Humphreys and I wrote together, we described faith as

> trust in God. Christian faith is trust in God as he revealed himself in Jesus Christ. Faith has two factors. The first is intellectual: one believes that God exists and that Jesus is his Son and humanity's Savior. The other factor goes beyond the intellectual to embrace the whole person: one believes in the God who acted in Jesus Christ.[89]

If one accepts that this is roughly what Paul had in mind by faith in 1 Corinthians 13, then it seems to be a very fine definition of what friendship between human beings and God would look like. It also describes the kind of trusting relationship that one would have with one's friends, a relationship in which one trusts the person to be honestly revealing of who he or she is and a relationship in which one commits one's whole self to the other person.

When Fisher and I defined hope, we described it this way:

> The Christian confidence that the future is in the hands of God. Christians have hope for themselves and for others because of what Jesus Christ accomplished in his life, through his death, and by his resurrection. This hope is normally thought of as hope for life after death and is assured to us by the presence of Christ in our lives."[90] Again, this appears to be the way one might describe the nature of a

---

[88] For example, Gene Outka, *Agape: An Ethical Analysis* (New Haven: Yale University Press, 1972).

[89] Fisher Humphreys and Philip D. Wise, *A Dictionary of Doctrinal Terms* (Nashville TN: Broadman Press, 1983) 35.

[90] Ibid., 55.

> Christian's friendship with God. Since God has made promises to Christians about the life to come, it is quite natural that they would put their hope in these promises and the one who issued them.

When one applies this definition of hope to one's friendship with another person, again it seems to be appropriate. The friendship with another is built on hope. That hope is based upon the person's trustworthiness and one's desire to believe the best about others. This hope is not frustrated by temporary setbacks but continues in spite of them. It is a hope that one's trust will be rewarded by a continuation of the friendship into eternity.

The definition of love is, surprisingly, shorter than the other two. We defined love as "devotion to another person. When you love someone, you want to be with that person and you act in that person's best interest. Love is the central attribute of God."[91]

Since this definition is not unlike the ones that earlier theologians used to establish that *agape* or *caritas* was like friendship, it is not difficult to think about our friendship with God in these terms. We are devoted to God and God is devoted to us. We want to be with (i.e., worship and pray to) God and God desires to be with us and communicate with us. God acts in our best interest and, when we are truly Christian, we act in God's best interest.

Taking that definition into human relationships is equally easy. We are devoted to our friends and they are devoted to us. We want to be with our friends and they want to be with us. We want to act in the best interest of our friends and they want to act in our best interest.

When taken together then, this picture of friendship, if raised to perfect proportions, becomes an explanation for what Paul had in mind when he argues that faith, hope, and love are the greatest Christian virtues. They are the virtues of God, and when combined as a blend of virtues, they become the ultimate Christian or theological virtue—friendship. When we respond to God or to others with faith, hope, and love, we will have established the kind of relationship with others that Paul envisioned, a perfect friendship.

---

[91] Ibid., 68.

I do not want to suggest that my friendship with Fisher Humphreys or the friendship that he has with others rises to this standard, but I do want to suggest that his effort to live by such a high standard has affected his theology and the lives of his friends. His theology is written for friends. It is not bombastic or confrontational. John Pierce, editor of *Baptists Today*, says that "Fisher has the ability to speak and write about complex and controversial issues without malice."[92] His style of argument is found in a phrase I have heard him use many times, "This is the way I see it; can't you see it this way, too?" If the answer is "no," the friendship is unaffected. Ralph Wood, Fisher's colleague at Samford University for only a few months, illustrates this perfectly. When asked to comment on his friendship with Fisher, he wrote, "Suffice it to say that he was ever so generous in inviting me, a reconstructed Calvinist and Barthian, to enter his Arminian circle of theologians!"[93] Randall O'Brien, the Provost at Baylor University adds, "Bertrand Russell wrote that he might have become a Christian had he ever met one. I've thought about that. Were it in my power I would have, with every sense of urgency and expectancy, introduced Russell to Fisher."[94]

Fisher's theological writings are substantial. He has written two dissertations; fourteen books; over seventy journal articles; and countless other contributions to collections, encyclopedias, and *Festschriften*. In all of these there is a clarity and simplicity that can be misleading. Because he writes so clearly, you have the feeling that you have always thought what he has written. This feeling might lead you to assume that Fisher's writings are simplistic, when in fact they are very dense. Only when one has studied theology carefully can one see the complex issues he addresses "between the lines" and appreciate the craftsmanship in his work. Fisher wants to be understood. This is what a friend will do. A friend will explain things in a way that does not make you feel ignorant. Fisher has always written theology to help ordinary people become better Christians

[92] John D. Pierce, e-mail to Philip Wise, 25 May 2006.
[93] Ralph Wood, e-mail to Philip Wise, 26 May 2006.
[94] Randall O'Brien, e-mail to Philip Wise, 27 May 2006.

and church members, not to impress other theologians. This is the reason why the title of this *Festschrift*, *Theology in the Service of the Church*, is so very appropriate.

I will conclude this chapter with some stories by Fisher's friends to illustrate how one theologian has practiced friendship as a theological virtue. Let me begin with one of his seminary classmates, Bob Powell, who says, "Over forty-five years, I haven't seen too many changes in Fisher. He was very intelligent then, as he is now. He had a very Christ-like spirit then, as he does now."[95] James Reed, a student and later a colleague of Fisher's at the New Orleans Baptist Theological Seminary, remembers Fisher's unpretentiousness: "Any professor who will admit his joy of Pac Man and play between classes with his students is my kind of friend."[96] Joe Trull, another New Orleans Seminary colleague, appreciated Fisher's collegiality: "Although we had a very diverse faculty, even the most ardent fundamentalist respected Fisher as a kind and fair colleague who would never do them harm."[97] For another of his students, missionary professor Lamon Brown, it was Fisher's ability and willingness to listen which he most treasured: "Fisher has always made time to visit with me.... When I talked, he focused, he listened. That is a sign of a good friend."[98] For Sheri Adams, Fisher's cousin and fellow theologian, Fisher's friendship was found in his encouragement to remain a Baptist when she was contemplating leaving the denomination.[99] For my wife, Cynthia, it was Fisher's generosity and sensitivity that is most appreciated. She writes about a time of "great spiritual anxiety" in her life. What she remembers was his gift to her of his own devotional guide, John Baillie's *A Diary of Private Prayer*.[100]

Another longtime friend, Walter "Buddy" Shurden, praises Fisher's style of correspondence. "He begins almost all of his emails

---

[95] Robert Z. Powell, e-mail to Philip Wise, 6 June 2006.
[96] James Reed, e-mail to Philip Wise, 25 May 2006.
[97] Joe E. Trull, e-mail to Philip Wise, 30 May 2006.
[98] R. Lamon Brown, e-mail to Philip Wise, 25 May 2006.
[99] Sheryl Dawson Adams, e-mail to Philip Wise, 11 June 2006.
[100] Cynthia A. Wise, e-mail to Philip Wise, 8 June 2006.

with 'Dear Buddy,' not just 'Buddy,' and not without any salutation at all.... A communication from Fisher is usually colored with encouragement, affirmation, and gratitude. Like a kid who made perfect grades on your report card, you want to put Fisher's words on your refrigerator door for all to see." He adds in his characteristically humorous way, "I am sure that there are people who do not like Fisher Humphreys, but I have never bumped into them in my whole life. And if I do, I will, in unFisher like fashion, zap them!"[101]

I first met Fisher Humphreys in his office at the New Orleans Baptist Theological Seminary in August 1970. Although I had enrolled in the seminary as a Th.M. student, I had not registered or attended any classes. My professors at Samford University had encouraged me to go to Southern Seminary, but I had chosen to go to New Orleans because of the influence of my former pastor Robert Marsh, who had completed two degrees at that institution. It was Dr. Marsh who first mentioned his brother-in-law, Fisher Humphreys, to me.

Fisher had just returned to the seminary to teach theology. He had been serving as a pastor in northwest Alabama and had not yet completed his doctoral dissertation. Because of some theological unrest at the seminary, Fisher was the only theology professor on campus. I remember vividly our first encounter. I walked into his office, told him who I was, and explained my connection to his brother-in-law. Not knowing what else to say to a theologian, I asked, "So, what do you think of Bultmann?"

I don't remember what Fisher said, but I do remember how he said it. Although my knowledge of Bultmann was marginal at best, he took my question very seriously. He began to talk in his characteristically slow and earnest way that showed he cared about me and was interested in my question. From that day forward, Fisher Humphreys has been my mentor and closest friend. That friendship has spanned thirty-five years and many challenges, disappointments, and joys. One of those joys is the opportunity to participate in this *Festschrift* and to reflect on my assigned topic, "Friendship as a

---

[101] Walter B. Shurden, e-mail to Philip Wise, 25 May 2006.

Theological Virtue," and through that reflection to treasure once again the friendship that I and others have shared with Fisher Humphreys.

The Writings of Fisher Humphreys: An Annotated Bibliography, 1972–2007

ERIC F. MASON

It has been my privilege to read—and in many cases, reread—the works of Fisher Humphreys for the preparation of this annotated bibliography.[1] It has been a rewarding experience to work through his writings in a systematic way, and I repeatedly have been reminded of how influential Fisher's theology has been on my own. At times I was even surprised by this, as I occasionally encountered verbatim phrases that I had spoken to my own students just days earlier without realizing that I had so internalized Fisher's words and ideas.

When reading Fisher's published works, one is struck by a number of characteristics that mark his writings. One could comment on the care with which he writes, organizing his material so that his arguments unfold gracefully and logically. Similarly, one could note the clarity of his language and his care to illustrate his positions with lucid analogies. Fisher's literary style is precise and concise.

One could also comment on the tone of Fisher's writings. I can think of no better term to describe this quality than irenic. Fisher has the profound ability to tackle the most sensitive subjects with a calm, engaging approach. He expresses appreciation for the intentions and contributions of opposing persons and views, yet he

---

[1] I am indebted to Charlene Thompson and Rebecca Koga of the Benjamin P. Browne Library, Judson University, for their diligent work obtaining many of the materials relevant to this chapter. Thanks also are extended to Joe E. Trull (*Christian Ethics Today*) and J. Randall O'Brien (Baylor University) for their assistance with particular items.

gently and fairly engages and illuminates their less persuasive points. He lives and writes as a man of peace.

The significance of Fisher's irenic tone is magnified because of the era in which he has ministered and the topics that he has addressed. One could scarcely imagine a major theological issue in Southern Baptist life since 1972 that Fisher has not addressed in a book, article, or both, be it speaking in tongues, dispensationalism, inerrancy, women in ministry, Calvinism, or fundamentalism. Given Fisher's personality, it is the greatest of ironies that his has been a prominent voice in the denominational dispute that flowered in 1979. Though Fisher's convictions have been clear and his concerns prescient, they consistently have been expressed with charity and moderation. As editor of *The Theological Educator*, the journal of New Orleans Baptist Theological Seminary, during the crucial years of that debate, Fisher boldly yet fairly addressed the controversy, especially with thematic journal issues on the key points of contention and interviews with major denominational figures, including Paul Pressler and Adrian Rogers. He also was a key contributor to official denominational conversations on inerrancy; several of his publications address that issue. The diversity of contributors to this *Festschrift* is a fitting tribute to Fisher's congenial manner in the midst of these disputes.

Fisher writes as a dedicated churchman, devout minister of the gospel, and academic theologian. His love for Baptists, their doctrines, and their polity is unmistakable. Fisher's faith, education, and ministry were nurtured by a loving Baptist congregation in Mississippi, and their investment in him has reaped a manifold harvest. He taught for two decades at a Southern Baptist seminary, then for almost two more decades at a divinity school of a Baptist university. He edited and frequently published in a Baptist seminary journal, and many of his other writings have been in Baptist journals or books published by Baptist presses. Several of his books specifically address Baptist readers.

While his Baptist convictions are indisputable, Fisher is first and foremost a Christian. From his earliest publications he has emphasized the relationship of Baptists to historic, orthodox Christianity. This is seen clearly in the recurring emphasis in his writings (developed most fully in his book *The Way We Were*) on the doctrines Baptists share with all orthodox Christians, with other Protestants, and with the Revivalist tradition. This strong emphasis in his theology made him an ideal participant in a decade of Roman Catholic-Southern Baptist ecumenical dialogue, also a subject of several of his published articles.

Perhaps the most important thing one could say about Fisher's works, though, is that he writes for the church. Indeed, this commitment is reflected in the theme and title of this volume in his honor. Fisher has written theological monographs like *The Death of Christ* and published in numerous academic journals, but his goal always has been to undertake theological study for the service of the church. His own words, from the opening chapter of the revised edition of *Thinking about God*, express this best:

> My theology is church theology. I do thinking about God in the fellowship of the church. And I do it for the church. It is possible to do theology in settings other than the church and for persons other than the church. I appreciate the work of people who do their thinking about God primarily as scientists, or as therapists, or in the setting of a secular university. And I appreciate the work of those who write about God for the benefit of persons in other religions, or for those who doubt the existence of God. But my theology is written from within the fellowship of the church, and for the use of persons who are, like myself, committed in faith to Jesus Christ.[2]

Without question, Fisher has done this exceedingly well.

Fisher is a prolific writer, as the bibliography that follows demonstrates. The items listed below include books, journal articles, contributions to volumes of essays, articles in dictionaries and encyclopedias, and a theological pamphlet. Omitted here by necessity are numerous other published works, including Bible study

---

[2] Fisher Humphreys, *Thinking about God: An Introduction to Christian Theology*, rev. ed. (New Orleans: Insight Press, 1994) 12.

curricula for various age groups; articles in magazines, newspapers, and newsletters (usually denominational or Baptist-related); book reviews (other than two major review essays); contributions to a local church history volume and other projects with very limited circulation; editorial notes in *The Theological Educator*; and the aforementioned interviews with denominational figures that Fisher conducted as editor of the journal.

1972

The Doctrine of the Church. Kansas City: Onesimus Incorporated, 1972. Written to emphasize the importance of the church to Christians normally inclined to stress the individual nature of Christian faith. Addresses the nature of the church as the body of Christ, the importance of the local church as the presence of the church in the world, various missions of the church (worship of God, evangelism, service to others, and edification of believers), and the ordinances of the church (baptism and Lord's Supper). The church, its mission, and its ordinances are not optional for believers but instead are God's intentions for his people. Reprinted as *The Christian Church* (1974).

1973

With Malcom Tolbert. *Speaking in Tongues*. New Orleans: Insight Press, 1973. Examines the phenomenon of glossolalia, its significance in Pentecostal and neo-Pentecostal (charismatic) contexts, practitioners' claims about its significance, biblical texts (especially in Acts and 1 Corinthians) normally cited in such discussions, and potential problems when the practice is introduced in traditional churches. Speaking in tongues is recognized as a legitimate spiritual practice that some Christians find very meaningful, but it is not a biblical norm for all believers as a sign of reception of the Holy Spirit distinct from conversion.

1974

The Christian Church. New Orleans: Insight Press, 1974. Reprint of *The Doctrine of the Church* (1972).

Thinking about God: An Introduction to Christian Theology. New Orleans: Insight Press, 1974. A systematic theology written for the church, engaging both traditional theological issues and matters of contemporary Christian living. Loci of discussion include revelation, God, man, Jesus, atonement, the Holy Spirit, salvation, Christian living, the church, Christian hope, and the Trinity. A significantly revised edition appeared in 1994.

1975

"The Hartford Seminary Heresies." *The Theological Educator* 6/1 (Fall 1975): 14–17. Explains the origins of the document "An Appeal for Theological Affirmation," which was produced at an ecumenical gathering of theologians at the Hartford Seminary Foundation in January 1975. The document includes thirteen "superficially attractive" but ultimately harmful ideas for churches, headed by the assertion that modern thought is preferable to anything previous.

1976

The Almighty: Who God Is and How to Relate to Him. Elgin IL: David C. Cook Publishing, 1976. Addresses several issues concerning the identity and purposes of God. God is both transcendent and personal. God is a friend who is characterized by love and goodness, best exemplified by the cross. God communicates with humans through ordinary experiences but does so most fully through the revelation of Jesus; God also listens to human concerns in prayer. God's purpose is to create a people who freely choose to love God and other people, and this is achieved because God acted through Christ to deliver humans from sin and transforms humans by the Holy Spirit. The doctrine of the Trinity reflects the biblical presentation of God as Father, Son, and Holy Spirit—how God has acted in history and is experienced by believers.

"An Apologetic Armoury." *The Evangelical Quarterly* 48 (1976): 90–95. Surveys and critiques eight approaches to apologetics, including appeals on traditional grounds like logic and philosophy; evidences from miracles and the fulfillment of prophecy; testimonies from religious experience; eristics, or arguments exposing the fallacies of opposing systems such as atheism and secularism; arguments based on the historicity of events like the resurrection and the birth of the church; presentation of Christian faith as the solution to cultural yearnings or ills; claims that pointers to Christian faith can be found in unexpected aspects of secular society; and explanations of Christian faith that correct misconceptions.

"Dispensationalism and Baptists." *The Theological Educator* 6/2 (Spring 1976): 13–17. Briefly explains the major tenets of dispensationalism and traces the movement from its nineteenth-century British origins with J. N. Darby to its popularization in the United States, especially through C. I. Scofield's reference Bible (1909) and Hal Lindsey's novel *The Late Great Planet Earth* (1970). Though very popular in some Baptist circles, dispensationalism ultimately is incompatible with Baptist thought because of its rigid literalism, pessimistic view of the church, and patchwork eschatology.

1977

"On Being Evangelized." *The Theological Educator* 8/1 (Fall 1977): 10–13. Reflections on what Christians might learn from being the object of evangelism efforts, based on experiences with Buddhist neighbors in Britain.

"Understanding the Cross." *The Theological Educator* 7/2 (Spring 1977): 89–95. Argues for the model of costly, or cruciform, forgiveness as the best means to understand the meaning of the cross. This model goes beyond the ideas that in the cross God simply expressed love or set an example; instead, God is understood as having provided forgiveness "by experiencing from within a human life the worst effects of the very sins for which, in so doing, he offers pardon to us" (92). The model is further explained as presenting Christ's work as objective; effective; universal (yet calling for human response); and vicarious, victorious, and a powerful moral influence. See also *The Death of Christ* (1978) below.

1978

"The Baptist Faith and Message." *The Theological Educator* 8/2 (Spring 1978): 9–10. A call at the fifteenth anniversary of the 1963 Baptist Faith and Message statement for revisions that would make the definition of the gospel more explicit in the document.

The Death of Christ. Nashville: Broadman Press, 1978. A book-length treatment of the theme of "Understanding the Cross" (1977). Numerous models for understanding the atonement are presented in the New Testament, including that it marks the dawning of a new age, it provides justification in a legal setting, and it provides sacrificial cleansing. Such models only function properly in a culture in which such language is understood; thus new, more relevant models have been proposed in subsequent eras of the church, and several of these are surveyed and critiqued. The model of costly (or cruciform) forgiveness is relevant in the modern era, and previous proposals of similar models are analyzed. The thesis is that "God in Christ accepted suffering as his way of forgiving the men whose sins caused him to suffer" (116). See also "Christ Died for our Sins according to the Scriptures" (1989) below.

1980

"Current Theological Trends among Southern Baptists." *Baptist History and Heritage* 15/3 (July 1980): 43–48. Briefly situates and critiques Southern Baptist theology in the context of broader Christian thought as theology done obliquely with practical, evangelistic motives, often derived directly and unmethodically from biblical texts rather than through systematic reflection. An emerging trend of greater influence by theologies of other Christian groups on Southern Baptists is noted, as are issues arising from the presence of five significant minority traditions within the SBC: Calvinists, Landmarkists, Fundamentalists, neo-Pentecostals, and the avant-garde (called progressives in later developments of this subject, as in the 1994 book *The Way We Were*). The article concludes with a proposed agenda for future developments in Baptist theology and recommended resources for further reading.

"A Dialogue with Roman Catholics." *The Theological Educator* 10/1 (Fall 1980): 6–7. Personal reflections on motivations for participating in the official Roman Catholic-Southern Baptist ecumenical dialogue and a brief report of the points of agreement and disagreement evident by the dialogue's midpoint. See also several articles below arising from these dialogues.

The Heart of Prayer. Nashville: Broadman Press, 1980. Reprint, New Orleans: Insight Press. Addresses various aspects of prayer, defined as communication with a transcendent yet personal God. As such, prayer differs from meditation, or reflection on spiritual matters. The purpose of prayer is not to marshal one's own power or to capture God's power; instead, a loving God listens and responds to our requests in light of God's "divine flexibility." Prayer can include various types of language (questions, requests of various sorts including those for forgiveness, expressions of appreciation and honor, promises) and can take various forms (personal or public/corporate; spontaneous or written, including use of others' prayers), but sincerity is extremely important, as is a commitment to pray and serve in accordance with God's purpose of creating a people for himself.

1981

"Anniversary of a Creed." *The Theological Educator* 12/1 (Fall 1981): 5–6. Reflections on the 1600th anniversary of the Council of Constantinople, where both the full divinity (against Arianism) and humanity (against Apollinarianism) of Jesus were affirmed along with the appropriateness of worshiping the Holy Spirit as divine (against Macedonianism). Brief comments on the relationship between the council and the Nicene Creed follow, as does a standard translation of the creed.

"A Theology of Salvation." *One in Christ* 17/3 (1981): 219–30. A description and evaluation of the consensus Southern Baptist understanding of salvation. Southern Baptist theology has eclectic influences but strongly emphasizes conversion and evangelism, approaching other aspects of Christian faith and life through these lenses. Baptist thought could be enriched and reconstructed with increased emphasis on the fundamental Christian beliefs in a personal God, the self-revelation of God's purposes through Jesus Christ, God's activity through Christ in history to achieve these purposes, and believers' experience of the Spirit of God in their personal lives and in their faith community. The article's origins are in the Roman Catholic-Southern Baptist ecumenical dialogues held 1978–1980. See also "Salvation: A Southern Baptist Perspective" (1982) below.

1982

"Call and Ordination: Commissioned to Ministry." In *God-Called Ministry*. Edited by Morris Ashcraft. Carey NC: Baptist State Convention of North Carolina, 1982. Examines understandings of the will of God and the call to ministry, the biblical basis for ordination, and four traditional categories (sacrament, authorization, installation, and confirmation and blessing) for understanding the practice of ordination. Ordination is affirmed as a rite of installation for service in the institutional church but more significantly as a congregation's communal expression of approval and support as one enters a new phase of ministry. Reprinted in *The Minister and the Ministry* (1989) and *The People of God* (abridged revision; 1991).

"Father, Son, and Holy Spirit." *The Theological Educator* 12/2 (Spring 1982): 78–96. An address on the Trinity to the faculty of the New Orleans Baptist Theological Seminary. Examines the biblical roots for the doctrine and its development in the experiences of the early church, ways the doctrine has been understood or explained in the history of the church, and the doctrine's continuing relevance for Christian unity, evangelism, and worship.

"Salvation: A Southern Baptist Perspective." *Review and Expositor* 79 (1982): 279–89. A light revision of "A Theology of Salvation" (1981) included in a thematic journal issue devoted to Roman Catholic-Southern Baptist ecumenical dialogue. A brief response to this and an accompanying article on salvation from a Roman Catholic perspective followed in the journal as Fisher Humphreys and Mark Heath, O. P., "Salvation: An Epilogue," *Review and Expositor* 79 1982): 290–92.

"The Theological Educator." Volume 4 of *Encyclopedia of Southern Baptists*. Edited by Lynn E. May. Nashville: Broadman Press, 1982. A brief history of the journal formerly published by the New Orleans Baptist Theological Seminary.

1983

With Philip Wise. *A Dictionary of Doctrinal Terms*. Nashville: Broadman Press, 1983. A concise treatment of 100 significant theological terms, intended for ministers, students, and lay readers. Entries are included for biblical terms (such as covenant and justification) and concepts important in historical Christian theology (such as creeds and Trinity). Entries typically are about a page in length, with glosses followed by a few paragraphs of elaboration.

"The Most Dangerous Conversation: A Review Article." *Perspectives in Religious Studies* 10/1 (Spring 1983): 63–73. A review of David Tracy, *The Analogical Imagination: Christian Theology and the Culture of Pluralism*. New York: Crossroad Publishing, 1982.

(Edited.) *Nineteenth Century Evangelical Theology*. Nashville: Broadman Press, 1983. An anthology of fifty-six readings from thirty-two authors, providing insights for modern evangelicals on evangelical thought (defined broadly) from 1800 through the end of World War I. An introduction provides a historical and socio-religious context for the era and brief biographies of the excerpted authors.

1984

"Altar Call (Invitation)." In *Encyclopedia of Religion in the South*. Edited by Samuel S. Hill, 24–25. Macon GA: Mercer University Press, 1984. A brief discussion of the practice from its roots in nineteenth-century revivalism to contemporary Southern church life. When practiced in the latter, it—rather than baptism or recitation of the Apostles' Creed—functions as the initial public confession of faith and the most anticipated aspect of the worship service. The article was reprinted in *Encyclopedia of Religion in the South*. Edited by Samuel S. Hill and Charles H. Lippy. 2nd edition, 50–51. Macon GA: Mercer University Press, 2005.

"Conversion." In *Encyclopedia of Religion in the South*. Edited by Samuel S. Hill, 184–85. Macon GA: Mercer University Press, 1984. Emphasizes the significance of the concept for revivalism, where it provides the sense of a personal relationship with God, separation to a community with transformed values, and a bond of ecumenical experience for persons of revivalist denominational traditions. The concept invites questions, however, about the respective divine and human roles in conversion, the personal responses that should accompany and flow from conversion, the proper role of the church in seeking conversions, and whether conversion is the normative experience for Christian initiation. The article was reprinted in *Encyclopedia of Religion in the South*. Edited by Samuel S. Hill and Charles H. Lippy. 2nd edition, 233–34. Macon GA: Mercer University Press, 2005.

(Edited with Thomas A. Kinchen.) *Laos: All the People of God*. New Orleans: New Orleans Baptist Theological Seminary, 1984. A volume of thematic essays addressing "the theology of the non-ordained" and emphasizing the importance of the ministry of the laity. The essays originally were presented at the Convocation on the Laity at New Orleans Baptist Theological Seminary in December 1983. Topics include salvation, spiritual gifts, and various aspects of ministry.

"Salvation." In *Laos: All the People of God*. Edited by Fisher Humphreys and Thomas A. Kinchen, 20–38. New Orleans: New Orleans Baptist Theological Seminary, 1984. An examination of various facets of salvation. Past, present, and future aspects of salvation are discussed systematically, with each aspect examined in terms of God's initiative, the human response, pictures or images describing salvation, and contemporary difficulties (or misunderstandings).

1985

"The Dynamics of Ministry." *The Theological Educator* 31 (Spring 1985): 57–61. Briefly addresses five questions: Who ministers? To whom? What kinds of ministry? What resources are available for ministry? What kind of person should a minister be?

The Nature of God. Layman's Library of Christian Doctrine 4. Nashville: Broadman Press, 1985. Explores the doctrine of God with biblical, doctrinal, and relational approaches. God created a covenant people in the Old Testament and revealed himself in history. Jesus was the major revelation of God's nature and announced the kingdom of God. God is both transcendent and personal, like us and unlike us, and can be trusted. God created humanity with free will, and his purpose is that humans relate to him and each other in love. God fulfills the human longing for ultimate reality, and in Christ God reveals his understanding of human suffering and ultimate victory over evil. God is revealed and experienced as Triune by believers.

1986

"Living as a Disciple." *Southwestern Journal of Theology* 28/2 (Spring 1986): 79–84. A description and analysis of Christian living in Southern Baptist contexts, addressing both what is encouraged and what is actually practiced. Major themes in discipleship include moral integrity, church loyalty, devotional life, personal growth (in aspects of life other than spiritual), and service. Points of consensus and diversity are noted, as are the practical implications of Baptist beliefs on issues such as grace and eternal security.

La naturaleza de Dios. Biblioteca de Doctrina Cristiana. Translated by Arnoldo Candlini. El Paso TX: Casa Bautista de Publicaciones, 1986. The Spanish translation of *The Nature of God* (1985).

"Prayer and Praise." *The Theological Educator* 34 (Fall 1986): 68–72. Addresses responses to good and evil in life. Both are real and incline humans toward different responses to God, but God's act through Christ assures God's trustworthiness. Believers are to call on God in both circumstances and to share in the joys and sorrows of others.

1987

"The Baptist Faith and Message and the Chicago Statement on Biblical Inerrancy." In *The Proceedings of the Conference on Biblical*

Inerrancy 1987, 317–29. Nashville: Broadman Press, 1987. Compares the discussions of Scripture in the 1963 Southern Baptist confession and the 1978 statement drafted by the evangelical International Council on Biblical Inerrancy. While the documents have much in common on issues such as the origin, authority, and message of Scripture, the *Chicago Statement* is more specific with its claims for inerrancy and plenary verbal inspiration. The definition of inerrancy, however, is heavily qualified and appeals to the autographs of Scripture rather than existing copies. Other critiques of the statement include its divisiveness, lack of clarity on the purpose of God in Scripture, and insistence on terminology not present in Scripture itself.

"Biblical Inerrancy: A Guide for the Perplexed." In *The Unfettered Word: Southern Baptists Confront the Authority-Inerrancy Question*. Edited by Robison B. James, 47–60. Waco TX: Word Books, 1987. Offers a generous, nuanced explanation of the key tenets and motivations of persons who hold to biblical inerrancy, followed by ten concerns common to persons who reject the term "inerrant" but stress Scripture's authority and inspiration. The thesis is that "when inerrancy is qualified carefully, [Humphreys is] unable to detect any substantial differences between it and the high view of Scripture offered by many noninerrantists" (49). Particular difficulties with the inerrancy position include its primary concern with the autographs rather than the present state of the biblical texts and the numerous qualifications of the inerrancy position that significantly mitigate the original assertions.

"The Mystery of the Cross." *Perspectives in Religious Studies* 14/4 (Winter 1987): 47–52. A brief discussion of the meaning of Jesus' death. Numerous Old Testament images were used in the New Testament to explain the cross, and this lack of exclusivity allows other metaphors appropriate to various situations to be utilized in subsequent generations. Such images serve to convey the meaning of Christ in relevant ways, authorize social change, and address the human need to understand and believe.

1988

"Believing in the Church." In *Professors Can Preach: Sermons from Leavell Chapel*. Edited by Joe E. Trull, 58–65. New Orleans: Insight Press, 1988. A sermon on the church, emphasizing its importance—despite human failures—for proclamation of Jesus, worship, and fellowship.

"The Holy Spirit." In *Disciple's Study Bible*. Edited by Johnnie Godwin and Roy Edgemon, xiv, 1668–69, and passim. Nashville: Holman Bible Publishers, 1988. Study Bible commentary on the Holy Spirit, including an outline of themes, summary of doctrine, and numerous notes keyed to appropriate biblical texts.

"The Humanity of Christ in Some Modern Theologies." *Faith and Mission* 5 (Spring 1988): 3–13. Examines four attempts to emphasize the humanity of Jesus, which historically has tended to be minimized in Christian theology in favor of stressing his divinity. The four approaches surveyed are the life of Jesus by John Robert Seeley, the kenotic Christology of Charles Gore, the psychological approach of W. R. Matthews, and the liberation theology of Jon Sobrino.

"Modest Proposals for Aspiring Theologians of the New Southern Baptist Establishment." *The Theological Educator* 37 (Spring 1988): 154–64. Concludes a thematic issue of the journal on "Polarities in the Southern Baptist Convention" with suggestions for those who have gained leadership in the SBC, including calls that they take seriously the theological heritage shared with other Christians, consider the human character of Scripture along with the divine, hold firmly to historic Baptist tenets, respect those whom they criticize, remember that all theological systems change and are fallible, seek exploration rather than indoctrination in theological education, and be active contributors for the good of denominational life.

1989

"Being a Christian Disciple." *The Theological Educator* 39 (Spring 1989): 37–49. Compares Baptist and Catholic thought and approaches to leading the Christian life. While the traditions have very much in common, they differ on issues concerning the security and assurance of salvation, sources of moral teaching and some particular activities, emphasis on the church as local or worldwide, particular devotional practices, forms of Christian service, and means of receiving God's help for living. The article appears in a thematic journal issue on ecumenical dialogue titled "To Understand Each Other: Roman Catholics and Southern Baptists."

"Call and Ordination: Commissioned to Ministry." In *The Minister and the Ministry*. Edited by Daniel O. Aleshire and George W. Knight, 24–31. Nashville: Seminary Extension Department, 1989. Reprint of the article of the same title from *God-Called Ministry* (1982).

"Christ Died for Our Sins According to the Scriptures." *Criswell Theological Review* 3/2 (1989): 295–305. Emphasizes the diversity of biblical images for understanding the nature of atonement. The penal substitutionary view is sometimes understood as the major model to the detriment or exclusion of others, but this is not the historic Christian position. While it has biblical basis, its preeminence over other understandings in the Bible is debatable, and its contemporary prominence is attributed to the influence of John Calvin's theology and interpretations of one's personal experience of salvation. The article is a response to criticisms of *The Death of Christ* (1978).

"Leonard Hodgson." *The Theological Educator* 40 (Fall 1989): 20–24. A brief survey of Hodgson's theology, summarizing his thought on revelation, God, Christ, the Trinity, and atonement.

"The Roman Catholic-Southern Baptist Scholars Dialogue." *Ecumenical Trends* 18 (December 1989): 172–74. A brief report on three series of ecumenical dialogues spanning 1978–1988, including comments on the nature of the meetings, published papers from the dialogues, and selected comments from the summary statement adopted at the conclusion of the meetings.

Southern Baptist Heritage. Nashville: Seminary Extension Department, 1989. A study guide for the SBC seminary extension diploma program, providing overviews, study questions, and supplemental materials (including a significant contribution by Albert McClellan on issues facing Southern Baptists in the decade of 1978–1987) to be read alongside assigned textbooks. The topics (especially doctrines Baptists share with other Christians and Baptist distinctives) anticipate the much fuller treatment of these issues in *The Way We Were* (1994).

1990

"E. Y. Mullins." In *Baptist Theologians*. Edited by Timothy George and David S. Dockery, 330–50. Nashville: Broadman Press, 1990. A biographical sketch and evaluation of the writings and significance of the important Baptist figure. Examines his responses to the major issues of his era and analyzes six of his books (those considered most important by his peers). Mullins is most distinguished by his moderation and positive use of the category of experience in his theology. This article was lightly revised and expanded for *Theologians of the Baptist Tradition* (2001).

"Publicans." In *Mercer Dictionary of the Bible*. Edited by Watson E. Mills et al., 724. Macon GA: Mercer University Press, 1990. A brief article on tax collectors in the gospels.

"The Star of Bethlehem." In *Mercer Dictionary of the Bible*. Edited by Watson E. Mills et al., 856. Macon GA: Mercer University Press, 1990. Discusses the star of Matthew's narrative of the birth of Jesus, emphasizing its nature as a miraculous event with theological meanings.

"Thomas." In *Mercer Dictionary of the Bible*, ed. Watson E. Mills, 911. Macon GA: Mercer University Press, 1990. A brief discussion of the apostle Thomas, especially as presented in the gospel of John.

1991

"Kingdom of God." In *Holman Bible Dictionary*. Edited by Trent C. Butler, 843–45. Nashville: Holman Bible Publishers, 1991. A brief examination of the major statements in the gospels on the subject, emphasizing the identification of the kingdom as God's reign (and thus not something built by humans) and various aspects of the nature of the kingdom.

"Ordination." In *The People of God: Essays on the Believers' Church*. Edited by Paul Basden and David S. Dockery, 288–98.

Nashville: Broadman Press, 1991. Abridged revision of "Call and Ordination: Commissioned to Ministry" (1982; 1989).

"Spiritual Gifts." In *Holman Bible Dictionary*. Edited by Trent C. Butler, 1300–1301. Nashville: Holman Bible Publishers, 1991. A brief survey of New Testament discussions of spiritual gifts, addressing similarities and differences concerning gifts of the Spirit in the Old and New Testaments.

1992

"The Name, Contents, and Characteristics of the Bible." In *Holman Bible Handbook*. Edited by David S. Dockery, 2–4. Nashville: Holman Bible Publishers, 1992. A basic introduction to literary and theological issues concerning the Christian Scriptures.

"A Neo-Evangelical Systematic Theology: A Review Article." *Perspectives in Religious Studies* 19/2 (Summer 1992): 217–25. A review of Paul K. Jewett, *God, Creation, and Revelation: A Neo-Evangelical Theology*. Grand Rapids: William B. Eerdmans Publishing Company, 1991.

1994

"The Bible and the Formation of Our Lives." In *Proclaiming the Baptist Vision: The Bible*. Edited by Walter B. Shurden, 87–95. Macon GA: Smyth & Helwys Publishing, 1994. Addresses the significance of the Bible as a "mirror" and "window," influencing both the Christian's worldview and self. It instructs readers on how to understand the nature of human existence and God's purposes, provides practical guidance and aid for understanding one's own identity and destiny, and shapes persons to be participants in the community of faith and to experience God. One may benefit from the Bible by studying, reading, listening, memorizing, singing, praying, and meditating in various ways.

"The Christian Life." In *Has Our Theology Changed? Southern Baptist Thought Since 1845*. Edited by Paul A. Basden, 135–58. Nashville: Broadman & Holman, 1994. Examines interpretations of topics relevant to Christian living (such as repentance, justification, sanctification, and prayer) in the writings of nine major Southern

Baptist theologians spanning 1857–1984 (Dagg, Boyce, Mullins, Connor, Stagg, Stevens, Roark, Moody, and Ashcraft).

Thinking about God: An Introduction to Christian Theology. Revised edition. New Orleans: Insight Press, 1994. A thorough revision, expansion, and updating of the 1974 book. Most chapters are significantly reworked, often reflecting the themes emphasized in publications in the intervening two decades.

"Trends in Studies in Theology Today." *The Theological Educator* 49 (Spring 1994): 69–76. Surveys ten trends in theology since the early 1960s, including the vitality of Roman Catholic theology, the renaissance of evangelical theology, interest in theological method, the debate on whether theology should be written for the public or the church, the rise of advocacy theologies, the interest of feminist theologians in the doctrine of the Trinity, the abiding strength of process theology, continuing challenges to the Enlightenment and liberalism, the flourishing of philosophical theology, and the renewed emphasis on writing systematic theologies.

The Way We Were: How Southern Baptist Theology Has Changed and What It Means to Us All. New York: McCracken Press, 1994. Addresses changes in the Southern Baptist Convention since 1979 by examining the beliefs of Southern Baptists in the years shortly before the controversy erupted in terms of "majority" and "minority" positions. The former were consensus positions in the SBC and are classified as those shared with all Christians, shared with Protestant Christians, unique to Baptists, or shared with other Revivalist Christians. Minority traditions are those of subgroups within the SBC, including Anabaptist, Calvinistic, Landmark, Deeper Life, Fundamentalist, and Progressive. Discussions frequently are illustrated with references to The Baptist Faith and Message (1963) and hymns familiar to Baptists. The book concludes with an examination of how particular majority and minority positions are faring in the post-1979 SBC compared to the previous consensus. The thesis is that a comparison of trends before and after 1979 reveals that the changes have been negative. (A revised edition appeared in 2002.)

1995

"All Creatures of Our God and King." *The Theological Educator* 51 (Spring 1995): 49–58. Reviews ten biblical themes for thinking Christianly about the earth: it is God's good creation, it exists to glorify God, humans are the greatest of God's creations, humans were created from the earth to live on it, God has given the earth to humans as a gift and blessing, creation points humans to know and praise God, humans are entrusted to care for the earth, human sin negatively impacts the earth, God has acted to deliver both humans and the earth, and ultimately both humans and the earth will be redeemed.

"Feminism and the Christian Faith." *The Theological Educator* 52 (Fall 1995): 15–20. Addresses issues concerning women and Christianity. Feminism is affirmed when defined as the pursuit of equality and fairness, but examples are given of ways it may become radical. The appropriateness of women in ministry is affirmed, as is retention of the Bible's masculine language for God.

1996

"Baptist." In *Dictionary of Ethics, Theology and Society*. Edited by Paul Barry Clarke and Andrew Linzey, 76–78. New York: Routledge, 1996. A brief survey of Baptist origins in English Puritanism, theological tenets and polity, stances toward government and societal issues, and future prospects.

1997

"Theodore R. Clark." In *Dictionary of Heresy Trials in American Christianity*. Edited by George H. Shriver, 88–93. Westport CT: Greenwood Press, 1997. Examines the dismissal of Clark from the faculty of New Orleans Baptist Theological Seminary in 1960 after the publication of his book *Saved by His Life* (1959) in the context of other events at the seminary.

"New Orleans Baptist Theological Seminary." In *Encyclopedia of Religious Controversies in the United States*. Edited by George H. Shriver and Bill J. Leonard, 324–26. Westport CT: Greenwood Press, 1997. A brief survey of controversies at the seminary, including its progressive policies toward women and African Americans in the 1940s and early 1950s, charges against Frank Stagg in 1956, the dismissal of Theodore Clark in 1960, the departure of three theologians in 1969, and issues relating to controversies in the Southern Baptist Convention after 1979.

"*Saved by His Life.*" In *Encyclopedia of Religious Controversies in the United States*. Edited by George H. Shriver and Bill J. Leonard, 409–10. Westport CT: Greenwood Press, 1997. A brief entry that summarizes the thesis of this 1959 book (the church has overemphasized the significance of Jesus' death to the detriment of appreciation of his life; the title is drawn from Romans 5:10), which contributed to the dismissal of Clark from the faculty of New Orleans Baptist Theological Seminary the following year.

"Southern Baptists and Calvinism." *The Theological Educator* 55 (Spring 1997): 11–26. An irenic analysis and response to Calvinism. The theology of John Calvin and his theological predecessors is examined briefly, followed by a short survey of the presence of Calvinism in Baptist history. The five-point presentation of Calvinism articulated at Dort is summarized, followed by comments on the strengths of Calvinism and its adherents (including a strong biblical focus and emphasis on humility, piety, and mission). A rebuttal of Calvinism is offered, critiquing its biblical claims, the five points of Dort, and understanding of God's sovereignty.

"Frank Stagg." In *Dictionary of Heresy Trials in American Christianity*. Edited by George H. Shriver, 388–92. Westport CT: Greenwood Press, 1997. Examines the investigation and vindication of Frank Stagg in 1956 at New Orleans Baptist Theological Seminary, including the theological and social issues at hand and a false legal accusation fabricated by a third party.

"Frank Stagg." In *Encyclopedia of Religious Controversies in the United States*. Edited by George H. Shriver and Bill J. Leonard, 456–59. Westport CT: Greenwood Press, 1997. A shorter version of the previous article on charges against Stagg and his vindication.

1998

"Community and Liberty." *Perspectives in Religious Studies* 25/1 (Spring 1998): 93–97. Addresses the two major contributions of Baptists to the wider church, an intentional church whose members practice baptism only of believers and religious liberty through the separation of church and state. Both traditions offer much for the current era but must be preserved from indifference and misunderstanding.

"A Man and His Church: Mission." In *God's Man: A Daily Devotional Guide to Christlike Character*. Edited by Don M. Aycock, 97–102. Grand Rapids: Kregel Publications, 1998. Seven devotional entries on various biblical passages. The volume was revised in 2000.

"Teaching Theology to Ministers." *The Theological Educator* 57 (Spring 1988): 53–61. Discusses a professor's goals for his theology students—that they be trustworthy theologians who are confident, humble, truthful, and loving; knowledgeable about the Bible, historic Christian orthodoxy, and modern academic theology; and focused on Jesus.

1999

"A Baptist Theology of the Lord's Supper." In *Proclaiming the Baptist Vision: Baptism and the Lord's Supper*. Edited by Walter B. Shurden, 117–28. Macon GA: Smyth & Helwys Publishing, 1999. Addresses five answers to the question "What does the Lord's Supper mean?" Its observance is an act of obedience by the church to Christ, a reminder of his sacrificial death, a visible proclamation of his death and anticipated return, a joyous expression of thanksgiving, and a meal of communion with Christ and his church. Interpretations of earlier Baptists are considered, especially on the issue of Christ's presence.

2000

"Baptists and Their Theology." *Baptist History and Heritage* 35/1 (Winter 2000): 7–19. Examines major figures and theological issues for Baptists in the seventeenth, eighteenth, and nineteenth centuries. Most Baptist theology has been folk theology produced by ministers rather than academics, and often it has been formulated in response to issues arising in other groups (such as the Calvinism-Arminianism debate). The seventeenth century saw emphases on believer's baptism, sectarianism, and religious freedom and varying Baptist stances toward predestination. This diversity continued in the eighteenth century and was impacted by revivalism, though the appropriateness of the latter and evangelism remained debated. Major issues in the nineteenth century were relations with non-Baptists and the rise of liberal Protestantism.

With Paul E. Robertson. *God So Loved the World: Traditional Baptists and Calvinism*. New Orleans: Insight Press, 2000. Asserts that Calvinism is a departure from traditional Southern Baptist theology. Addressed specifically to non-Calvinistic Baptists, brief surveys of the history and tenets of Calvinism and Baptist history (opposing the claim that Calvinism is the historic Baptist position) are followed by discussions of the major biblical emphases and interpretations claimed by Calvinists and traditional Baptists. A traditional Baptist theology is then articulated, emphasizing God's sovereign choice to grant humans free will and save those who respond in faith; this best accords with the biblical claim of the book's title and provides the proper rationale for missions and evangelism.

2001

"Edgar Young Mullins." In *Theologians of the Baptist Tradition*. Edited by Timothy George and David S. Dockery, 181–201. Nashville: Broadman & Holman Publishers, 2001. A lightly revised and expanded version of the article "E. Y. Mullins" (1990) included in this updated and reconfigured abridgement of *Baptist Theologians*.

2002

"Faith and Higher Education." *Christian Ethics Today* 8/1 #38 (2002): 15–18. An address to professional educators at the 2001 national meeting of the Cooperative Baptist Fellowship. Emphasizes respect for students, best expressed through a professor's humility, and that education is best understood as the formation of persons.

"Theological Variety in the Baptist Experience." *Baptist History and Heritage* 37/3 (2002): 48–61. An abridged presentation of the majority and minority traditions discussed in *The Way We Were*, adding Pentecostalism as a minority tradition.

The Way We Were: How Southern Baptist Theology Has Changed and What It Means to Us All. Revised edition. Macon GA: Smyth & Helwys Publishing, 2002. An updating of the 1994 book, incorporating a new foreword by Walter B. Shurden, revision of statistics, minor rewordings in the first ten chapters, and expansion of the final two chapters in light of the 2000 revision of The Baptist Faith and Message and other actions of the SBC and its leaders since the mid-1990s.

2003

"Women in Christian Ministry." In *Putting Women in Their Place: Moving beyond Gender Stereotypes in Church and Home*. Edited by Joe E. Trull and Audra E. Trull, 137–46. Macon GA: Smyth & Helwys Publishing, 2003. Affirms the appropriateness of women in ministry. Despite the patriarchy of ancient biblical societies, several women are prominent in the Old Testament, and Jesus displays a progressive attitude toward women disciples. Other New Testament teachings affirming women in ministry include the priesthood of all believers and the possession of spiritual gifts. Ordination indicates a church's confirmation and blessing of one called to ministry rather than granting authority, and the prohibition against women in ministry in 1 Timothy 2 is best understood as culture-specific for patriarchal societies.

2004

With Philip Wise. *Fundamentalism*. Macon GA: Smyth & Helwys Publishing, 2004. An irenic examination and critique of Christian fundamentalism. Considers common characteristics of fundamentalist movements in various religions and then examines the history, theological tenets, and attitudes of Christian fundamentalism. The second half of the book more closely considers fundamentalism in Baptist life, addressing the influence of the movement in the Southern Baptist Convention and offering advice on how progressive Baptists should respond. The final chapter elucidates the book's thesis—the emphases of fundamentalism are not the actual fundamentals of the Christian faith.

"Traditional Baptists and Calvinism." *Baptist History and Heritage* 39/2 (Spring 2004): 56–60. A brief presentation of the thesis of *For God So Loved the World* (2000), contrasting the theological tenets and core assumptions of Calvinists and traditional, non-Calvinistic Baptists. While both groups make strong appeal to the Bible, Calvinists emphasize foreordination of particular persons as an essential feature of God's sovereignty, whereas traditional Baptists understand God's sovereignty as including both human freedom and God's desire that all experience salvation through Christ.

2005

"Fundamentalism [2005 T. B. Maston Lecture]." *Carson-Newman Studies* 10/4 (2005): 101–13. Discussion of Christian fundamentalism abridged from the 2004 book.

I Have Called You Friends: New Testament Images that Challenge Us to Live as Christ Followers. Birmingham AL: New Hope Publishers, 2005. A devotional study of ten selected personal images of Christians in the New Testament, examining various facets of each image relevant for Christian living. The images are disciple, servant, steward, soldier, athlete, traveler, priest, child, friend, and guest.

2006

"The Revelation of the Trinity." *Perspectives in Religious Studies* 33/3 (Fall 2006): 285–303. Addresses whether the fourth-century formulations of Trinitarian theology properly reflect the faith of the New Testament era. While it is true that the New Testament lacks explicit articulation of Trinitarian theology, passages specifically addressing the doctrine, rebuttals of positions later declared heretical, or the precise vocabulary subsequently employed to describe the Trinity in these later formulations, it nevertheless points to existence of the Trinity. This may be observed in four stages traced in reverse: passages in the New Testament that associate the Father, Son, and Spirit; use of Trinitarian language in the life of the church; Trinitarian faith; and the revelation of God to Israel, Jesus in the Incarnation, and the Spirit at Pentecost. Implications of this New Testament evidence are addressed. This is the lead article in a thematic journal issue on the Trinity edited by Fisher Humphreys.

2007

Baptist Theology: A Really Short Version. Brentwood TN: Baptist History and Heritage Society, 2007. A pamphlet addressing the origins and theological traditions of Baptists (adapted from *The Way We Were*). In addition, several urgent theological issues, classified as issues in society (religious freedom, the new atheism, relationships between science and Christian faith, status of women in society, and racial justice), in the church (believers' baptism, Calvinism, Fundamentalism, Pentecostalism, the ecumenical movement, and trends in worship), and perennial issues (suffering and Christian faith, the Trinity, and published volumes of systematic theology by Baptists) are surveyed. As they continue to make theological judgments, Baptists are encouraged to appeal to their traditional norms of the Bible, the various historic theological traditions that have shaped Baptists' religious experience (things shared with all Christians, with other Protestants, and with other groups influenced by the evangelical awakenings, along with Baptist distinctives) and reason.

Contributors

Thomas E. Corts, president emeritus of Samford University, is a graduate of Georgetown College of Kentucky and holds Master's and Doctor of Philosophy degrees from Indiana University. Dr. Corts has served as chair of the Commission on Colleges of the Southern Association of Colleges and Schools, as president of the Southern Association of Independent Colleges and Universities, and as president of the National Fellowship of Baptist Educators. He has won numerous honors including the Outstanding Educator Award in Alabama and the Citizen of the Year Award. He is the editor of *Henry Drummond: A Perpetual Benediction* (Edinburgh: T&T Clark, 1999), and his published articles and essays include "D. L. Moody: Payment on Account," in *Mr. Moody and the Evangelical Tradition*, ed. Timothy George (Edinburgh: T&T Clark, 2004). His most recent publication is *Deo, doctrinae, aeternitati—For God, for Learning, Forever*, ed. Jack E. Brymer (Birmingham: Samford University Press, 2006).

J. Norfleete Day is associate professor of Divinity at Beeson Divinity School, Samford University, where she teaches in the areas of spiritual formation and New Testament. Dr. Day holds degrees from Samford University (BA), the University of Alabama (MLS), Beeson Divinity School (M.Div.), and Baylor University (Ph.D.). Formerly associate director of the Birmingham Public Library, she was a member of the charter class at Beeson Divinity School and has the distinction of being the only Beeson graduate to serve as a member of the teaching faculty. She is author of *The Woman at the Well: An Interpretation of John 4:1–42 in Retrospect and Prospect* (Leiden: Brill, 2002) and has written curriculum and devotional materials for multiple publications. Dr. Day is a deacon and active member of Vestavia Hills Baptist Church in Birmingham.

Stephen J. Duffy (deceased) was ordained a priest on 2 February 1957 and served the Archdiocese of New Orleans for many years. He received a licentiate in theology from the Pontificia Università Gregoriana in Rome and a doctorate in theology from the Catholic

University of America. Professor of religious studies at Loyola University, New Orleans, for many years, he wrote articles, books, and reviews throughout his career, including "Interreligious Dialogues: the Theological and Comparative Components" in *Ecumenical Trends* and "A Theology of the Religions and/or a Comparative Theology" in *Horizons*. His books included *The Quest for Freedom in a Culture of Choice* (Chicago: Loyola University Press, 2001) and *Encountering the Stranger: Christianity in Dialogue with the World Religions* (Chicago: Loyola Religious Studies, 1994).

Curtis W. Freeman is research professor of theology and director of Baptist House of Studies at Duke University Divinity School. Dr. Freeman holds degrees from Baylor University (BA and Ph.D.) and Southwestern Baptist Theological Seminary (M.Div.). He has edited two books, *Ties That Bind* (with Gary Furr) (Macon GA: Smyth & Helwys, 1994) and *Baptist Roots: A Reader in the Theology of a Christian People* (with James Wm. McClendon Jr. and C. Rosalee Velloso Ewell) (Valley Forge: Judson, 1999). He writes articles that seek to describe the development of a distinctly Baptist theological tradition as well as articles relating to Baptist and Free Church theology. Dr. Freeman is a series editor of *Studies in Baptist History and Thought* (Paternoster Press) and serves on the Baptist World Alliance Doctrine and Interchurch Cooperation Commission.

Gary Furr has served as pastor of Vestavia Hills Baptist Church in Birmingham, Alabama, since 1993. Prior to moving to Alabama, his pastoral experience spanned more than twenty-six years in churches in Texas and Georgia. He holds degrees from Carson-Newman College (BA), Southeastern Baptist Theological Seminary (M.Div.), and Baylor University (Ph.D. in religion). Dr. Furr often speaks at conferences and retreats in the areas of worship and spiritual formation. He co-authored *The Dialogue of Worship* with Milburn Price (Macon GA: Smyth & Helwys, 1998), and he co-edited (with Curtis Freeman) and contributed to *Ties That Bind: Life Together in the Baptist Vision* (Macon GA: Smyth & Helwys, 1994) He served as editor and contributor to the *Library of Distinctive Sermons* series (Multnomah Books) and is an adjunct professor of religion at Samford University and Beeson Divinity School.

Timothy George is the founding dean of Beeson Divinity School of Samford University. He holds degrees from the University of Tennessee at Chattanooga (AB), Harvard Divinity School (M.Div.), and Harvard University (Th.D.). He taught at Southern Seminary for many years before coming to Samford University. He serves as senior editor for *Christianity Today* and is a member of the editorial board of *First Things*. He also serves on numerous advisory boards. A prolific author, he contributes regularly to scholarly journals. His books include *Galatians*, New American Commentary (Nashville: Broadman & Holman, 1994), *Theology of the Reformers* (Nashville: Broadman, 1988), and *Is the Father of Jesus the God of Muhammad?* (Grand Rapids: Zondervan, 2002). He is editor of the Beeson Divinity Studies series (Baker Academic), including *Pilgrims on the Sawdust Trail* (2004) and *God the Holy Trinity* (2006).

Steven R. Harmon is associate professor of Christian Theology at Campbell University Divinity School, Buies Creek, North Carolina. He holds degrees from Howard Payne University (BA) and Southwestern Baptist Theological Seminary (M.Div. and Ph.D.), and he received a dissertation fellowship for study at Westfälischen-Wilhelms Universität, Münster, Germany. In addition, Dr. Harmon has studied at the Catholic University of America, University of Dallas, and Duke Divinity School (sabbatical research). His writings include *Towards Baptist Catholicity: Essays on Tradition and the Baptist Vision* (Carlisle: Paternoster, 2006) and *Every Knee Should Bow: Biblical Rationales for Universal Salvation in Early Christian Thought* (University Press of America, 2003). Dr. Harmon serves as vice chair of the Doctrine and Interchurch Cooperation Commission of the Baptist World Alliance and book review editor for *Perspectives in Religious Studies*.

Richard Land has degrees from Princeton University (AB) and the University of Oxford (D.Phil.). He has served as president of the Southern Baptist Convention's Ethics and Religious Liberty Commission since 1988. Dr. Land has represented Evangelicals before Congress and US presidents and as a commissioner of the US Commission on International Religious Freedom. In 2005 *Time* named him one of "The Twenty-five Most Influential Evangelicals." Dr. Land has worked as a pastor, theologian, and public policy maker, and his most recent book is titled *The Divided States of America? What Liberals AND Conservatives Are Missing in the God-and-Country Shouting Match!* (Nashville: Thomas Nelson, 2007).

Wanda S. Lee has served as executive director of Woman's Missionary Union (an auxiliary of the Southern Baptist Convention) since 2000. A nurse by profession for thirty years prior to coming to WMU, she received her education at Ida V. Moffett School of Nursing (now part of Samford University) and received an honorary doctorate in public administration from Campbellsville University. She has written numerous articles for Christian journals and is the author of *Live the Call: Embrace God's Design for Your Life* (Birmingham: New Hope, 2006).

Bill J. Leonard is founding dean and professor of church history at Wake Forest University Divinity School. Dr. Leonard holds degrees from Texas Wesleyan College (BA), Southwestern Baptist Theological Seminary (M.Div.), and Boston University (Ph.D.). He is author or editor of fifteen books, including *God's Last and Only Hope: The Fragmentation of the Southern Baptist Convention* (Grand Rapids: Eerdmans,1990) and *Dictionary of Baptists in America* (Downers Grove: InterVarsity Press, 1994). Before arriving at Wake Forest in 1996, he served as professor of church history at the Southern Baptist Theological Seminary (1975–1992) and chair of the department of religion and philosophy at Samford University (1992–1996). He has also taught at Yale Divinity School and Seinan Gakuin University, Fukuoka, Japan.

Eric F. Mason is associate professor of Biblical Studies at Judson University, Elgin, Illinois. He holds degrees from Union University (BA), Beeson Divinity School (M.Div.), and the University of Notre Dame (MA, Ph.D.), and he was the recipient of a graduate school fellowship from the Pew Younger Scholars Program. He was honored as a 2007 Regional Scholar by the Society of Biblical Literature for his paper titled "Melchizedek in Hebrews and the Dead Sea Scrolls," and he was selected to participate in a National Endowment for the Humanities Summer Seminar on the history of Mormonism in 2005. Dr. Mason is the author of *'You are a Priest Forever': Second Temple Jewish Messianism and the Priestly Christology of the Epistle to the Hebrews* (Leiden: Brill, 2008) and is an associate editor for the journal *Henoch: Studies in Judaism and Christianity from Second Temple to Late Antiquity.*

Samuel J. Mikolaski was born in Yugoslavia and reared in Canada. He is the former president of Atlantic Baptist University (Moncton, New Brunswick) and Pioneer McDonald Professor at Carey Theological College and Regent College (Vancouver). He holds degrees in philosophy from the University of Western Ontario (BA and MA), University of London (BD Honors), University of Oxford (D.Phil.), and Acadia University (DD *Honoris Causa*). Earlier he was professor of theology and convener of the theology department in the New Orleans Baptist Theological Seminary, and he also taught for several years as adjunct professor for Fuller Theological Seminary and Golden Gate Baptist Seminary/Saddleback Church Seminary. In addition, he has served as a pastor in Canada, England, and the United States.

Robert Smith Jr., professor of Christian Preaching at Beeson Divinity School, received his education from God's Bible College (AS), Cincinnati Bible College (BS), and the Southern Baptist Theological Seminary (M.Div.and Ph.D.). He also was granted an honorary Doctor of Sacred Theology by the Temple Community Bible College. He is a contributing editor for *Preparing for Christian Ministry*, and he received Beeson's "Teacher of the Year Award" in 2005. He is a member of the Academy of Homiletics and serves on the Board of Consulting Editors for *Preaching* Magazine. He co-edited (with Timothy George) *A Mighty Long Journey: Reflections on Racial Reconciliation* (Nashville: Broadman & Holman, 2000). His newest book, *Doctrine That Dances: Bringing Doctrinal Preaching and Teaching to Life* (Nashville: Broadman & Holman, 2008) has been chosen as the annual Book of the Year for *Preaching Magazine*.

Frank Thielman is professor of divinity at Beeson Divinity School of Samford University, where he has taught New Testament since 1989. He was educated at Wheaton College (BA), Cambridge University (BA and MA), and Duke University (Ph.D.) and holds memberships in the Evangelical Theological Society, the Institute for Biblical Research, the Catholic Biblical Association, the Society of Biblical Literature, and Studiorum Novi Testamenti Societas. His books include *From Plight to Solution: A Jewish Framework to*

Understanding Paul's View of the Law in Galatians and Romans (Leiden: Brill, 1989), *Paul and the Law: A Contextual Approach* (Downers Grove: InterVarsity Press, 1994), *Philippians*, NIV Application Commentary (Grand Rapids: Zondervan, 1995), *The Law and the New Testament: The Question of Continuity* (New York: Herder & Herder, 1999), and *Theology of the New Testament: A Canonical and Synthetic Approach* (Grand Rapids: Zondervan, 2005).

Philip Wise has served as senior pastor of Second Baptist Church in Lubbock, Texas, since 2003. He has co-authored two books with Fisher Humphreys, *A Dictionary of Doctrinal Terms* (Nashville: Broadman, 1983) and *Fundamentalism* (Macon GA: Smyth & Helwys, 2004). He is a graduate of Samford University and received his Th.D. in systematic theology from the New Orleans Baptist Theological Seminary. In addition, he undertook three years of postgraduate study at the University of Oxford. He serves on the Doctrine Commission of the Baptist World Alliance and the National Coordinating Council of the Cooperative Baptist Fellowship.

Ralph C. Wood, University professor of theology and literature at Baylor University in Waco, Texas, holds degrees from Texas A & M University-Commerce (BA and MA), and from the University of Chicago (MA and Ph.D.). From 1971 to 1997 he taught on the faculty of Wake Forest University, where he was the John Allen Easley Distinguished Professor of Religion. Dr. Wood serves as an editor-at-large for *The Christian Century* and as a member of the editorial board of the *Flannery O'Connor Review*. His first major book, *The Comedy of Redemption: Christian Faith and Comic Vision in Four American Novelists* (examining F. O'Connor, W. Percy, J. Updike, and P. De Vries), was published by the University of Notre Dame Press (1988). Other books include *Contending for the Faith: The Church's Engagement with Culture* (Waco: Baylor, 2003), *The Gospel According to Tolkien: Visions of the Kingdom in Middle-earth* (Louisville: Westminster John Knox, 2004), and *Flannery O'Connor and the Christ-Haunted South* (Grand Rapids: Eerdmans, 2004).